COUNSELING AND DEVELOPMENT SERIES
ALLEN IVEY, Editor

RESEARCH AS PRAXIS
Lessons from Programmatic
Research in Therapeutic Psychology
Lisa Tsoi Hoshmand & Jack Martin, Editors

**THE CONSTRUCTION
AND UNDERSTANDING OF
PSYCHOTHERAPEUTIC CHANGE**
Conversations, Memories, and Theories
Jack Martin

Research as Praxis

Lessons from
Programmatic Research in
Therapeutic Psychology

Edited by

LISA TSOI HOSHMAND   JACK MARTIN

Teachers College, Columbia University
New York and London

Published by Teachers College Press, 1234 Amsterdam Avenue, New York, NY 10027

Copyright © 1995 by Teachers College, Columbia University

All rights reserved. No part of this publication may be reproduced or transmitted in any form or by any means, electronic or mechanical, including photocopy, or any information storage and retrieval system, without permission from the publisher.

Library of Congress Cataloging-in-Publication Data

Research as praxis : lessons from programmatic research in therapeutic
  psychology / Lisa Tsoi Hoshmand, Jack Martin, editors.
      p. cm. — (Counseling and development series)
    Includes bibliographical references and index.
    ISBN 0-8077-3427-6 (paper : alk. paper). — ISBN 0-8077-3428-4 (cloth : alk. paper)
    1. Clinical psychology—Research. 2. Psychotherapy—Research.
  I. Hoshmand, Lisa Tsoi, 1947–   . II. Martin, Jack, 1950–   .
  III. Series.
    [DNLM: 1. Psychology, Clinical. 2. Research—methods.
  3. Psychotherapy.   WM 105 R4318 1995]
  RC467.8.R47   1995
  616.89'0072—dc20
  DNLM/DLC
  for Library of Congress   94-42581

ISBN 0–8077–3427–6 (paper)
ISBN 0–8077–3428–4 (cloth)

Printed on acid-free paper
Manufactured in the United States of America

02 01 00 99 98 97 96 95   8 7 6 5 4 3 2 1

Contents

Preface vii

Part I   The Epistemology of Research and Issues of Method

1. Method Choice 3
    Lisa T. Hoshmand and Jack Martin
2. The Inquiry Process 29
    Lisa T. Hoshmand and Jack Martin
3. Research on Psychological Practice 48
    Jack Martin and Lisa T. Hoshmand

Part II   Reflective Accounts of Research Programs in Therapeutic Practice

4. Musings About How to Study Therapist Techniques 81
    Clara E. Hill
5. How Does Psychotherapy Work? A Personal Account of Model Building 104
    Jack Martin
6. The Poetics of Science: Creativity in the Construction of Causality 127
    George S. Howard
7. Methods and Metaphors: The Study of Figurative Language in Psychotherapy 153
    Linda M. McMullen
8. On the Process of Studying the Process of Change in Family Therapy 171
    Myrna L. Friedlander
9. Strategic Choices in a Qualitative Approach to Psychotherapy Process Research 198
    David L. Rennie

Part III Toward a Model of Knowledge for Research on Practice

10.	Summary and Analysis *Lisa T. Hoshmand and Jack Martin*	223
11.	Concluding Comments on Therapeutic Psychology and the Science of Practice *Lisa T. Hoshmand and Jack Martin*	235

Postscripts	242
Author Index	253
Subject Index	259
About the Contributors	263

Preface

This book is based on a project that began almost 3 years ago with a number of questions and concerns that we had about inquiry in psychology. In discussing the nature of research methods in the social sciences and their applications and limitations, particularly in the practicing areas of psychology, we became aware of a critical need for knowledge about diverse methods, as well as ways of overcoming the confusion that seems to have resulted from an increasingly pluralistic orientation to psychological inquiry. It was our impression that few resources are available to researchers, methodologists, instructors, and students in psychology that would meet these needs at both a conceptual and a practical level. We also felt that the standard modes of research reporting found in the professional literature do not provide sufficiently realistic accounts of the inquiry process and how researchers shape this process in thought and action, accounts that could be helpful to other researchers and students of inquiry. Questions arose as to the contexts in which method choices are made and the cognitive and social factors that enter into the manner in which inquiry is conducted. We wanted to explicate these contexts and factors in order to achieve a more complete understanding of the nature of the research craft and our knowledge enterprise.

Our questions and concerns were accompanied by a sense of uncertainty about the extent of progress in our profession's inquiry into such areas as therapeutic practice. It appeared that many persistent issues of psychological inquiry and concomitant problems with method choice are experienced by researchers of therapeutic practice. We wanted to understand how these researchers have dealt with such issues and made methodological decisions, and to describe the inquiry process intertwined with their research praxis. To this end, we enlisted the cooperation of a group of colleagues from whom we asked for personal accounts of their own programs of research in therapeutic psychology. Against their experiential accounts and the lessons they were willing to share, we attempted to articulate the issues concerned and to develop possible frameworks for their analysis. Our hope has been to develop a contingent vision of what may constitute progressive psychological inquiry in this and other human domains. Whether this goal has been realized is for the reader to judge.

This book is organized into three parts. In Part I we present the problems of method choice and a working conception of the inquiry process. We also discuss a variety of issues and challenges of research in therapeutic practice. A conceptual framework and method for understanding the inquiry practices and methodological reasoning of researchers are provided. This is followed in Part II by several accounts of programmatic research in different areas of therapeutic practice. A summary and analysis of these cases are presented in Part III, concluding with our comments on how to evaluate progress in the research praxis under consideration. Additional recommendations are offered on the uses of a pragmatic framework for integrating methodological understanding across diverse method choices and philosophical commitments. Further reflections by the authors are included in the postscripts.

A project such as this undertaking would not have been possible without the goodwill and efforts of colleagues who share our concern for improving psychological inquiry and a special interest in the domain of therapeutic practice. Perhaps none of us realized from the outset how this project would unfold and what it might yield; its developmental nature is reflective of the organic potentials of all inquiry. As editors, we are grateful for the intellectual gifts and personal insights that our colleagues have contributed. The high quality of the collaboration that we experienced has made this endeavor personally and professionally rewarding.

Lisa T. Hoshmand and Jack Martin
March, 1994

PART I

The Epistemology of Research and Issues of Method

CHAPTER 1

Method Choice

LISA T. HOSHMAND AND JACK MARTIN

Our purpose in this book is to learn about the research craft as applied by psychological researchers and to derive general understandings about the factors entering into choice of research methodology and development of the inquiry process. By presenting and examining the personal accounts of a select group of programmatic researchers in psychotherapy practice, we hope to convey a view of research practice that is more realistic and informative than what typically can be inferred from published reports in the professional literature. To set the stage for studying the lessons to be shared by these researchers in Part II of this book, concepts and issues relevant to research in psychology and other human sciences will be presented within a heuristic framework here in Part I and will be revisited in our concluding section of Part III.

The most basic task that confronts researchers once they have determined the purpose of their research is to choose a method for their inquiry. In this initial chapter, we address the topic of method choice by first defining the nature of method and explaining the necessity of choice. Philosophical concepts and considerations relevant to the study of methods of inquiry are examined. Paradigmatic commitments and the implications of multiple available alternatives are discussed. We then propose an evolving framework for examining issues of method preference and selection, exploring the conditions and criteria for the evaluation of method choices. A number of hypotheses are entertained regarding the basis on which researchers make decisions about method. In our attempt to understand method choice and the inquiry process in research on psychotherapeutic practice throughout this book, we will draw upon philosophical and methodological work on science in general, and psychology as a social science and human practice in particular.

THE DEFINITION OF METHOD

The term *method* is used here to refer to any ordered set of activities and practices, the planful use of which yields data. Method involves the use of both conceptual and procedural tools. Ideas and concepts are as much a part of method as the means by which we gather and evaluate information to answer the research questions that we pose. Thus, method is more than a set of techniques and procedures. It can be regarded as a means of ordering and embedding observations and meanings in a particular network of relationships to other observations and meanings. All applications of methods of inquiry, like other human practices, are social in nature. The means that researchers typically follow communally established guidelines that are understood explicitly or implicitly by other users of the same methods. The methods we have in psychology are part of the symbolic resources and conventions shared by our professional community in obtaining and communicating knowledge.

Methodology refers to the reasoning involved in designing a particular approach to inquiry and selecting particular methods. Research methodologies can be understood in terms of their logic in use and the context of usage. Philosophers of science historically have viewed method as the logic by which we investigate a phenomenon of interest and draw conclusions about it. The nature of that logic is the substance of the rationality attributed to science, or what we need to understand as the cognitive aspects of science. Early empirical scientists of the eighteenth century advocated the use of inductive reasoning in inferring generalities from the observation of multiple instances. Based on this inductive logic, statements were made about the regularities and lawfulness of an observed phenomenon. During the nineteenth century, the need to postulate theoretical entities as the causal base of observed phenomena that seem to be governed by unobservable forces led to the use of the hypothetico-deductive logic. Scientists engaged in theory-testing by confirming or refuting hypotheses that are logically deduced from a theory that can have a broad range of manifestations. Thus, two types of logic are involved in research, each associated with a different function.

Reichenbach (1938) distinguished between the context of discovery and the context of justification. In these two contexts, research activities may be aimed, respectively, at the generation of theories and the testing of theories. In the former case, method serves to create an empirical domain for which a theory or working model is constructed to give meaning to our findings. For example, descriptive data from clients' recollections of the experience of therapy may be used to construct an experiential model of therapy. In the latter case, method provides the conditions for witnessing the application of a theory or demonstration of a model. For example, the conditions can be set up to test the hypothesis of mutual influence between therapist and client as deduced from an interpersonal theory of counseling. Although the distinction between discovery and justification as different phases of inquiry is probably an oversimplification of the research process, one may regard the two contexts as each having different methodological requirements. The methodological strategy applied to serve the purpose at hand in each case entails the use of particular research methods and designs.

In actual practice, researchers utilize both discovery-oriented methods and theory-testing methods, as each type of strategy is incomplete by itself. Inductive inquiry leads to an open-ended search for possible conclusions or plausible interpretations of an emergent picture, a picture for which all constitutive elements can never be examined exhaustively. Deductive theory-testing seems to be an equally endless activity in that it may take an indeterminate number of observations to overturn the explanatory claims of a theory because so much rests on how observations are interpreted. In other words, theory tends to be underdetermined by data. There is a degree of uncertainty and incompleteness in the use of both theory-building and theory-testing methods. Added to this uncertainty are our own limitations in applying reasoning to the inquiry process. In that knowledge acquisition is mediated by human judgment, we must consider personal and environmental factors that have an impact on such judgment. Contrary to former beliefs in the rationality and neutrality of method, method is viewed by contemporary philosophers of science as non-neutral and theory-laden (Hanson, 1958; Hesse, 1981; Shapere, 1984). There is no presuppositionless method. Differences in method choice in psychology have been associated with non-accidental theoretical differences and philosophical differences (Danziger, 1988; O'Donohue, 1989).

Inevitably, the methods endorsed by a profession are partially a function of the ideology and social organization of the discipline, reward systems, and professional training and socialization. This non-neutrality of method and the socially and professionally embedded nature of its use make it necessary to consider method choice as more than a matter of technical consideration. It involves complex and weighted decisions. In view of the role of human judgment and the social factors surrounding the selection and usage of methods of inquiry, one may expect the logic used by researchers to be more functional than formal. The nature of method choice in a given domain of inquiry may be clarified with conceptual effort and illuminated by empirical study.

Method choice is inherent in any research process. Researchers aim to maximize credible findings, and the desiderata for appropriate research procedures and arrangements often conflict. For instance, in choosing units of observation, simplicity of a unit lends itself more readily to an adequate operational definition and reliable use, whereas complexity of a unit presents problems of definition and reliable observation. It is easier to observe the frequency of a certain type of statement by a therapist to a client than to observe the therapeutic and communication context in which such statements occur. The relative advantage of the former, however, has to be weighed against its potentially lower meaningfulness compared with the latter. More meaningful and possibly more valid information may be gained by placing the statement in context, even though doing so would involve a more difficult and complex observation task. "Trade-offs" between reliability and validity in the choice of units of analysis are encountered frequently in psychological research that aspires to inform practice, given that validity is impossible without reliability. Similarly, precision and control are easier to achieve in a confined setting such as the classic psychological laboratory. On the other hand, generalizability to the context of practice seems to require naturalistic approaches that may not permit the same degree of precision and control. The fact that it is not possible for a researcher to maximize all aspects of method that potentially could enhance the credibility of a study creates many occasions for weighted decisions. The methodological implications of considering issues such as unit of analysis, the simultaneous requirements of reliability and validity, and choice of discovery versus theory-testing strategies in psychotherapy research will be discussed at length in Chapter 3.

The appropriateness of method choice is always an issue. Although method choice should be guided by one's research purpose, in practice method often dictates the selection of problems and the structure of the empirical domain that results from inquiry. Neimeyer and Resnikoff (1982) likened the effects of using different methods to casting different fishing nets, with nets of varied mesh resulting in different types of catch. They advocated the use of multiple methods, or triangulation of methods, to increase the variety and span of information gain. Using a similar fishing analogy, Howard (1982) pointed out that the fruitfulness of each method can be empirically investigated, just as the type and size of catch from different netting procedures can be compared. We propose that the soundness of method choice should itself be a subject of study. Going beyond research on individual methods, we probably can learn more by looking at a series of method choices made by researchers involved in a variety of research programs. It is our belief that research programs, more than single studies, provide researchers with greater latitude in method choice and the opportunity to reap the benefits of complementary methods. Part II of this book consists of an examination of sequential method choices in a diverse set of research programs on therapeutic practice.

To study the nature of method choice, such as is attempted in this volume, there has to be a working framework. To pave the way for the introduction of such a framework, we will use a number of relevant concepts and consider certain philosophical issues.

PHILOSOPHICAL CONCEPTS AND CONSIDERATIONS IN THE STUDY OF METHOD

There are many assumptions about the proper form and uses of method. These assumptions are linked to larger belief systems and scientific models referred to as paradigms (Kuhn, 1962). Historically, different paradigms have been associated with particular scientific world views. The system of empirical science practiced during the nineteenth century, and further formalized in the 1920s and 1930s, is referred to as the positivistic tradition (Hanfling, 1981). Positivistic science is based on the philosophical view that objective methods can provide knowledge of reality, and that cognitive certainty with respect to such knowledge may be guaranteed by a universal system of rationality. This doctrine is referred to as "foundationalism." Although postpositivistic writers have added other nuances to this earlier thesis, the positivistic methodological stance tends to promote a formalistic conception of research practice. Researchers are expected to apply the scientific method in establishing networks of lawful statements about nature, based on logical steps of hypothesis-testing and falsification that are found in standard practice.

A different scientific world view is constructionism (Gergen, 1985). The constructionist view is that methods of knowledge consist of the symbolic tools employed to construct and represent meanings, and are relative to cultural and historical context. In this view, there is no privileged access to reality or cognitive certainty through the application of a universal method of knowledge. Accordingly, research paradigms based on the positivistic foundation differ from those of a constructionist orientation. Whereas in positivistic science, methods of knowledge are presumed to follow a universal logic based on a shared foundation of rationality, the constructionist view is that human knowledge is varied in rationale and socially embedded. (For an overview of paradigmatic positions pertinent to therapeutic psychology, the reader can refer to a history of ideas such as given in Mahoney, 1991.)

The point to recognize is that methods are linked to philosophical assumptions in the underlying model of knowledge to which we subscribe (Hoshmand, 1994). One type of assumption is concerned with *ontology* or the nature of things (such as the mind and reality). Our ontological assumptions about ourselves and the world affect what we consider to be appropriate methods of knowing. The branch of philosophy that historically has been concerned with questions of what is knowable, how one can access knowledge, and what are appropriate conditions for knowledge, is *epistemology* (Campbell, 1988; Goldman, 1986). Although epistemological assumptions are clearly behind the fashioning of methods, epistemology cannot be dissociated from ontology in the human quest for knowledge about ourselves and our social and physical worlds. How we gain knowledge of the world depends on the nature of the mind as manifested in perception and learning. Our process and criteria of knowing invoke assumptions about the relationship between the knower (or knowing mind) and the known. Thus, we need to examine both ontological and epistemological assumptions in the study of method in the human sciences.

Chapter 3 will present methodological issues in research on therapeutic practice in relation to ontological assumptions in current conceptions of this substantive domain, and a number of associated epistemological difficulties. As explained in Hoshmand (1994), methods of psychological research, like methods of practice, can be understood in terms of presuppositions about the subject matter and the implications they carry for appropriate ways of understanding it.

The discussion and evaluation of methods require some additional concepts. Philosophers of science have concentrated their efforts on specifying the conditions for accepting knowledge claims. Justifications of given claims of valid knowledge are referred to as "epistemic warrants." A warrant is a belief that certifies the acceptability of a claim based on relevant information. Epistemic warrants involve the application of cognitive, epistemic values or rules and criteria that govern the evaluation of methods of knowledge acquisition and the results claimed. Questions that we raise about epistemic warrants as well as the ontological nature of our subject matter are second-order or meta-level questions, as distinguished from substantive or empirical questions that we ask about a phenomenon of interest. We suggest that these philosophical questions should be the subject of reflection by researchers and students of inquiry. This is because the methods that we use in research, and the knowledge that we claim in therapeutic and other areas of psychological practice, involve such philosophical considerations and evaluations.

Our profession uses standards of validity upheld in the social sciences, for the most part, to adjudicate psychological research on practice.

There have been various seminal works on the subject of validity, including those of Campbell and Stanley (1963), Cook and Campbell (1979), Brinberg and McGrath (1985), Cronbach (1982, 1988), and Messick (1989). Recent views on validity in psychological inquiry have emphasized the functional value of methods in a given context of usage. Validity is no longer considered to be the property of a method, separate from how it is used. The discussion of validity issues has come to be centered on the question of meaning. Furthermore, the consequential nature of method choice is evaluated by its human and social impact. Such impact is judged by social values apart from the cognitive values involved in epistemic warrants. Thus, both epistemic and non-epistemic values are involved in the evaluation of methods of inquiry (Howard, 1985b). We cannot neglect the moral context and axiological dimensions of research in psychological practice. Concerns have been raised about how we are treating our human clientele (Koch, 1981), the power implications of our methods and theoretical models (Hare-Mustin & Maracek, 1988; Taggart, 1985), and the relevance of the research findings to practitioners and the clients they serve (Howard, 1985a; Sarason, 1981). Although such discussions about non-epistemic values tend to be separate from the discussion of cognitive criteria and epistemic standards, they, together with epistemic values, will constitute the basis on which method choice and inquiry practices are considered in this volume.

The context of inquiry is set by the researcher's purpose. Research on practice can include in principle both theory-testing and the discovery of new formulations and hypotheses. It follows that research methods and findings should be evaluated with respect to each of these purposes. Due to the historical emphasis on theory-testing or disconfirmation in positivistic science (Popper, 1934, 1981), however, philosophers and methodologists have neglected developing criteria for evaluating research in the discovery context (Nickles, 1980). Royce (1988) suggested that exploratory and descriptive research can have heuristic value, and should be evaluated for the extent to which useful classification of conceptual alternatives may result and whether acceptable patterns of inference are used in hypothesis generation. Certain criteria have been proposed for the evaluation of research methods that are generally associated with descriptive and discovery strategies, and as a basis for judging the findings they yield (e.g., Kvale, 1989; Lincoln & Guba, 1986). These criteria are less codified at this point than those used to warrant knowledge claims made on the basis of theory-testing.

Given the diversity of inquiry purposes, there need to be diverse criteria and standards for evaluating different methods and claims of knowledge. A question that has concerned philosophers of science is whether the criteria and standards of knowledge we use constitute a universal system of rationality. This question is relevant to all psychological inquiry, including research on therapeutic practice, as there are ongoing debates in our profession about the appropriate warrants to apply to different research approaches. Under traditional foundationalism in positivistic science, scientific methods are considered to be governed by a universal set of rules and standards. The successful application of methods according to these prior standards is presumed to provide access to a knowable world. However, since the work of Kuhn (1962) and others (Merton, 1973; Mulkay, 1979) who adopted a sociological view of knowledge, rules and standards for warrants have assumed a modified role. Rather than being universal givens, they appear to be negotiated among members of a community of scholars. There is a social designation of authority and a shared cultural understanding of the process by which knowledge claims are considered warranted or acceptable. Recent studies further suggest that although scientists have learned to work in a rule-governed fashion to some extent, they are open to persuasion by the presented evidence. Simons (1989) presented a rhetorical perspective on the construction of knowledge, with examples of the use of rhetoric in the human sciences. Polkinghorne (1991) cited several other sources on the rhetoric of science in support of the view that judgments about knowledge claims are hinged on the persuasiveness of arguments presented by those making the claims. In other words, human judgment enters into every point in the process of establishing knowledge.

Under the post-Kuhnian view of science, methods no longer may be brought under the same set of rules and standards, or a state of commensurability (Kuhn, 1962). When members of a profession disagree about the types of warrant for their knowledge enterprise, it becomes difficult to adjudicate the work of researchers with different epistemic and methodological orientations. This problem is compounded in the human and social sciences by a lack of clarity on the kinds of argumentation logic involved in judging the strength of evidence. For example, different types of findings are yielded by quantitative studies of groups and by qualitative case studies. In addressing the question of the validity of findings from these two approaches, we have to distinguish between the respective types of arguments used. In the former case, the argumentation logic is based on statistical sampling and aggregation, whereas in the latter, assertorial arguments are made on the basis of theoretical sampling and the logic of parts to a whole or comparison to a prototype (Polkinghorne, 1991; Yin, 1989). To apply formal statistical logic and argumentation to the evidence produced by case studies would seem an inappropriate use of warrant and argumentation logic. In effect, we would be using the warrants and logic employed in one approach to adjudicate a different approach. This type of confusion needs to be avoided. At present, there is greater shared understanding in psychology about standards of judgment for research in the quantitative, experimental tradition than for research representing non-experimental and qualitative alternatives.

The prospect of using increasingly pluralistic methods means that our profession must deal with questions regarding the appropriate warrants and standards to adopt with different methods, as well as how they are to be applied and argued for (Hoshmand, 1994). These issues follow us into the judgment of progress on a larger scale. The question of what constitutes progress in a given area of inquiry has been a subject of philosophical debate. Scientific progress was couched previously as a matter of falsification or rejection of theories (Popper, 1934). More recent views rejected the theory-testing conception of scientific advancement in favor of the notion of *progressive research programs* capable of accommodating novel facts and anomalies in a problem context (Kuhn, 1962; Lakatos & Musgrave, 1970). Toulmin (1972) expressed a *pragmatic* view of scientific rationality by which theories and methods can be appraised by their problem-solving effectiveness as concepts and methods are revised in the light of problem-solving experience. Laudan (1977) further argued that scientific progress should be measured not so much by the number and importance of solved problems, but by the balance between solved and unsolved problems of a conceptual as well as an empirical nature. According to historians of science such as Berkson (1984), examples of scientific creativity illustrate a fruitful interaction of research programs with problem situations, whereby new problems are identified and investigated in new ways.

Thus, under a problem-solving view of science, we may expect progressive research programs to be characterized by (1) appropriate changes in method choice over time, and (2) a pattern of effective problem finding and problem solving. We consider this heuristic, pragmatic view of science to be appropriate for psychology as a science of practice. Its practical implications will be further expounded subsequently as we examine examples of research programs in therapeutic practice.

This brief overview of philosophical issues is intended to provide a backdrop for the present study of method choice in relation to the inquiry process. In spite of differences in opinion among philosophers of science, advances in knowledge have been linked to the cognitive limits of researchers and the types of rationality they are supposed to follow. Whether researchers actually act in ways consistent with their cognitive values and epistemic goals is an empirical question. During our journey into the methodological courses taken by a group of researchers of therapeutic practice, we hope to identify those functional criteria and conditions for sound method choices. To evaluate these method choices in context, we plan to entertain the notion of progressive research programs as well as embed the choices in the intentions and values (of both an epistemic and a non-epistemic nature) of the researchers involved. We will attempt to understand researchers' method choices in relation to their apparent philosophical commitments and the meta-goals of their research programs.

PARADIGMS AND THEIR IMPLICATIONS FOR METHOD

As stated previously, the inquiry practices of researchers reflect their commitment to particular paradigms. Paradigms are systems of inquiry with particular underlying ontological, epistemological, and axiological assumptions. If method choice is based on personal values and philosophical commitments, we have to be aware of the range of available paradigm choices and their implications. It is not our purpose to provide a comprehensive review of the major paradigms that constitute systems of belief and practice germane to our field. For a description of emergent paradigms in psychology and the social sciences and the arguments surrounding alternative paradigm choices, the reader can refer to a number of sources (Guba, 1990; Hoshmand, 1989; Lincoln & Guba, 1985; Polkinghorne, 1983; Reason & Rowan, 1981). Our comments here are concerned mainly with the methodological implications for research in psychological practice of prevailing paradigms in psychology and some of the emerging alternatives (see also Hoshmand, 1994).

Psychological science, in striving for scientific status, has adopted a positivistic model of knowledge for most of its history. Researchers utilized operationalization, quantification, and experimentation, following the methodological principles of objective science. With the rise of behaviorism, reductionistic experimental paradigms were developed for theory-testing whereby psychological phenomena were reduced to simple units of observable behavior that could be operationalized and measured with precision. These methodological preferences resulted, however, in dissatisfaction with experimental research and the relationship of psychological science to practice. Many feel that operationalism and measurement have imposed constraints on the meaningful study of phenomena of interest in therapeutic practice. The notion of a universal logic of inquiry and the preference for a mathematical language have further contributed to a relative neglect of the knowledge of practice and other forms of knowledge that can be constructed with natural language (Hoshmand & Polkinghorne, 1992).

In view of such dissatisfaction, attempts have been made to improve the applicability of the prevailing research paradigm to problems of practice. Methodological extensions include quasi-experimental designs and case study methods. Analogue studies of counseling and therapy have given way to the naturalistic observation of therapeutic interactions. There has been more attention to assessing the clinical significance of criterion behaviors and events relevant to therapeutic actions and proximal outcomes (Elliott & Shapiro, 1992; Jacobson & Truax, 1991; Mahrer & Nadler, 1986). Increased efforts also have been made to draw upon the experience of practice to inform research (Elliott, 1983; Kazdin, Siegel, & Bass, 1990). Nonetheless, an increasing number of researchers believe that the nature of phenomena such as therapists' intentions, clients' subjective experiences and meanings, as well as the interaction of couples and families, require alternative research paradigms that are based on philosophical assumptions fundamentally different from those of traditional reductionistic research.

The gradual emergence of alternatives to the reductive experimental methodology associated with a positivistic model of knowledge has paralleled the influences of contextualism and systems theory in psychology and other social sciences (Altman & Rogoff, 1987; Bateson, 1972; Gibbs, 1979; Sarbin, 1977). Individual actions and interpersonal phenomena are conceived in terms of complex interactive, embedded systems. Holistic, contextualist, and dialectical conceptions of theory and practice require a move away from narrowly defined categories of meaning and reductionistic methods of inquiry. The cybernetic framework (Keeney & Morris, 1985) and the study of therapeutic process in context (Greenberg, 1986; Rice & Greenberg, 1984) represent examples of holistic, contextualist paradigms of interest to researchers of therapeutic practice.

Other major research paradigms distinct from reductive experimentation include the phenomenological (Giorgi, 1985; Kvale, 1983; Merleau-Ponty, 1962; Misiak & Sexton, 1983), the ethnographic (Geertz, 1973; Goetz & LeCompte, 1984; Jorgensen, 1989; Lincoln & Guba, 1985; Sanday, 1983; Spradley, 1979; Van Maanen, 1983), grounded theory (Glaser & Strauss, 1967; Rennie, Phillips, & Quartaro, 1988), and the narrative-hermeneutic (Howard, 1991; Polkinghorne, 1988; Sarbin, 1986). These have been described in terms of their philosophical and conceptual underpinnings, methodological characteristics, and the types of research questions they can address (Hoshmand, 1989, 1994). Although they tend to have different origins and communities of users, these paradigms share many common characteristics in terms of purpose, mode of inquiry, presumed structure and process, strategies of data collection and analysis, and procedural rules and standards of knowledge. Inquiry is aimed at understanding lived meanings and experiences, as well as reciprocal intentions and perceptions in human action. It is dependent on mutual exchange between researcher and subject as co-constructors of the data. The inquiry process tends to be open and adapted to the realities of naturalistic contexts. Findings are evaluated by the intelligibility of the interpretive process, the coherence of the researcher's arguments, and the viability and usefulness of the interpretations to the parties involved.

Yet another approach to inquiry is the practice of deconstruction, using largely hermeneutic methods. This practice of examining and critically questioning the underlying assumptions of existing paradigms is referred to as critical theory analysis (Popkewitz, 1990). It is generally consistent with the social constructionist world view in its rejection of the positivistic foundation as an authoritative basis of knowledge. It has been employed in the feminist critique of psychological theory and therapeutic practice (Chodorow, 1989; Gavey, 1989). Additional research approaches with constructionist and non-positivistic foundations include methods used by personal construct theorists (Bannister & Fransella, 1986; Neimeyer, 1993) and modes of personological and experiential inquiry promoted in humanistic psychology (Allender, 1987; Moustakas, 1990; Patton, 1990).

As noted by Hoshmand (1989), different classifications and terminologies have been used to refer to the growing diversity of methods. It is important to specify the type of epistemological stance and methodological approach represented by a given alternative when we refer to inquiry strategies by terms such as "qualitative methods." There is a continuum of methods, serving descriptive-discovery purposes as well as theory-probing purposes, that can be considered alternatives to the experimental paradigm. The epistemic criteria and logic of their use and evaluation also vary (Miles & Huberman, 1984; Packer & Addison, 1989; Polkinghorne, 1991; Stiles, 1993). Notwithstanding occasional lack of clarity and consensus, the possibility now exists of a broader choice of research paradigms, or *methodological pluralism,* in the study of psychological practice. For instance, Toukmanian and Rennie (1992) presented examples of research on therapeutic practice based on a variety of paradigms.

Whether researchers in therapeutic psychology are beginning to practice methodological pluralism is a question of critical importance at this juncture. Methods are linked to paradigms, and particular paradigmatic or philosophical commitments can continue to result in the predominant use of a particular set of methods. Research related to therapeutic psychology, like many other areas of psychological research, has been dominated by the reductionistic form of hypothesis-testing (McKay, 1988). This has been in spite of the fact that not all paradigms of practice are philosophically congruent with the reductive research paradigm, and few models of practice have the status of well-developed theories. As a result, only a portion of working theories and models in therapeutic psychology have been subjected to systematic investigation. The perpetual use of restrictive research paradigms has contributed to a sense of insufficient progress in research on therapeutic practice (Gendlin, 1986; Mahrer, 1988). It is our belief that part of the answer to this problem might come from broadened choices of methods in extended research efforts. A crucial part of our project involves determining the extent of pluralism in the method choices demonstrated by our selected group of researchers of therapeutic practice who are engaged in extended inquiry.

As mentioned previously, methodological diversity presents certain problems. Philosophers of science have pondered the relationship between method and theory, especially the question of whether or not systems of inquiry can be free standing. Just as practitioners would not use interventions that are in conflict with their therapeutic orientation, there is a limit to the range of research methods that are consistent with the theoretical framework inherent in a given paradigm and its intended focus and underlying ontological assumptions. This congruence can be gauged at several levels. The concept of commensurability (Kuhn, 1962) has been used to refer to congruity at the level of theory, method, and world views, as well as findings, dimensions on which systems of inquiry can differ. This congruity may be considered a meta-level concern, as reflected in the overall rationale and goals that constitute a researcher's *meta-reasoning*. We believe that the meta-reasoning applied by a researcher is central to understanding methodological decisions in a given research program.

Given the above concepts, it may be helpful to clarify what it means to have a broad as opposed to a narrow choice of method. Flood (1989) distinguished between the positions one can take with respect to the commensurability of theories and methodologies. An isolationist position implies commitment to a single paradigm to the exclusion of alternative paradigms. Theoretical isolationism promotes theoretical incommensurability. It often involves the use of a universal rationale for methodology across all contexts, as defined from one theoretical world view. Behaviorism has had this type of impact on our field, at least in North America from approximately 1930 to 1960. Methodological isolationism further endorses a single in-house methodology that is subjected only to internal analysis and minor revision. Even in extreme cases of lack of progress, other forms of rationality are not considered. Isolationism can create problems for intellectual and social integration in a profession.

Pluralism, on the other hand, is antithetical to isolationism. It is a conciliatory position that encourages openness to alternative forms of rationality and the interchange of world views. Pluralistic paradigm choices entail diverse epistemic warrants and some degree of congruity between one's ontological and theoretical assumptions and overall methodological approach. In order for it to be different from simple pragmatism, which can run the risk of theoretical contradiction by the trial and error use of different methods for practical reasons, pluralism must involve meta-reasoning of a theoretically reflexive nature (Flood, 1989; Rescher, 1977). Diverse methods may be used in a series of studies that are conceptually linked, under a methodological rationale that is congruent with the researcher's ontological assumptions. Pluralistic method choice should be guided by a higher order rationale that is open to scrutiny. With theoretical commensurability at the meta-level, researchers can pursue common goals in conceptualizing related studies while maintaining methodological selectivity by always linking method to context. In other words, a full range of methodological possibilities is considered, but only those most fitting within a given problem context will be used.

Under methodological pluralism, no *a priori* assumption is made about the universal applicability of a given logic of inquiry or the superiority of a given paradigmatic view. Furthermore, one does not subscribe to the use of a single standard for assessing different methodologies (as in isolationism), or one form of validation of knowledge. The spirit of pluralism and a *meta-methodological* perspective were expressed by Brewer and Hunter (1989) as:

> the challenge to state new problems (or restate old ones) in terms that make them susceptible to study by different methods, to find common ways of comparing and evaluating the results of different methods, and to reconcile the contradictions that the application of different methods may produce. (p. 24)

Methodological pluralism could strengthen research programs in psychological practice by endorsing the comparative advantage of multiple methods and perspectives. The meta-reasoning developed and modified by the experience of application may lead to increasingly progressive method choices.

We advocate the use of *pluralistic research programs* in areas of psychological practice because research in these areas is beset by tensions that cannot be resolved adequately through the conduct of single, isolated studies that employ only a single set of methods. Tensions in our field (such as those to be discussed in Chapter 3) have not been resolved as they are embedded in the motives and intentions of researchers and practitioners. The likelihood that these tensions will continue to be the subject of philosophical debates within the discipline demands that researchers negotiate between seemingly incompatible warrants and world views. Pluralistic programs of research can pursue different, but conceptually related, studies that reflect diverse intentions and inform different poles of such classic tensions across different studies and phases of such research programs. Consequently, programmatic research of this kind may contribute to a progressive research praxis supported by various sets of epistemic warrants. More will be said concerning our concept of the pluralistic research program in Part III, following several illustrations of programmatic research in therapeutic practice that will be presented in Part II of this volume.

Whereas how methodological decisions are to be evaluated has been a function of the basic paradigmatic position adopted, with separate criteria proposed under different paradigms, the rejection of positivism as the sole methodological doctrine has opened up new discussions on the standards for method choice. Howe (1990) suggested that with the changing discourse from paradigm conflicts between the positivistic model and its alternatives to the possibility of methodological pluralism, a new perspective is needed on the issue of standards. He argued that epistemic criteria should be concerned with the logics in use and the judgments, purposes, and values that make up research activities. In other words, the criteria involved in a researcher's applied epistemology may be deduced from the actual research practice. We shall examine research methods in our domain of study by their functional logic, the purposes they serve, and the judgments and values that inform their choice during extended research practice.

THE BASIS OF METHOD CHOICE: SOME HYPOTHESES

Questioning method choices requires us to be reflexive or willing to refer to ourselves and our own working assumptions. Reflexivity in the study of methods is predicated on an ontological assumption of embeddedness. We cannot separate methods of knowing from the human mind and the social context of knowledge. Too often in professional training, we are encouraged to assume an objective attitude of rationality without sufficiently accounting for personal factors that enter into our actions. Method choice should therefore begin with self-reflection on one's orientation to knowledge, personal world views, and preferred style of inquiry (Hoshmand, 1994). Through reflective study, one may bring to greater awareness the assumptions and constraints of one's preferred methodological paradigm. Hopefully, a better appreciation for the constraints of a given orientation may lead to more openness to alternative choices.

When immersed in the planning and execution of a study, a researcher must set up appropriate conditions for reflection on the ongoing inquiry process and the method decisions made at each point in time. Pressures of time, funding, and other demands can affect the research agenda in ways that are not conducive to such reflection. Phenomenological researchers practice reflection as a built-in part of the research process, to help themselves with "bracketing" or suspending preconceptions about the subject of inquiry (Colaizzi, 1973). Reflection on one's own contribution to and choice of a method probably should become an inherent part of the inquiry process. Morgan (1983) provided excellent examples of how researchers can reflect on their philosophical assumptions as well as the social and political implications of their methods. Berg and Smith (1988) addressed the use of self in inquiry. By considering the researcher's involvement in the research process, the personal contribution to method is brought to greater awareness. This reflective capacity is what we believe to be fundamental to effective inquiry, in allowing researchers to maintain a critical stance with respect to their own work. In our attempt at understanding method choice in programmatic research on therapeutic practice, we will rely on the researchers' own reflections and their constructions of the research process as experienced. This is not to presume that all method choices are always the result of conscious reflection. The extent to which informed and self-conscious choices are made should be an issue in professional training and development (Hoshmand, 1994).

Not having a complete understanding of how researchers make decisions about methods, we venture only to propose a number of hypotheses. These hypotheses can serve as windows on the process undertaken by the researchers of therapeutic practice as described in their personal accounts in Part II of this volume. The easiest assumption to make is that method choice is a function of one's learning history and the repertoire one has developed, shaped by modeling and reinforcement from teachers and peers in academic and professional settings. In addition, method choice has been linked to paradigmatic commitments and the epistemic style of the researcher. Krasner and Houts (1984) found consistent paradigmatic commitments among behavioral psychologists. The academic culture and its socialization of future researchers will moderate the types of scientific world view and paradigmatic commitment brought to method choices.

Mitroff and Kilmann (1978) proposed a classification of inquiry styles by researchers' temperament and scientific world view. They suggested that each inquiry style is governed by different rules and criteria, and unless all possible rules are identified, only those codified to the greatest extent would continue to be adopted. (Recall our earlier comment on epistemic criteria and the fact that standards for experimental methods are more established than those associated with the use of alternative research paradigms.) Granting a range of epistemic styles permits a broader conception of science than represented in traditional norms that reflect a particular style. Krathwohl (1985) proposed a continuum of epistemic orientations, from those closest to the natural sciences to those closest to the humanities. He argued that each type of researcher will emphasize a different set of criteria of knowledge and thus have different orientations to method. Salner (1988) as well as Krathwohl speculated that there may be a developmental progression toward orientational maturity for both researchers and psychological science itself. These formulations may be explored in our study of the accounts provided in Part II, by paying attention to the epistemic criteria used by the various researchers and placing them in the developmental context of each research program.

If the epistemic orientation and paradigmatic commitment of the investigator can influence decisions on method, method choice must be understood as a phenomenon that is determined not entirely by technical considerations. Even judgments about the requirements of a study can be only reasoned judgments mediated by personal values and orientations to knowledge. Since Kimble's (1984) study of the epistemic values of psychologists, little documentation of the epistemic preferences of psychological researchers has occurred. It would seem important to consider a broad range of epistemic orientations and their foundation. Aesthetic preference and ontological assumptions can play a critical role in the selection of method, as emphasized in cybernetic models of research and practice in family therapy (Keeney, 1983; Keeney & Morris, 1985; Keeney & Sprenkle, 1982). Such aesthetically based method choice appears to be illustrated in an example of frame analysis of discourse (Chenail, 1990/1991). How best to characterize the epistemic orientation of a given researcher may also be open to debate (see, for example, Keeney, 1982). To the extent that the interpretation of epistemic orientation is a function of our conceptual lenses, it will be advisable to continue to put forth multiple hypotheses.

Much discussion of issues of method choice tends to emphasize reasoned decisions premised on various scientific standards. There are practical constraints on method choice. Contrary to the scientific ideal of endless testing and replication, most research efforts are limited by available time and resources. Naturalistic methods that require long-term investment of time and resources in the field setting may not be chosen for this reason. Survey methods and time-limited studies are often preferred for their relative ease of execution. Non-epistemic factors such as reward systems and political pressure also can be part of the bounded rationality that drives actual research programs. Program development and evaluation research, for instance, are especially in need of a stable source of funding. Funding issues may create greater vulnerability to political pressure. Unless the investigator has full evaluation authority, the rationality of method choice can be undermined (Tharp & Gallimore, 1982). Political constraints and survival agendas can mitigate against programmatic research, the type of research we believe makes it feasible for an investigator to maximize on method choice.

Research cannot be divorced from its embedding social context. The fact that professional practice has to demonstrate accountability can be both an incentive and a constraint in research on practice. Research on therapeutic practice must be rigorous and at the same time meet ethical standards. In a treatment setting, the requirements of informed consent and clients' self-selection can make it impossible to achieve ideal randomization. Thus, a methodological compromise such as the use of matching may be used in some studies. Method choices are similarly limited by the possibility of negative reactivity and potential harm to subjects. The challenge becomes one of finding research methods that are consistent with good therapeutic practice. The popularity of qualitative methods among certain researchers of therapeutic practice seems partly due to their intended egalitarian treatment of the human subject.

Our interest is in placing method choices in the temporal and developmental context of progressive inquiry. Brinberg and McGrath (1985) and Krathwohl (1985) attempted to explicate the nature of decision making with respect to the method requirements of a given stage of research. The maturity of judgment of an investigator is considered a major factor in the meta-reasoning applied, as informed by prior experience with related research or actual knowledge of the substantive field. Tharp and Gallimore (1982) included personal knowing and experienced judgments as a critical part of their meta-model for methodological choice in program development and evaluation research. It would appear that the ability to make appropriate method choices is a function of experience and might improve as one continues to inquire into an area of interest. This inference is consistent with a pragmatic view of the inquiry process.

A PRAGMATIST FRAMEWORK AND CONSTRUCTIONIST LENSES

The foregoing definition of method as heuristic, value-laden, and personally and professionally embedded points to many issues of method choice. We propose that these issues can be understood from a constructionist perspective in which knowledge is regarded as a human construction, always culturally embedded, subject to human judgment, and informed by socially derived beliefs and values. We also consider a pragmatist framework to be useful in understanding the practical uses of research methods, which we believe to be the appropriate context for evaluating any human practice. The fact that there is always an element of trial and error in the practical application of method makes it appropriate to think of method as evolving. An evolutionary conception of method and method choice has precedent in evolutionary ideas of science (Campbell, 1988; Popper, 1979; Toulmin, 1972). It is also supported by pragmatic conceptions of science in general (Laudan, 1984; Margolis, 1986; Okrent, 1988; Rorty, 1991). Tharp and Gallimore (1982), for example, used an organic metaphor for their meta-methodology of program development and evaluation research by referring to it as a "seral" (as in seres) model. Our position is that the wisdom of the researcher that grows with experience critically informs pragmatic decisions on method.

A pragmatist views scientific method in terms of heuristics rather than formal logic (Nickles, 1987). The assumption of a universal logic in the application of method goes counter to cultural and contextual variability. A heuristic view of science regards method as bound to its context of usage. The choice of method depends on the purpose for which it is intended and the types of data that are sought. Strauss (1987) stated:

> Researchers need to be alive not only to the constraints and challenges of research settings and research aims, but to the nature of their data. They must also be alert to the temporal aspects or phasing of their researches, the open-ended character of the "best research" in any discipline, the immense significance of their own experience as researchers, and the local contexts in which the researches are conducted.... Methods, after all, are developed and changed in response to changing work contexts. (pp. 7–8)

Thus, the application of method must be understood in relation to the ongoing inquiry process, a topic to be covered in Chapter 2.

Part II of our volume will supply a set of detailed cases in which researchers of therapeutic practice discuss their method choice in the context of their continuing program of research. We believe that a varied basis for method choices may be uncovered if we allow researchers to reflect on both the cognitive, epistemic and the non-epistemic, social values that enter into their own method decisions within their program of inquiry. Reflexivity is required as the researchers engage in their self-study. The embedded narratives given will be treated as personal constructions anchored in events with certain objective referents. We invite the reader to join us in putting on pragmatically tinted constructionist lenses when viewing the different researchers' attempts at making sense of their choices and actions as documented in the second part of this book.

In the heuristic view, research is regarded as a form of problem solving. Method includes the conceptual and methodological tools brought to bear on a given problem. How problem situations are constituted has implications for method and scientific creativity (Nersessian, 1987). Normally, researchers guided by their theoretical interest and allegiance to particular world views may follow a given program of research to the extent that it provides an opportunity to derive research questions and empirical hypotheses within the working system. Problems that originate from outside the system may be interpreted with the concepts within the preferred theoretical system and investigated with the methodological tools of the system. The issue becomes whether the concepts and tools can bend to the nature of the problem and whether the research program can be shaped by interaction with the problem situation. Flexible interaction between a research program and the problem to be addressed seems to be a minimal requirement for productive inquiry.

Whereas in most hypothetico-deductive research, novel formulations of researchable questions are made within the confines of a given theoretical system, problem solving in the setting of practice has to transcend the limits of a particular theory. Method has to be extended conceptually and strategically in order to open the investigator to the fullest possible implications of the problem situation. Rather than relying on a preformulated research program, a researcher needs to apply methods flexibly and critically, based on an appropriate reading of the requirements of the problem context. In other words, the pragmatic use of method involves a creative response in problem finding and problem solving, thus allowing for a dialectical interplay of discovery and verification. It involves learning to make sound decisions or learning to learn. In the subsequent chapters, we will take a closer look at the inquiry process in terms of how problem definition interacts with the sequential choice of methods by each researcher. We will consider the researchers' accounts of their journeys from the standpoint of how they have learned from experience to solve problems.

A derivative from the non-neutral, pragmatic conception of method is that it has to be specific to the domain and context of application. Research techniques share ontological presuppositions with the theories used to construct particular empirical domains (O'Donohue, 1989). A methodological approach that is incongruent with a given theory and domain of study will not be considered appropriate for use. For instance, few reductive experimental methods are suited for use with existential theory and its domains of interest. This consideration argues against the universal application of methods regardless of domain and context. Method should be matched with the particular assumptions and goals of inquiry in a given context of usage. Thus, researchers interested in inquiry related to therapeutic practice need to consider the nature of the therapeutic domain and the professional and social setting of practice. In research on family therapy process, for instance, it is essential to capture the systemic nature of familial interactions. Linear, mechanistic methodology will not meet the needs of a researcher with a cybernetic view (Keeney & Morris, 1985; Schwartzman, 1984), not only because of technical difficulties, but also because of its violation of the conceptual and philosophical assumptions of the model of practice involved. In Chapter 3, we will review the ontological, epistemological, and axiological issues entailed in researchers' conceptualization of therapeutic phenomena. These issues should be kept in mind as we learn about how research problems are selected and framed in the various programs described in the chapters in Part II.

REFERENCES

Allender, J. S. (1987). The evolution of research methods for the study of human experience. *Journal of Humanistic Psychology, 27*, 458–484.

Altman, I., & Rogoff, B. (1987). World views in psychology: Trait, interactional, organismic, and transactional perspectives. In D. Stokolis & I. Altman (Eds.), *Handbook of environmental psychology* (pp. 1–40). New York: Wiley.

Bannister, D., & Fransella, F. (1986). *Inquiring man*. Beckenham, England: Croom-Helm.

Bateson, G. (1972). *Steps to an ecology of mind*. New York: Ballantine.

Berg, D. N., & Smith, K. K. (1988). *The self in social inquiry* (2nd ed.). Newbury Park, CA: Sage.

Berkson, W. (1984). *Learning from error: Karl Popper's psychology of learning*. LaSalle, NY: Open Court.

Brewer, J., & Hunter, A. (1989). *Multimethod research: A synthesis of styles*. Newbury Park, CA: Sage.

Brinberg, D., & McGrath, J. E. (1985). *Validity and the research process*. Newbury Park, CA: Sage.

Campbell, D. T. (1988). *Methodology and epistemology for the social sciences*. Chicago: University of Chicago Press.
Campbell, D. T., & Stanley, J. C. (1963). *Experimental and quasi-experimental designs for research*. Chicago: Rand McNally.
Chenail, R. J. (1990/1991). Bradford Keeney's cybernetic project and the creation of recursive frame analysis. *The Qualitative Report*, Vol. 1. Fort Lauderdale, FL: Nova University and Northern Illinois University.
Chodorow, N. J. (1989). *Feminism and psychoanalytic theory*. New Haven, CT: Yale University Press.
Colaizzi, P. F. (1973). *Reflection and research in psychology*. Dubuque, IA: Kendall Hunt.
Cook, T. D., & Campbell, D. T. (1979). *Quasi-experimentation*. Chicago: Rand McNally.
Cronbach, L. J. (1982). *Designing evaluations of educational and social programs*. San Francisco: Jossey-Bass.
Cronbach, L. J. (1988). Five perspectives on validity argument. In H. Wainer & H. I. Braun (Eds.), *Test validity* (pp. 3–17). Hillsdale, NJ: Lawrence Erlbaum.
Danziger, K. (1988). On theory and method in psychology. In W. J. Baker, L. P. Mos, H. V. Rappard, & H. J. Stam (Eds.), *Recent trends in theoretical psychology* (pp. 87–94). New York: Springer-Verlag.
Elliott, R. (1983). Fitting process research to the practicing psychotherapist. *Psychotherapy: Theory, Research, and Practice, 20*, 47–55.
Elliott, R., & Shapiro, D. A. (1992). Client and therapist as analysts of significant events. In S. G. Toukmanian & D. L. Rennie (Eds.), *Psychotherapy process research: Paradigmatic and narrative approaches* (pp. 163–186). Newbury Park, CA: Sage.
Flood, R. L. (1989). Six scenarios for the future of systems "problem solving." *Systems Practice, 2*, 75–100.
Gavey, N. (1989). Feminist poststructuralism and discourse analysis. *Psychology of Women Quarterly, 13*, 459–475.
Geertz, C. (1973). *Interpretation of cultures*. New York: Basic Books.
Gendlin, E. T. (1986). What comes after traditional psychotherapy research? *American Psychologist, 41*, 131–136.
Gergen, K. J. (1985). The social constructionist movement in modern psychology. *American Psychologist, 40*, 266–275.
Gibbs, J. C. (1979). The meaning of ecologically oriented inquiry in contemporary psychology. *American Psychologist, 34*, 127–140.
Giorgi, A. (1985). *Phenomenology and psychological research*. Pittsburgh, PA: Duquesne University Press.
Glaser, B., & Strauss, A. (1967). *The discovery of grounded theory*. Chicago: Aldine.
Goetz, J. P., & LeCompte, M. D. (1984). *Ethnographic and qualitative design in educational research*. New York: Academic Press.
Goldman, A. I. (1986). *Epistemology and cognition*. Cambridge, MA: Cambridge University Press.
Greenberg, L. S. (1986). Change process research. *Journal of Consulting and Clinical Psychology, 54*, 4–9.

Guba, E. G. (Ed.). (1990). *The paradigm dialog*. Newbury Park, CA: Sage.
Hanfling, O. (1981). *Logical positivism*. New York: Columbia University Press.
Hanson, N. R. (1958). *Patterns of discovery*. Cambridge: Cambridge University Press.
Hare-Mustin, R. T., & Maracek, J. (1988). The meaning of difference: Gender theory, postmodernism, and psychology. *American Psychologist, 43*, 445–464.
Hesse, M. (1981). Theory and value in the social sciences. In S. Brown, J. Fauvel, & R. Finnegan (Eds.), *Conceptions of inquiry* (pp. 309–326). New York: Methuen.
Hoshmand, L. T. (1989). Alternate research paradigms: A review and teaching proposal. *The Counseling Psychologist, 17*, 3–79.
Hoshmand, L. T. (1994). *Orientation to inquiry in a reflective professional psychology*. Albany: State University of New York Press.
Hoshmand, L. T., & Polkinghorne, D. E. (1992). Redefining the science-practice relationship and professional training. *American Psychologist, 47*, 55–66.
Howard, G. S. (1982). Improving methodology via research on research methods. *Journal of Counseling Psychology, 29*, 318–326.
Howard, G. S. (1985a). Can research in the human sciences become more relevant to practice? *Journal of Counseling and Development, 63*, 539–544.
Howard, G. S. (1985b). The role of values in the science of psychology. *American Psychologist, 40*, 255–265.
Howard, G. S. (1991). Culture tales: A narrative approach to thinking, cross-cultural psychology, and psychotherapy. *American Psychologist, 46*, 187–197.
Howe, K. R. (1990, May). Standards for qualitative (and quantitative) research: A prolegomenon. *Educational Researcher*, 2–9.
Jacobson, N. S., & Truax, P. (1991). Clinical significance: A statistical approach to defining meaningful change in psychotherapy research. *Journal of Consulting and Clinical Psychology, 1*, 12–19.
Jorgensen, D. L. (1989). *Participant observation: A methodology for human studies*. Newbury Park, CA: Sage.
Kazdin, A. E., Siegel, T. C., & Bass, D. (1990). Drawing on clinical practice to inform research on child and adolescent psychotherapy. *Professional Psychology: Research and Practice, 21*, 189–198.
Keeney, B. P. (1982). Not pragmatics, not aesthetics. *Family Process, 21*, 429–434.
Keeney, B. P. (1983). *Aesthetics of change*. New York: Guilford.
Keeney, B. P., & Morris, J. (1985). Family therapy practice and research: A dialogue. In L. Andreozzi (Ed.), *Integrating research and clinical practice* (pp. 98–107). Rockville, MD: Aspen.
Keeney, B. P., & Sprenkle, D. H. (1982). Ecosystemic epistemology: Critical implications for the aesthetics and pragmatics of family therapy. *Family Process, 21*, 1–19.
Kimble, G. A. (1984). Psychology's two cultures. *American Psychologist, 39*, 833–839.
Koch, S. (1981). Psychology and its human clientele: Beneficiaries or victims? In R. A. Kasschau & F. S. Kessel (Eds.), *Psychology and society: In search of symbiosis* (pp. 30–60). New York: Holt, Rinehart & Winston.

Krasner, L., & Houts, A. C. (1984). A study of the "value" systems of behavioral scientists. *American Psychologist, 39,* 840–850.

Krathwohl, D. R. (1985). *Social and behavioral science research.* San Francisco: Jossey-Bass.

Kuhn, T. S. (1962). *The structure of scientific revolutions.* Chicago: University of Chicago Press.

Kvale, S. (1983). The qualitative research interview: A phenomenological and a hermeneutical mode of understanding. *Journal of Phenomenological Psychology, 14,* 171–196.

Kvale, S. (Ed.). (1989). *Issues of validity in qualitative research.* Lund, Sweden: Studentlitteratur.

Lakatos, I., & Musgrave, A. (Eds.). (1970). *Criticism and the growth of knowledge.* Cambridge: Cambridge University Press.

Laudan, L. (1977). *Progress and its problems: Toward a theory of scientific growth.* Berkeley: University of California Press.

Laudan, L. (1984). *Science and values.* Berkeley: University of California Press.

Lincoln, Y. S., & Guba, E. G. (1985). *Naturalistic inquiry.* Beverly Hills, CA: Sage.

Lincoln, Y. S., & Guba, E. G. (1986). But is it rigorous? Trustworthiness and authenticity in naturalistic evaluation. In D. D. Williams (Ed.), *Naturalistic evaluation* (pp. 73–83). San Francisco: Jossey-Bass.

Mahoney, M. J. (1991). *Human change processes: The scientific foundations of psychotherapy.* New York: Basic Books.

Mahrer, A. R. (1988). Discovery-oriented psychotherapy research: Rationale, aims, and methods. *American Psychologist, 43,* 694–702.

Mahrer, A. R., & Nadler, W. P. (1986). Good moments in psychotherapy: A preliminary review, a list, and some promising research avenues. *Journal of Consulting and Clinical Psychology, 54,* 10–15.

Margolis, J. (1986). *Pragmatism without foundations: Reconciling realism and relativism.* New York: Basil Blackwell.

McKay, D. G. (1988). Under what conditions can theoretical psychology survive and prosper? Integrating the rational and empirical epistemologies. *Psychological Review, 95,* 559–565.

Merleau-Ponty, M. (1962). *Phenomenology of perception* (C. Smith, Trans.). New York: Humanities Press.

Merton, R. K. (1973). *The sociology of science.* Chicago: University of Chicago Press.

Messick, S. (1989). Validity. In R. L. Linn (Ed.), *Educational measurement* (3rd ed., pp. 13–103). New York: Macmillan.

Miles, M., & Huberman, A. (1984). *Qualitative data analysis.* Beverly Hills, CA: Sage.

Misiak, H., & Sexton, V. S. (1983). *Phenomenological, existential, and humanistic psychologies: A historical survey.* New York: Grune & Stratton.

Mitroff, I., & Kilmann, R. H. (1978). *Methodological approaches to social science.* San Francisco: Jossey-Bass.

Morgan, G. (Ed.). (1983). *Beyond method.* Beverly Hills, CA: Sage.

Moustakas, C. (1990). Heuristic research: Design and methodology. *Person-Centered Review, 5,* 170–190.

Mulkay, M. (1979). *Science and the sociology of knowledge.* London: Allen & Unwin.
Neimeyer, G. (Ed.). (1993). *Constructivist assessment: A casebook.* Newbury Park, CA: Sage.
Neimeyer, G., & Resnikoff, A. (1982). Qualitative strategies in counseling research. *The Counseling Psychologist, 10,* 75–85.
Nersessian, N. J. (Ed.). (1987). *The process of science.* Dordrecht, N. Holland: Martinus Nijhoff.
Nickles, T. (Ed.). (1980). *Scientific discovery, logic, and rationality.* London: D. Reidel.
Nickles, T. (1987). 'Twixt method and madness. In N. J. Nersessian (Ed.), *The process of science* (pp. 41–67). Dordrecht, N. Holland: Martinus Nijhoff.
O'Donohue, W. (1989). The (even) bolder model: The clinical psychologist as metaphysician-scientist-practitioner. *American Psychologist, 44,* 1460–1468.
Okrent, M. (1988). *Heidegger's pragmatism.* Ithaca, NY: Cornell University Press.
Packer, M. J., & Addison, R. B. (1989). Evaluating an interpretive account. In M. J. Packer & R. B. Addison (Eds.), *Entering the circle: Hermeneutic investigation in psychology* (pp. 275–292). New York: State University of New York Press.
Patton, M. Q. (1990). Humanistic psychology and humanistic research. *Person-Centered Review, 5,* 191–202.
Polkinghorne, D. E. (1983). *Methodology for the human sciences: Systems of inquiry.* Albany: State University of New York Press.
Polkinghorne, D. E. (1988). *Narrative knowing and the human sciences: Systems of inquiry.* Albany: State University of New York Press.
Polkinghorne, D. E. (1991, April). *Generalization and qualitative research: Issues of external validity.* Paper presented at the annual meeting of the American Educational Research Association, Chicago.
Popkewitz, T. S. (1990). Whose future? Whose past? Notes on critical theory and methodology. In E. G. Guba (Ed.), *The paradigm dialog* (pp. 46–66). Newbury Park, CA: Sage.
Popper, K. (1934). *The logic of scientific discovery.* (English translation, 1959). New York: Basic Books.
Popper, K. (1979). *Objective knowledge: An evolutionary approach* (5th ed.). Oxford: Clarendon Press.
Popper, K. (1981). Against methods of discovery. In S. Brown, J. Fauvel, & R. Finnegan (Eds.), *Conceptions of inquiry* (pp. 82–88). New York: Methuen.
Reason, P., & Rowan, J. (Eds.). (1981). *Human inquiry: A sourcebook of new paradigm research.* New York: Wiley.
Reichenbach, H. (1938). *Experience and prediction.* Chicago: University of Chicago Press.
Rennie, D. L., Phillips, J. R., & Quartaro, G. K. (1988). Grounded theory: A promising approach to conceptualization in psychology. *Canadian Psychology, 29,* 139–156.
Rescher, N. (1977). *Methodological pragmatism.* Oxford: Basil Blackwell.
Rice, L. N., & Greenberg, L. S. (Eds.). (1984). *Patterns of change: Intensive analysis of psychotherapy process.* New York: Guilford.
Rorty, R. (1991). *Objectivity, relativism, and truth: Philosophical papers* (Vol. 1). Cambridge: Cambridge University Press.

Royce, J. R. (1988). Theory appraisal and the context of discovery. In W. J. Baker, L. P. Mos, H. V. Rappard, & H. J. Stam (Eds.), *Recent trends in theoretical psychology* (pp. 59–64). New York: Springer-Verlag.

Salner, M. (1988). Epistemic beliefs and their developmental relationship to post-positivist psychology. In W. J. Baker, L. P. Mos, H. V. Rappard, & H. J. Stam (Eds.), *Recent trends in theoretical psychology* (pp. 65–76). New York: Springer-Verlag.

Sanday, P. R. (1983). The ethnographic paradigm. In J. Van Mannen (Ed.), *Qualitative methodology* (pp. 19–36). Beverly Hills, CA: Sage.

Sarason, S. B. (1981). *Psychology misdirected.* New York: The Free Press.

Sarbin, T. R. (1977). Contextualism: A world view for modern psychology. In A. W. Landfield (Ed.), *The 1976 Nebraska symposium on motivation* (pp. 1–42). Lincoln: University of Nebraska Press.

Sarbin, T. R. (1986). *Narrative psychology: The storied nature of human conduct.* New York: Praeger.

Schwartzman, J. (1984). Family theory and the scientific method. *Family Process, 23,* 223–236.

Shapere, D. (1984). *Reason and the search for knowledge.* Dordrecht, N. Holland: Reidel.

Simons, H. W. (1989). *Rhetoric in the human sciences.* Newbury Park, CA: Sage.

Spradley, J. P. (1979). *The ethnographic interview.* New York: Holt, Rinehart & Winston.

Stiles, W. B. (1993). Quality control in qualitative research. *Clinical Psychology Review, 13,* 593–618.

Strauss, A. (1987). *Qualitative analysis for social scientists.* Cambridge: Cambridge University Press.

Taggart, M. (1985). The feminist critique in epistemological perspective: Questions of context in family therapy. *Journal of Marital and Family Therapy, 11,* 113–126.

Tharp, R. G., & Gallimore, R. L. (1982). Inquiry process in program development. *Journal of Community Psychology, 10,* 103–118.

Toukmanian, S. G., & Rennie, D. L. (Eds.) (1992). *Psychotherapy process research: Paradigmatic and narrative approaches.* Newbury Park, CA: Sage.

Toulmin, S. (1972). *Human understanding: The collective use and evolution of concepts.* Princeton, NJ: Princeton University Press.

Van Maanen, J. (Ed.). (1983). *Qualitative methodology.* Beverly Hills, CA: Sage.

Yin, R. K. (1989). *Case study research: Design and methods* (2nd ed.). Newbury Park, CA: Sage.

CHAPTER 2

The Inquiry Process

LISA T. HOSHMAND AND JACK MARTIN

In Chapter 1, we defined method and its use in general terms. Here, we examine method in relation to the process of inquiry. Although the selection of method is critical at the initiation of a study, decisions about method are encountered throughout an investigation. The inquiry process, with many potential choice points, can be characterized partly as a series of judgments and decisions. These judgments and decisions constitute the functional logic in use. From a pragmatic standpoint, this functional logic is considered to be determined by the interaction between a problem context and the methods brought to bear on the problem. The problem context is in turn embedded in a larger professional and social context. Thus, we are interested in understanding the cognitive and social values as well as other contextual factors that inform the choices of researchers in the practice of inquiry. It is our belief that such information on research practice may help us eventually to construct criteria for progressive inquiry in our domain of study.

THE NATURE OF THE INQUIRY PROCESS

How the research process is conceived is partly a function of the paradigm of knowledge on which research models are based. Traditional experimental research is presumed to follow a more or less preplanned sequence, with a logical structure that corresponds to what we have come to know as the standard structure of the scientific report. Professional writing reinforces the uniformity of that structure in the reporting of research. The research questions, procedures, and units of analysis are predetermined, to be followed by results couched in the expected terms. This type of presentation, although somewhat modified for applied studies, continues to give the impression of a simple, linear progression in inquiry. The logical sequence implied is based on the formal reconstruction of the dominant research practice adopted by the scientific community. This idealized normative reconstruction tends to differ from the actual functional logic in use (Kaplan, 1964). In reference to psychological science, Skinner (1956) asserted that our scientific practice should not be equated with the formalized constructions of scientific method and statistics. Speaking of scientific training and what can be learned from the practicing scientist, in contrast to logicians and methodologists, he stated:

> He cannot refer the young psychologist to a book which tells him about how to find out all there is to know about a subject matter, how to have the good hunch which will lead him to devise a suitable piece of apparatus, how to develop an efficient experimental routine, how to abandon an unprofitable line of attack, how to move on rapidly to later stages of his research.... We must keep in mind that some very important parts of the scientific process do not now lend themselves to mathematical, logical, or any other formal treatment. (p. 221)

After referring to personal notes and records and reviewing his earlier publications, Skinner concluded from his own case that actual research practice is not the same as the reconstructions of formalized scientific method.

In practice, most research efforts probably involve processes more complex than the picture given in a scientific report that reflects the formal, normative logic of inquiry in the discipline. Field research conducted with alternative approaches, such as the ethnographic paradigm, follows a much more open-ended process than the planned experiment, with the possibility of emergent questions and the need to change a course of inquiry in the light of field realities (Hoshmand, 1989). It does not correspond as closely as the laboratory experiment to the normative logical structure in which most psychological researchers are trained. We conjecture that an alternative characterization of the research process may be more fitting for naturalistic or field research on practice.

The logic of inquiry, understood in a functional as opposed to a formal sense, depends critically on the purposes of the researcher. Different inquiry methods and processes are usually needed to achieve different goals. In the testing of a specific hypothesis in a narrowly defined context, an experimental paradigm that involves a relatively limited number of steps may be used. On the other hand, the discovery of new concepts for program development and the evaluation of overall program effects requires a continuous process of data monitoring in combination with focal testing (Tharp & Gallimore, 1982). This often involves a more differentiated sequence of decisions and inferences. Programmatic research of the type presented in this volume is also more likely than single studies to involve a series of methodological decisions.

Due to the common distinction between the context of discovery and the context of justification, the research process is held to be different for those who have theory-testing as a goal as opposed to those interested in the discovery of new formulations. In the former case, the rules of justification that govern the process of inquiry are relatively formalized, giving the impression of a more predictable process. In the latter, the rules of inquiry are functionally related to an emerging, yet to be known context that calls for activities that cannot be preplanned. Philosophers of science have generally conceded that it is easier to construct a logic of hypothesis-testing than to construct a logic of discovery (Gutting, 1980; Lakatos & Musgrave, 1970; Nickles, 1980). This is perhaps because the circumstances of discovery are more elusive and the cognitive processes involved are less amenable to formalization. This issue of discovery versus justification will be discussed further in Chapter 3.

The literature on creativity in science points to a number of interesting observations and conclusions (Kneller, 1967; Koestler, 1964). One view is that creativity involves divergent thinking and the ability to entertain multiple possibilities. Important discoveries are sometimes made without a research plan (Richter, 1953). Another view attributes discoveries to convergent and highly focused work. Klemm (1977) inferred from the biographies of successful researchers that inductive process, a long incubation period, and the recycling of the inquiry process to refine hypotheses contribute to major breakthroughs in biology. Citing another set of case studies, Mansfield and Busse (1981) concluded that successful scientists were engaged in certain common processes, including the selection of problems, extended efforts at problem solving, and setting constraints of an empirical, theoretical, or methodological nature. Of interest to our project is the finding that discoveries seem to occur when researchers change earlier constraints, and engage in programmatic efforts to verify and elaborate their methodology. How researchers are led to modify their conceptual and methodological constraints, and how they evolve a program of research from initial efforts, are instructive to other researchers.

The course of inquiry cannot be separated from the judgments and intentions of the person conducting the inquiry. In searching for rationality, many of us wonder if researchers always make reasoned choices and whether there is a higher order reasoning or meta-reasoning involved in the execution of an extended program of research. As readers of research articles published in professional journals, we are seldom able to see beyond the apparent reconstructed process to the inner workings of the researcher's mind. However, if we were to follow a collection of studies by the same researcher(s) in the same area of inquiry, we might be able to discern a pattern of thinking and questioning as well as a style of investigation. It is our hope that the stories told by programmatic researchers, along with documents of their work, will reveal to us their applied epistemology and any non-epistemic factors behind their actions.

In reflecting on his own career, Skinner (1956) applied a psychological view of the scientist's work, concluding that the scientist will find certain practices to be more appropriate than others as a function of his or her history. He further cautioned that until we have an adequate empirical understanding of the behavior of scientists, we should not try to fit all scientific practices into a single mode. Probably, no naturalized study of research, including our own attempt, can provide a complete understanding of the workings of science. Ziman (1978), a distinguished physicist and scientific administrator, stated:

> We cannot learn the art of research by reference to the formal philosophies, sociologies and psychologies of science. . . . We read our Popper and our Kuhn, our Merton and our Polanyi, not for rules and laws and formulae and proofs, but for maxims and insights and understanding. (p. 185)

Our own efforts are aimed at deriving insights and understanding, rather than at evolving meta-methodological principles that would become yet another set of rigid formalisms. The project is exploratory and the analysis intended to be tentative. The researchers' accounts presented in Part II of this book will be examined individually and collectively for insights into the basis of method choice. The results of our search for meta-reasoning in programmatic research will be presented in Part III. In this effort, the pragmatist conception of inquiry as problem solving provides a working framework for our analysis.

A Problem-Solving View of Method Choice and the Inquiry Process

Just as the research process is a function of the goals of investigation, the choice of methods is a function of the research problem to be addressed. A researcher's perceptions as to which particular aspects of a phenomenon are problematic or worthy of focus depend on his or her substantive knowledge and theoretical views. As schematized by Brinberg and McGrath (1985, p. 22), research involves an interaction of three domains or levels of concerns, the conceptual (ontological), the methodological (epistemic), and the substantive (empirical). All three domains are involved in determining the design of a study and the methods to be used. In addition, we have indicated that there are non-epistemic values and ideological issues that constitute a fourth level of concern. A given researcher's choice of approach may be informed by knowledge and interest in any of these domains or levels at which questions may be posed. Simultaneously, there may be constraints due to limited understanding and limiting assumptions about any of these domains. Too often, it is presumed that a researcher has sufficient understanding of the phenomenon in question to make initial choices of method that set the course of inquiry. In practice, this initial understanding may be limited by personal knowledge of the substantive domain. Practitioners who are experts in a substantive field, or researchers' own experience of therapeutic practice, can inform the choice of method in research on therapeutic practice. Having some sense of the nature of the problem from related research into the particular domain also can help an investigator select appropriate units of analysis and research strategies.

The ability of the researcher to adapt to the needs of a problem situation may be a matter of training and experience. A researcher who has learned to be flexible and open to modifying an existing program of research to suit a problem situation may be more likely to abort a line of inquiry, or to find new ways of approaching the situation when necessary. In practice, however, most researchers bring their theoretical world views and preferred research protocols into the situation of problem selection. Theory or conceptual frames with particular ontological suppositions, and methodological repertoire with related epistemological assumptions, contribute to the direction and course of inquiry by shaping the research questions posed. The power of the research question stems from its selective focus. It sets the figure against the ground of uncertainty. One may consider question framing as a skill in itself, initially directed by one's conceptual and paradigmatic preferences, and gradually informed by the benefits of experience. We learn from experience that research questions should be formulated in such a way as to illuminate the problem of interest or make it more amenable to intelligent study.

Basing method choices on the nature of the problem at hand implies an open attitude toward the presenting information while undertaking a continuous search. The researcher has to modify preconceptions and resist premature cessation of the search for the best possible way of formulating and investigating a problem. Research problems vary according to their history in the discipline or stage of development in a research program. Temporally, a given problem unfolds as the inquiry process evolves. This is demonstrated often in field research where the original conception of a problem becomes modified with increased understanding brought about by the initial findings. In therapeutic research as well, the human subject and the focal phenomenon may present qualitatively different problems than originally conceived. This calls for flexibility in the approach to inquiry.

The dynamic relationship between problem formulation and an open selection of methods is described by Brewer and Hunter (1989), drawing upon the ideas of Dewey.

> As research into a problem proceeds, with researchers posing it in different ways, the problem ideally (as Dewey implied) unfolds to reveal new dimensions that facilitate the problem's solution. The variety of available research methods is a key element in this process in that it provides researchers with a multifaceted empirical view of the phenomena and the theories in question. This enables researchers to formulate problems in a manner that does greater justice both to the complexity of social phenomena and to the complex implications of our theories. (p. 65)

In that problems of practice constitute the context of inquiry for applied researchers, the choice of conceptual and methodological tools should be guided by consideration of the complexities of these problems (as will be discussed in the next chapter). Such consideration may require a broad range of methods, including methods not normally preferred. A knowledge of diverse research paradigms is needed for a problem-based orientation to method choice.

In the case of programmatic research in the areas of practice, the problem at hand changes as inquiry continues. In other words, the requirements of the research task vary as a function of where one is in the inquiry process. It is generally believed that discovery calls for more inductive and descriptive methods of data gathering, whereas justification calls for focal testing and controlled experimentation. This could be an oversimplification as far as being a guideline for method choice. Brewer and Hunter (1989) cautioned that research is not so orderly and unidirectional that only certain methods are best suited for a certain phase. They noted, for instance, that the combined use of field research and survey methods can be appropriate in both the exploratory and verification phases of a study (Seiber, 1973). It may also be misleading to classify an entire study as either generative or verificational in that these two contexts of inquiry may be interchangeable at any given point of an integrated research process. As a researcher moves from a generative to a verification context, there is a shift in problem formulation. New methods introduced to meet the requirements of the modified nature of research tasks may not be appropriate to the original theory or substantive question. An integrative process of inquiry would entail redefining the conceptual and methodological requirements as the problem at hand is reformulated. Being able to move flexibly between different strategies of task identification enables a researcher to keep alive a program of research.

In many instances, a program of research may have reached a point of verification of some of its elements, yet the results of verification tests can reveal anomalies that require a return to exploratory methods. At this juncture, it behooves the researcher to adopt a more descriptive and discovery-oriented strategy in order to redefine and reconceptualize the phenomenon. Such work often leads to a reformulation of the original research question(s) or the generation of new questions. In this way, a contribution is made to inquiry into the domain of interest. Strong (1991) gave a condensed account of his decisions on method in researching the interpersonal dynamics of counseling, using an evolving conceptual framework of social influence. In this case, results that could not be accommodated by the conceptual model in use led to the search for new methods and the testing of new hypotheses.

The foregoing conception of the relationship between method choice and inquiry process leads us to the conclusion that pluralistic use of methods is preferable to monolithic choices of method in programmatic research. Methodological pluralism has the merit of increasing the scope of research questions and preventing premature closure to the investigative process. It also allows the investigator to respond flexibly to the research task at hand. Reciprocally, the application of pluralistic methods can change the course of inquiry and open the investigation to a broader range of possibilities.

Although the problem-solving view of research can be captured by the interaction among the conceptual, the methodological, and the substantive, as mentioned earlier, it is important to distinguish further between substantive problems (which are addressed by theoretical and empirical research questions) and epistemic problems (which represent second-order or meta-level questions about justification of the inquiry methods and methodology used). As we try to understand the inquiry process in terms of the problem tasks encountered by researchers, we encourage the reader to keep these two levels of problem solving in mind. At one level, we will analyze how conceptual and methodological means are used by researchers to solve substantive problems, based on their particular ontological beliefs and epistemological or ideological commitments. At another level, we will consider how researchers seem to deal with epistemic problems of verifying their findings and justifying their approach. We make no presumption, however, as to the level of problem solving involved or the type of yield intended. The utility of this heuristic frame of analysis will be determined by our application of a broadly defined problem-solving view to the researchers' work.

The Researcher's Role in the Inquiry Process

In the previous chapter, we put forth the hypothesis that personal ideology and world views are part of the basis for method choice. There are other aspects of the researcher's makeup that enter into the research process. Personal and professional goals and one's sources of self-esteem may be related to the project undertaken or the manner in which it is conducted. The researcher's professional maturity and development over the period of inquiry are intertwined with the types of method choices made. We want to emphasize that in research on therapeutic practice, knowledge of the substantive domain as a function of personal experience with such practice probably is a major determinant of the perspective brought to the study.

Variables selected for focus by a researcher reflect patterns of understanding derived from practice as much as theoretical knowledge from one's academic training. Similarly, prior experience as a researcher in the field setting should prepare an investigator for the types of problems and obstacles encountered in a new project. Campbell (1974) acknowledged the place of qualitative knowing in action research. Tharp and Gallimore (1982) reported that in long-term program development and evaluation, the personal knowing of the researcher plays a central role in the identification of program elements, choice of methodologies, and decisions about the direction and course of inquiry. This personal knowing comes from immersion in the field and the experience of practicing inquiry. There is therefore a developing aspect to investigation, at the level of both the researcher and the research itself. The development of a researcher probably parallels the progression of inquiry. We would speculate that becoming a programmatic researcher involves this kind of maturing process. Hill's (1984) account of her development as a researcher of counseling process illustrates the personal insights that come with experience. The learning undergone by our group of researchers of therapeutic practice will be examined further in subsequent chapters.

Our search for answers to the question of what constitutes pragmatically sound method choices leads us to examine the logic in use or the applied epistemologies of researchers of practice. Part of the answer will become available as we gain an understanding of how the reasoning of programmatic researchers is informed by experience. We postulate that epistemic styles associated with sound method choices are open to revision and adaptive to the changing problem contexts of practice. Through learning to learn from the pragmatic consequences of selection and adaptation (Campbell, 1977; Toulmin, 1972), the researcher's epistemic strategies and skills evolve and become integrated as a form of personal knowledge. At its best, this personal knowing may serve as a kind of guiding wisdom, informed by values that are not only pragmatically sound but socially appropriate and progressive.

As acknowledged in Chapter 1, there are limits to human judgment such that even scientific rationality is a limited rationality. We are prepared to consider each researcher's account of inquiry as a human story of intricate intentions and interactions in particular social and historical locations. We further believe that progress is defined and evaluated in relation to the collective intentions and actions of any group of researchers and the professional community to which they belong.

Criteria for Progressive Inquiry

The question of how we should conceptualize progress in a human science of therapeutic practice is a complex one. Historical definitions of scientific progress have varied from the gestalt models of Hanson and Kuhn to the evolutionary models of Popper and Toulmin (Richards, 1981). Among the various ideas about scientific progress, Laudan's (1977) is representative of the pragmatist framework we wish to adopt. Laudan defined progress in terms of the problem-solving effectiveness of science. Scientific rationality consists in making choices that will maximize progress or the contribution of science to solving important problems. From our standpoint of evaluating method choice in research on psychological practice, those choices that increase the possibility of researchers solving problems and producing more informative accounts of phenomena relevant to a human science of practice can be considered "progressive."

Cronbach (1986) stated that progress in social and psychological inquiry is measured not so much by the cumulation of answers to fixed questions, but by an increased repertoire of questions. The creation of new meanings and processes constitutes progress in the sense of keeping alive an ongoing quest for potential knowledge. New meanings that set new directions for communal investigation are a contribution to research productivity. If we can demonstrate greater sophistication in the methodology and analytical processes we use during the course of continued inquiry, that too may constitute a type of progress. Within this kind of conceptual scheme, initial efforts at generating research questions and tentative hypotheses are just as important as the refinement of theoretical models and the testing of particular concepts in relation to evolving models. For discussion purposes, we will therefore distinguish between process-related criteria and outcome-related criteria for progressiveness.

If process criteria are important in the appraisal of progress, we must evaluate research programs not solely by the potential benefits to practice of their yield. Such process criteria as flexibility in problem solving and fruitfulness of questions in continuing inquiry should be used. Although progressiveness in terms of outcome or long-term yield will be reflected upon in Part III of this book, our study of method choice is aimed largely at determining what types of method choices we can regard as progressive in a process sense. In answering this question, we will evaluate the actions of the researchers who are responsible for the accounts given in Part II, by the extent to which their practice has shown the benefit of experience. We will also consider their own perceptions of progress.

As we have defined methods in terms of both conceptual and procedural tools, the relationship between method and theory (as defined in ordinary usage) has implications for the progressive use of methods. This relationship has been emphasized in the conception of validity in research. Wampold, Davis, and Good (1990) introduced the term *hypothesis validity* to refer to how well hypotheses are formulated to meaningfully test an aspect of theory. Thus, method choice is to be evaluated in relation to an investigator's rendering of theoretical understanding as much as in relation to the methodological approach for clarifying such understanding. This type of consideration may distinguish meaningful theory-guided research from hypothesis-testing that fails to contribute to the advancement of knowledge (McKay, 1988). In other words, our process criteria of whether new meanings and processes are generated are to be qualified by judgments of their contribution to good theoretical sense in current understanding.

The pragmatist framework is essential not only in providing us with a definition of progress, but in bringing some clarity to the current discourse about method choice and paradigms of knowledge. A central question for the profession concerns what kinds of paradigm and method choices are likely to contribute to progress in our human science of practice. Methodological pluralism, in contrast to isolationism that is associated with a universalistic position on the choice of method, may facilitate our movement toward progress. At the same time, we are aware that a divergent pluralism based on extreme relativism may not resolve paradigm clashes or reduce researchers' confusion about the appropriate criteria for adjudicating the work of their peers. As stated in Chapter 1, the presence of multiple paradigms and broadened choices has meant that there are multiple, seemingly incompatible criteria for warrants. Methodological pluralism needs to be guided by meta-level reasoning and cer-

The Inquiry Process

FIGURE 2.1 **Paradigmatic Positions, Method Choice, and Knowledge Criteria**

Paradigmatic Position	Basis & Nature of Method Choice	Criteria
Positivist--Single Dominant Paradigm	Technological Interest--Universal Method	Universal System of Justification (Formal Rules and Formal Logic)
Relativist--Multiple Paradigms	Diverse Knowledge Interests--Pluralistic Methods	Divergent Criteria for Warrants and Value Judgments
Pragmatist--Cross-Paradigm Methodology	Common Pragmatic Purpose--Pluralism Guided by Meta-reasoning	Superordinate Heuristic Criteria (Functional Rules and Logic in Use) Informed by Cognitive and Social Values

tain kinds of superordinate criteria in order for us to overcome the difficulties arising from a divergent pluralism. We believe that a pragmatist perspective can be of help in this regard.

Figure 2.1 illustrates how a pragmatist position differs from a universalistic or relativistic position with respect to method choice. By grounding the criteria for the evaluation of knowledge activities in their heuristic value and problem-solving effectiveness, the pragmatist view links method choice to problem context and the unique nature of a given domain of inquiry. Both cognitive and social values are probably involved in judging the selection of problems and the methods for problem solving. This meta-reasoning, as we indicated earlier, is selective and contrary to a non-discriminant stance of methodological anarchism.

We also indicated in Chapter 1 that we would apply the concept of scientific research programs (Lakatos & Musgrave, 1970) in viewing the work of researchers in the psychological science of therapeutic practice. It is probably overly ambitious for us to assume that the conceptual and research systems of our profession are ready for consideration as scientific research programs in the same way that certain physical sciences have been studied by historians of science. As a way of conceptualizing the progressiveness of scientific work, the notion of progressive research programs is used mainly to account for the rational status of a scientific discipline. Its merit consists in moving the evaluation of progress from the testing of single theories and ideas to considering the growth of larger systems of conceptually related research activities. It appears to us that the research activities of our field, being a conglomerate of more tentative and loosely connected theorizing and research, require this larger unit of analysis. Even if our substantive achievements are modest, programmatic research can be a guiding metaphor.

In practice, because method choices are embedded in the ongoing activities of a given program of research, their evaluation must be made within the context of the research program and its embedding factors, including the history of inquiry into the problem by the discipline and its community of researchers. Theories and hypotheses that have been developed within pluralistic programs of research grounded in systematic study of focal phenomena in context are more likely to be fruitful than those theories and hypotheses borrowed from other fields of study and sanctified through rigid paradigmatic preferences. This prediction, however, is open to empirical verification over time.

Our criteria for progressive method choices need to be linked to current understandings about validity of inquiry in the domain of interest. Research on therapeutic practice has certain unique problems and challenges, as will be discussed in Chapter 3. The validity issue, which should be part of any rational consideration of progress, has different meanings as a function of the nature of the research undertaken and the stage of inquiry. Earlier, we referred to the distinction made by Brinberg and McGrath (1985) among research that originates primarily from the conceptual, methodological, or substantive/empirical domain. They proposed different criteria for evaluating method choices, depending on the domain from which the research path originates. We have added the axiological domain to this conceptual scheme. As illustrated in Figure 2.2, a research path may begin with an empirical, ontological, epistemological, or axiological issue, and take the researcher into encounters with any level of questions associated with any of the domains or combination of domains.

According to Brinberg and McGrath (1985), for the substantive (empirical) domain, cost–benefit, system effectiveness, and feasibility may be appropriate standards for evaluation. For the conceptual (ontological) domain, such criteria as parsimony, internal consistency, and testability may be applied to the research methods and the results they yield. For the methodological (epistemological) domain, efficiency, power, explicitness,

FIGURE 2.2 Research Domains, Questions, and Research Paths

Domains	Level of Questions	Research Paths
A. Substantive	Empirical	A to B and/or C and/or D and return to any level or combination
B. Ontological	Conceptual	B to A and/or C and/or D and return to any level or combination
C. Epistemological	Methodological	C to A and/or B and/or D and return to any level or combination
D. Axiological	Ethical / Ideological	D to A and/or B and/or C and return to any level or combination

and reproducibility may be used as criteria. These authors did not address the nature of the axiological domain where ethical/ideological questions may arise, nor did they propose standards by which we could make judgments in relation to this domain. (These topics will be considered briefly in Chapter 3.)

In this proposed scheme, process criteria also vary by stage of inquiry. Initially, value or worth constitutes the criterion for selecting the elements and relations to be studied. Such initial judgment of value usually has to do with perceived importance, meaningfulness, or usefulness. In mid-stage, degree of fit between relations among elements from the different domains yields correspondence validity. The concern is with how well complementary networks of relations from two domains mesh with one another to build a structure that results in information gain. In later stages, generalization validities become more relevant. Here, robustness as a criterion entails replicability (between time periods, researchers, and sites), ecological validity (by convergence or triangulation of different methods, models, and occasions), as well as differentiation (by boundary search for the limits of the findings). We expect progressive method choices to be in harmony with such standards of inquiry as stipulated for the type of activity and stage of inquiry under consideration. In fact, they should be generally facilitative of the attainment of such standards.

There are different opinions on the type of yield that we should expect from research on practice. This issue, which bears on the question of progress, also will be discussed in Chapter 3. Our personal interest in the question of progress in a human science of practice goes beyond a process conception based on progressive method choices. The ultimate worth of a research program should be judged not only by its impact on the discipline and its knowledge enterprise, but on the actions that ensue and their social implications. We have to move from process criteria for scientific rationality to criteria for evaluating the consequences and social value of scientific activities.

Before moving into the domain of research in therapeutic practice, we wish to explain how the contributing researchers were instructed to write the accounts presented in Part II of this book and the approach we subsequently used in reading these accounts. This includes how we planned to analyze method choice and applied epistemology in the light of the researchers' apparent goals and intentions, as well as some of the criteria discussed in these first two chapters.

RECONSTRUCTING THE INQUIRY PROCESS

It is beyond the scope of this volume to try to identify and characterize those exemplary research programs in the entire field of therapeutic practice that may be most appropriately assigned the status of progressive research programs. All we could do is to study, on a more modest scale, a few cases of programmatic research and analyze the method choices made by the researchers involved for their contribution to the process of continuing inquiry. By programs of research, we mean sustained series of research studies that span several years and are associated with one or more active researchers. Selecting programs that meet these criteria helps ensure that the researchers involved will have experienced both successes and failures in their research efforts and probably will have reflected on the purposes, methods, and dilemmas associated with their work. We are especially interested in these researchers' experimentation with a variety of theoretical frameworks, inquiry methods, and epistemic principles during the course of their programmatic efforts.

By selecting a diverse set of such programs of research as cases within which to investigate the applied epistemologies (especially method choices and criteria of perceived progress) of these researchers, we hope that it will be possible to develop an understanding of the characteristics and conditions of pragmatically sound inquiry practices. The advantages of a case study approach consist in its versatility, depth, and contextual richness (Yin, 1989). In addition to empirical and theoretical papers written by the researchers themselves and by others that focus on the programs of research being studied, we have asked the contributing authors to attempt to examine such materials as project notes and files, pilot data, letters and communications with other scholars, and retrospectively to attempt to describe their own experiences within, and reactions to, their work as it has developed.

Whether one can "successfully" reconstruct an inquiry process has been questioned by sociologists of science in the post-Kuhnian era. There is no agreement on the criteria for evaluating reconstructed accounts or meta-analysis of such accounts. In our opinion, Latour (1980) and Woolgar (1988) have identified the most central issue in the social construction of science, namely, reflexivity. The written accounts have to be referred back to the researchers and their personal history and orientation to knowledge. Our analysis of their accounts must also be reflexive. A double reflexivity is involved, with researchers reflecting on their construction of their own work, and us reflecting on our understanding and analysis of their accounts. Sociologists have been criticized for being constructionist with respect to the work of scientists, while being realist in regard to their own interpretations. We stated at the outset that we would use constructionist lenses, constrained by a pragmatic form of critical realism. In social constructionist terms, the written accounts by the researchers are constitutive of their reality. These accounts represent historical reality to the extent that they are anchored in records of the researchers' work and verifiable events (such as interaction with colleagues). From a pragmatic standpoint, what the researchers have learned from their research practice is highly important. The present schemata they hold of their programmatic efforts are likely to be applied to continuing inquiry.

Our selected group of researchers had access to the first chapter of this book in its original draft form. The second and third chapters were written by us independently and preceded the submission of their accounts. The contributing authors were instructed to focus on their method choice in relation to the process of their inquiry and on the issues and problems they encountered in the course of their research. They were encouraged to write in a reflective, personal voice, with a teaching purpose in mind. We also asked these researchers to comment briefly on their criteria of progressiveness as they reviewed their own program of research.

The approach we used in the analysis of the accounts consisted of a combination of hermeneutic and propositional-analytical methods. Prior to reading a researcher's account, each of us wrote down our preunderstandings and preconceptions, any prior knowledge or opinions of the researcher's epistemological stance, and other relational and contextual factors deemed relevant to the project. Each account was first read in an open manner, followed by a holistic reading for voice, developmental themes, unifying purpose, and so forth. We looked for critical incidents and choice points, and attempted to discern their meanings as well as instrumental implications. Analytical questions posed to the text included the following:

- What was the nature of the described methodology? What were the apparent considerations in method choice? How did problem selection and the research task interact with the concepts and strategies used? How did the researcher attempt to address issues of validity?
- What were the circumstances of changes in method? What seemed to have been the consequences of method change? Were there new questions or inquiry processes following such changes?
- In what sense is the described research programmatic? What are the researcher's criteria for evaluating his or her progress? Is the described research progressive?
- What does the account reveal about the inquiry process and the problems of research in therapeutic practice? What has the researcher learned from his or her own research practice? How is this personal knowledge being applied to problem solving?
- Does the account fit with a heuristic interpretation? Are there discrepancies? What may be some alternative interpretations of the account?

Each researcher's account was read independently by us, and detailed notes were kept on our reactions, interpretations, and analyses. We then compared notes and discussed our respective impressions. A second set of notes was generated by each of us as meta-commentary on the first set of notes. Individual cases were analyzed in their own right as prototypes of particular research courses and personal epistemic commitments. Cross-case comparisons were made, in an attempt to discern common themes. Conclusions were arrived at through dialogue between us, but grounded as much as possible in the accounts and their supporting information.

We had a choice of entering into an active dialogue with each researcher during the process of their writing. We elected, however, not to unduly influence their own constructions of their research programs and inquiry processes. Editorial feedback on the initial drafts of the contributed chapters was limited to clarifying questions and stylistic suggestions. The amount of subsequent interaction with the contributing authors concerning their account was largely left to their initiative. We felt that our social contract with these colleagues did not entail an invitation for us to engage in what might have been experienced as excessive personal probing. After the final submission of their chapters, contributing authors were given an opportunity to read our analysis of their accounts as presented in Part III of this book, and to add a postscript, giving their reactions to our interpretations. We believe that each researcher should have the last word on his or her own experience, having courageously revealed personal struggles and dilemmas encountered in the pursuit of greater knowledge about therapeutic practice.

The present work involves several projects being analyzed within our larger project, and a meta-narrative being constructed from the various accounts given by the contributing researchers. We have to keep in mind the personal intentions and purposes embedded in these various narratives, and the fact that our judgments and values interact in socially and culturally designed ways to derive the kinds of understanding that we hope to provide. As co-editors and co-participants, we have tried to examine our own ontological, epistemological, and axiological stances in order to have a reflexive approach to this project. Both of us have been schooled in the prevalent methodologies of psychology and socialized in the scientist-practitioner era of our profession. One of us has a record of research activities founded on the hypothetico-deductive experimental paradigm and has been committed to theory-testing largely under a critical realist view. The other has taught and written about alternative research methods and has been supportive of qualitative modes of inquiry under a constructionist perspective. Although we are both interested in using a combination of pragmatist and constructionist ideas, qualified by a critical realism, it has taken considerable discussion to articulate our areas of differences and consensus. We have tried to deconstruct our own interpretations, identifying the underlying assumptions and values in our respective notes and studying the meta-commentary generated on these notes. It appears that we have each made shifts in our understanding, partly as a result of learning from the process of collaboration. Some of our reflections on our own biases and uncertainties will be shared in Part III as we discuss our analysis of the researchers' work.

The next chapter will set the stage for the presentation of researcher accounts, by providing an overview and discussion of problems and issues in research on psychological practice.

REFERENCES

Brewer, J., & Hunter, A. (1989). *Multimethod research: A synthesis of styles.* Newbury Park, CA: Sage.

Brinberg, D., & McGrath, J. E. (1985). *Validity and the research process.* Newbury Park, CA: Sage.

Campbell, D. T. (1974, September). *Qualitative knowing in action research.* Kurt Lewin Award Address, Society for the Psychological Study of Social Issues. Presented at the 82nd annual meeting of the American Psychological Association, New Orleans.

Campbell, D. T. (1977). Discussion comment on "The natural selection model of conceptual evolution." *Philosophy of Science, 44,* 502–507.

Cronbach, L. J. (1986). Social inquiry by and for earthlings. In D. W. Fiske & R. A. Shweder (Eds.), *Metatheory in social science* (pp. 83–107). Chicago: University of Chicago Press.

Gutting, G. (Ed.). (1980). *Paradigms and revolutions: Appraisals and applications of Thomas Kuhn's philosophy of science.* Notre Dame, IN: University of Notre Dame Press.

Hill, C. E. (1984). A personal account of the process of becoming a counseling process researcher. *The Counseling Psychologist, 12,* 99–109.

Hoshmand, L. T. (1989). Alternate research paradigms: A review and teaching proposal. *The Counseling Psychologist, 17,* 3–79.

Kaplan, A. (1964). *The conduct of inquiry: Methodology for behavioral science.* New York: Harper & Row.

Klemm, W. R. (Ed.). (1977). *Discovery processes in modern biology.* Huntington, NY: Krieger.

Kneller, G. F. (1967). *The art and science of creativity.* New York: Holt, Rinehart & Winston.

Koestler, A. (1964). *The act of creation.* New York: Macmillan.

Lakatos, I., & Musgrave, A. (Eds.). (1970). *Criticism and the growth of knowledge.* Cambridge: Cambridge University Press.

Latour, B. (1980). Is it possible to reconstruct the research process? Sociology of a brain peptide. In K. D. Knorr, R. Krohn, & R. Whitley (Eds.), *The social process of scientific investigation, Sociology of the Sciences Yearbook* (Vol. 4, pp. 53–73). Dordrecht, N. Holland: D. Reidel.

Laudan, L. (1977). *Progress and its problems: Toward a theory of scientific growth.* Berkeley: University of California Press.

Mansfield, R. S., & Busse, T. V. (1981). *The psychology of creativity and discovery.* Chicago: Nelson-Hall.

McKay, D. G. (1988). Under what conditions can theoretical psychology survive and prosper? Integrating the rational and empirical epistemologies. *Psychological Review, 95,* 559–565.

Nickles, T. (Ed.). (1980). *Scientific discovery, logic, and rationality.* London: D. Reidel.

Richards, R. J. (1981). Natural selection and other models in the historiography of science. In M. B. Brewer & B. E. Collins (Eds.), *Scientific inquiry and the social sciences* (pp. 37–76). San Francisco: Jossey-Bass.

Richter, C. P. (1953). Free research versus design research. *Science, 118,* 91–93.

Seiber, S. D. (1973). Integrating field work and survey methods. *American Journal of Sociology, 78,* 135–139.

Skinner, B. F. (1956). A case history in scientific method. *American Psychologist, 5,* 221–233.
Strong, S. R. (1991). Theory-driven science and naive empiricism in counseling psychology. *Journal of Counseling Psychology, 38,* 204–210.
Tharp, R. G., & Gallimore, R. L. (1982). Inquiry process in program development. *Journal of Community Psychology, 10,* 103–118.
Toulmin, S. (1972). *Human understanding: The collective use and evolution of concepts.* Princeton, NJ: Princeton University Press.
Wampold, B. E., Davis, B., & Good, R. H. (1990). Hypothesis validity of clinical research. *Journal of Consulting and Clinical Psychology, 58,* 360–367.
Woolgar, S. (Ed.). (1988). *Knowledge and reflexivity: New frontiers in the sociology of knowledge.* Newbury Park, CA: Sage.
Yin, R. K. (1989). *Case study research: Design and methods* (2nd ed.). Newbury Park, CA: Sage.
Ziman, J. (1978). *Reliable knowledge: An exploration of the grounds for belief in science.* Cambridge, UK: Cambridge University Press.

Chapter 3

Research on Psychological Practice

JACK MARTIN AND LISA T. HOSHMAND

In this chapter, the challenges of research on psychological practice will be examined, particularly in relation to therapeutic practice. Some of these problems are discussed frequently in the scholarly literature in applied psychology. Others are discussed frequently in the professional literature related to therapeutic practice. All of these problems relate to the diversity of purposes of researchers and the decisions they must make about how best to study those focal phenomena they hope to understand, and perhaps explain. These problems are separate from, yet highly interactive with, specific, substantive research questions. For example, psychotherapy researchers might share a substantive focus on clients' affective reactions to particular kinds of therapeutic interventions, yet make very different decisions with respect to methodology because of the assumptive frameworks they adopt in studying such client reactions. Later in this chapter this discussion of problems faced by researchers of psychological and other human practices will give way to a reconsideration of some basic ontological and epistemological issues endemic to research on therapeutic practices. This is followed by a brief acknowledgment of ethical issues and axiological/ideological matters. We conclude by reaffirming our belief in the utility of a pragmatist framework for addressing the problems of research on practice at the level of method choice, with a more open conception of the inquiry process than has been apparent in the published research literature in psychotherapy.

FREQUENTLY DEBATED ISSUES IN RESEARCH ON PSYCHOLOGICAL PRACTICE

Problems of research on psychological practice that are discussed frequently in the professional literature tend to revolve around debates about seemingly irreconcilable or oppositional positions. Chief among these are disputations about (1) the scientific rigor versus the practical relevance of research on practice, (2) the use of discovery versus verification strategies in research on practice, (3) underlying assumptions about deterministic versus agential conceptions of humans, their actions, and their psychological states, (4) the use of reductionistic versus holistic units of analysis in both theoretical and empirical work directed at understanding psychological practice and its effects, and (5) assumptions concerning the type of yield to be expected from research on practice: instrumental-prescriptive versus conceptual-informative. A brief consideration of each of these controversies highlights the currently fragmented character of psychological research on psychological practice.

Rigor Versus Relevance

There is a sense in which the very idea of research on psychological practice is recent in the history of psychology. The standard assumption that seems to have dominated that history (cf. Danziger, 1990) has not promoted research on psychological practice. Rather, primary attention has been given to work in determining (under tightly controlled, rigorous laboratory conditions) basic principles and mechanisms of human thought, behavior, and experience. It is assumed that knowledge of these principles and mechanisms can be used by psychological practitioners to affect and change the behaviors and experiences of individuals with whom they work in therapeutic, educational, and other applied settings. As many have argued (e.g., Hoshmand & Polkinghorne, 1992; Howard, 1985a), an important consequence of this assumption has been that practitioners (and studies of practitioners' activities) have been assigned a secondary role in the psychological research enterprise. Reliance has been placed on what research psychologists have considered to be the formal procedures of science as a means of securing accurate psychological knowledge that will be of direct use to psychological practitioners. In short, research removed from practice, but presumed to be scientifically rigorous, has attempted to inform practice. During the past 3 decades of psychology's 115 year history, there have been numerous calls from research psychologists to increase the relevance of psychological research to practice by moving it from isolated laboratory settings into actual practice contexts (e.g., Neisser, 1978; Wexler & Rice, 1974). Nonetheless, practitioners still perceive research on practice to be largely irrelevant and peripheral to their work (cf. Howard, 1985a).

In traditional psychological research, rigor is derived from the procedural achievement of adequate experimental control, while relevance refers to the generalizability of research findings to ecologically valid, natural settings. The question of rigor versus relevance has been formulated primarily as a sort of trade-off between the internal validity of research and its external validity. Internal validity most frequently is achieved through experimental control, such that it is possible to assign experimental effects of interest to specific levels of experimentally manipulated factors with some known degree of confidence. External validity most frequently is achieved by selecting experimental tasks, instructions, contexts, and participants to represent adequately the events, actions, contexts, and individuals to which generalizations are made. Ideal external validity might be obtained through the "non-interfering" study of naturally occurring events of interest, thus rendering generalization from "laboratory to field" unnecessary. (Of course, generalization to other and future, naturally occurring events of interest still would require the building of "inferential bridges"—cf. Cornfield & Tukey, 1956.) However, experimental control, and therefore internal validity, would seem to be compromised under this option. On the other hand, a reversed scenario of idealized experimental control and internal validity will be at the expense of "laboratory to field" generalizability and external validity. Consequently, the conduct of psychological research seems to necessitate a constant balance between competing desires for high levels of both internal and external validity, whereby any increment in one necessitates a decrement in the other.

The traditional approach to optimizing external and internal validity within psychology has been to emphasize internal validity. It has been assumed in this approach that the underlying, basic laws of cognition, perception, behavior, and so forth that are generated from such research will survive the journey from the laboratory to relevant practice settings (see Banaji & Crowder, 1989, for a contemporary rendering of this rationale). Opponents of this traditional strategy are becoming increasingly numerous and vocal. They argue that traditionalists' claims of progressive knowledge accumulation under this strategy apply only to contrived laboratory contexts that can reveal little about highly contextualized psychological phenomena of practical interest. A humorous example of this mounting concern is Neisser's (1978) description of the practical yield from decades of psychological laboratory research on perception and memory, as enabling individuals to read better during flashes of lightning in thunderstorms.

Frequently associated with debates over rigor versus relevance, whether or not cast as internal versus external validity, are related controversies concerning paradigms of inquiry (e.g., hypothetico-deductive approaches aimed at establishing causal relationships among variables of interest versus hermeneutic studies aimed at a more holistic understanding of focal phenomena), appropriate methodologies (e.g., quantitative versus qualitative methods), and "vantage point" (e.g., extraspective accounts of researchers versus introspective accounts of those actually participating in the psychological practices being studied). As discussed later in this chapter, the very nature of psychological phenomena may require greater emphasis on external validity; interpretive, qualitative methodologies; and phenomenological, introspective accounts than typically has been required to achieve progress in the physical, natural sciences (cf. Rennie & Toukmanian, 1992). Nonetheless, few psychologists, whatever their paradigmatic preferences, would deny the overall desirability of research that could demonstrate high levels of both scientific rigor and practical relevance.

It has been difficult to optimize both, under a prevalent positivistic, empiricist approach to psychological research that seems to require sacrificing one in favor of safeguarding the other. The inability of psychological scholars to make a decisive Alexandrian cut through this particular Gordian Knot, has led some noted psychologists, who actually were instrumental in framing psychology's traditional approach to questions of external and internal validity, to propose a new perspective on such questions (e.g., compare Cronbach, 1984, 1988, with Cronbach & Meehl, 1955; also see Messick, 1989). Under such proposals, traditional conceptualizations of validation (internal versus external validity of empirical studies, as well as other forms such as the content, predictive, concurrent, and construct validity of measures of psychological phenomenon) have been retooled to place issues of meaning and interpretation at the heart of the entire validation process. In so doing, these more recent proposals emphasize the need to become conceptually clear about the nature of the objects of psychological inquiry (human actions and experiences) and the extent to which our methods of study adequately explicate these focal phenomena. With respect to research for psychological practice, the primary message is that such research should be both rigorous and relevant. This ideal depends largely on the extent to which researchers succeed in studying those phenomena that occur in specific practical settings in ways that permit convincing interpretations of the results obtained. Under this formulation, what traditionally has been referred to as external or ecological validity becomes a necessary prerequisite, but not a sufficient condition, for internal validity. Rigor is impossible without relevance.

Related to the various matters we have discussed in connection with the frequently perceived tension between rigor and relevance is the complex issue of idiographic versus nomothetic approaches to the study of human psychology. Science, especially physical science, has been concerned primarily with generalities (i.e., covering laws expressed in terms of deductive-nomological models of explanation). However, in psychology, rigorous adoption of the old adage, *scientia non est individuorum* (science does not deal with individual cases), risks the creation of an aggregate psychology that reflects the actions and experiences of no single individual. Historically, many idiographically minded psychologists (e.g., Allport, 1962; James, 1907) have taken their cue from the European romantic tradition of Verstehen (understanding). This romantic tradition, especially popular in nineteenth-century Germany, represented a swing away from classical attachments to objectivity, materialism, and mechanism in the social sciences toward greater subjectivity, vitalism, and intuitionism. A central claim was that the social sciences were distinct from the natural sciences and that the former demanded methods of Verstehen. As Dilthey (1937/1989) argued, we explain nature, but we understand human beings. In this view, the rigor of traditional physical science must give way to an emphasis on establishing meaning and understanding at the level of individual experience. Whether or not such an idiographic approach can be scientific is much debated and obviously depends a great deal on one's conception of science, especially human science.

It is of particular interest to see the ways in which many contemporary researchers of psychotherapeutic practice, such as featured in Part II of this book, have attempted to balance the demands for general rigor and individual relevance in their programs of research. We encourage readers to make their own judgments as they read carefully the researchers' own accounts in the next part of this book.

Verification Versus Discovery

A second distinction, much discussed by researchers of psychological practice, is between research that aims to discover appropriate descriptions and conceptualizations of focal phenomena, and research that aims to verify or test theories based on such descriptions and conceptualizations. Since Reichenbach's (1938) distinction between the context of discovery and the context of justification (verification and falsification), it has been assumed by many that issues of knowledge generation and issues of knowledge testing should be separated. Consequently, many programmatic researchers of psychological practice have developed pluralistic research strategies that have advocated distinct, temporally sequenced phases of inquiry. Under this view, initial phases of empirical work employ methods appropriate to discovering and understanding more about the practice contexts and events of interest. Later phases of empirical work employ methods more appropriate to testing the theoretical models developed in the earlier phases (see Greenberg, 1986, for a contemporary rendering of such a "discovery to verification" strategy in research on psychotherapy).

However, both the possibility and desirability of maintaining the distinction between discovery and verification in psychological research have been questioned. As explained in Chapter 1, one problem with the traditional formulation of this distinction is the assumption that the context of discovery does not involve important methodological decisions and reasoning to the same extent as the context of justification. Gutting (1980) argued that it is a mistake to distinguish discovery from justification on this basis because the modes of cognitive activity involved in knowledge generation include those of evaluation and judgments about validity. Nickles (1980) also stressed the importance of processes of evaluation and decision making (about what line of inquiry to pursue, and so forth) in the process of discovery. Both argued against a simplistic distinction between discovery and verification. It is proposed that any formalized research strategy that separates them into tightly compartmentalized stages does not describe the manner in which programmatic researchers actually go about their work.

If psychological research is understood as a form of human problem solving, the research process must be adapted to the problem context. As researchers study contexts of interest, greater understanding of these contexts emerges, understanding that permits fuller descriptions and better articulated theories. As theories emerge and are tested, more is discovered about the problem context. Thus, the course of inquiry is shaped continuously by the perceptions and judgments that researchers develop as they go about their work in relevant problem contexts. It may be that the forms of judgment entailed do not consist of the rigid application of rules, but are themselves informed by experience gained as the research program is conducted. Wartofsky (1980) indicated that scientific inquiry requires craftsmanlike skill in judgment and tinkering. As we have stated in Chapter 2, the course of inquiry cannot be separated from the judgments and intentions of the persons conducting the inquiry. Advances seem to occur when researchers change certain constraints of a theoretical and/or methodological nature that permit them to address more adequately a variety of problems in the context of their overall programs of research. Obviously, to the extent that such a view of research practice is merited, any rigid distinction between, or sequencing of, the work of discovery and verification is unwarranted.

A second problem with the traditional discovery–verification distinction is that verification itself, at least as understood within positivist and neopositivist epistemologies, may be difficult to achieve in psychological science. A burgeoning literature in the human and social sciences has developed in the past 30 years that challenges the mainstream positivist assumption that the subject matter of psychological science (human actions and psychological states) can be studied "scientifically," in the sense of establishing and verifying causal laws that have general (as opposed to local) applicability. Because human actions and psychological states are both socially located and intentionally represented, they are not constituted atomistically in the manner of water, rocks, and daffodils.

Psychological phenomena exist only in their relevant social and intentional contexts and cannot be isolated for study in special "laboratory" conditions without being altered in significant ways. Since physical science strategies of validating causal claims require isolation of focal phenomena in tightly controlled, laboratory settings (so as to minimize interference from causal forces other than those under immediate study), they cannot be employed successfully in psychological science (cf. Bhaskar, 1989; Greenwood, 1991). From this point of view, the primary verification problem faced by researchers of psychological practice is that they cannot employ verification strategies of isolation and control, which seem to have worked reasonably well in physical sciences, without distorting the psychological phenomena of interest. On the other hand, to attempt to verify causal, lawful relations in the real-world settings in which these phenomena occur seems to be an impossible task because of the wide array of situational and intentional factors that potentially might affect the relations under study.

Given the seeming intractability of the foregoing difficulty, many philosophers and psychologists have advocated a more hermeneutic or interpretive approach to psychological science, one that effectively forgoes the establishment of causal, generalizable laws as a possible goal for psychology. Under many hermeneutic proposals for psychological and social science (e.g., Bernstein, 1983; Gadamer, 1960/1975; Gergen, 1982), psychology would become an almost exclusively discovery-oriented, constructive activity. Intensive descriptive, interpretive, and critical study of focal psychological phenomena in local contexts might yield meaningful understanding of these contexts. Such studies may be done without the necessary intent of generating generalizable (and certainly not universal) causal relationships (see Phillips, 1987, for a critical discussion of the hermeneutic case against positivist social and psychological science).

The primary implication of the hermeneutic critique of positivist psychological science with respect to the discovery–verification distinction has been to encourage a move away from verification testing, particularly as cast within traditional psychology's penchant for hypothesis-testing. With specific reference to research on psychotherapeutic practice, Mahrer (1988) and others have argued that the traditional approach encourages a poor articulation of the phenomena of practice, reducing them to trivial formulations that permit relatively facile (and somewhat mindless) use of hypothesis-testing strategies. The expressed concern is that psychology keeps putting its methodological cart before its phenomenal horse.

There probably is little doubt that discovery-oriented research that aims at a full description and interpretation of focal phenomena has been badly neglected in much psychological research on practice. It also may be the case that the relative absence of such thoroughgoing descriptive, interpretive work is especially problematic in psychological science, where it may be the only achievable form of scientific inquiry possible. Nonetheless, to give up on any sort of theory-verification or -testing in psychological science seems difficult. Even though there now is much debate about whether or not such testing is possible (especially with respect to causal claims), and what warrants of justification might be invoked to support theoretical formulations as more or less appropriate or progressive, some sort of testing of psychological theories seems necessary if we are to enhance our knowledge of psychological practice in general, and of psychotherapeutic practice in particular (cf. Martin, 1991a).

It appears to us that pragmatic proposals that argue for a more limited testing of the practical consequences of psychological practice with respect to specific purposes could offer a middle ground between traditional notions of highly general verification testing, and radical hermeneutic arguments that would seem to question the very notion of verification in favor of discovery work alone. One way of assessing the possible merits of the pragmatist framework we have adopted is to examine the inquiry practices and purposes of those engaged in programmatic research on psychological practice. What do researchers actually do at various phases of their programs of research? Can their actions, decisions, judgments, and choices at different phases in their work be captured by formal distinctions between stages of discovery and verification? If not, perhaps where formal epistemology has been stymied, less formal "epistemologies-in-action" might prevail. At least, such is part of the hope that drives our undertaking in this volume.

Having said this, it is not our intention that readers should be constrained to consider the researchers' accounts that follow in terms of the foregoing questions and framework. In a more general sense, we want to encourage readers to look carefully at each of these accounts with respect to determining whether each researcher tends to use strategies of verification or discovery, and when each kind of strategy is employed. Of course, either strategy may be used extensively, perhaps even exclusively, throughout a series of studies. It is also possible that both strategies may be found in a particular program of research because of its particular aims.

Determinism Versus Agency

A third oppositional dichotomy that has troubled researchers of psychological practice is that between human agency (freedom), on the one hand, and some variety of determinism, on the other. Adherents of the traditional or received view in psychology have tended to treat human agency as epiphenomenal or illusory (cf. Lefcourt, 1973). Set against this received wisdom is a large body of psychologically relevant literature that attests to the ubiquity of human agency or freedom (see Westcott, 1988, for a detailed review). Indeed, most legal and ethical practices in human societies are dependent on some notion of human freedom. That freedom is essential to meaning and morality was understood by the ancients (cf. Aristotle, 1987) very much as it is understood by most nonpsychologists today. An understanding of virtue requires a distinction between voluntary and involuntary emotions and actions, such that only the former are worthy of praise or blame. To deny human freedom to act and choose is to strip humanity of its moral dimension. And yet, this is precisely what deterministic psychology seems to do by placing human actions under the determination of physiology, environment, past experience, and/or current social, psychological projects. Further, as noted by Westcott (1988), human experience, at a personal as well as a social level, seems to reflect an ability to choose between what one does and other things that one might have done.

Throughout this century numerous attempts have been made to resolve the tension perceived by psychologists between the seeming requirements of a deterministic science and the apparent necessity of human agency. Williams (1992) has reviewed such attempts, concluding that none of them can save the idea of human agency as freedom of choice. For example, prominent psychologists such as Bandura (1989) have attempted to save the notion of freedom of choice by endowing the agent with some power or capacity to exercise agency. Although those attempts recognize the necessity for such a capacity, they proceed to ground it firmly in complex structures of causal necessity that lose the very notion of agency (as freedom of choice) they are trying to save. Also associated with many attempts to instill a free capacity or "will" in psychology are well-known problems of placing such capacities in some sort of "self" structure. These hypothesized structures then require explanation in turn, resulting in an infinite regress of explanations that themselves seem to require the same sort of explanation that they are intended to provide.

One way out of the agency versus determinism tangle may be to stop equating agency with indeterminism, and therefore as directly in opposition to the requirements of a deterministic science. Harré (1984), Hermans, Kempen, and van Loon (1992), and Williams (1992) take such an approach by adopting social constructionist, existential, or dialogical perspectives on the self that de-emphasize traditional dualisms between the personal, psychological and the social, collective. Harré, for example, holds that human agency arises from the holding of a theory about one's self that is appropriated from one's social, cultural conversations and practical activities. However, once appropriated, such theories permit moral assessments of individual actions in the appropriate social, cultural context. The likely constraints on individual action and self-interpretation that arise from these assessments may be seen as representing a kind of causal influence, albeit of a much more epistemic and moral order than the mechanistic and behavioristic conceptions of causality favored in most natural sciences. Rychlak (1988) makes a similar proposal, but is quick to point out that due to the often dialectical, highly personalized meanings resident in individuals' personal theories, any psychological science likely must settle for a much "softer," person-specific form of determinism than that sought in natural science.

Other psychologists, such as Howard and Conway (1986), have suggested that it might be possible to take a more empirical approach to the question of agency, perhaps even succeeding in quantifying the proportion of causal force attributable to the agential exercise of free will. (This approach receives considerable explication and elaboration in the chapter by George Howard in the second part of this volume, so it only is mentioned here in passing.)

At the heart of both the agency versus determinism and discovery versus verification debates is the larger controversy about whether or not the traditional attempt by psychologists to explain the human world in the same deterministic terms as physical scientists use to explain the natural world is appropriate and productive. Many Anglo-American analytical philosophers (e.g., Peters, 1958; Winch, 1958) have argued that the "fact" of human agency requires "reason explanations," not causal explanations, and that this requirement makes the human sciences (like psychology) fundamentally different from the natural sciences. From this point of view, an adequate explanation of human actions is held to be non-causal because such explanations are essentially interpretations of human action in terms of shared reasons, purposes, values, and beliefs. Because this type of explanation involves the critical explication of the meanings of shared concepts, the basis of human science may be more philosophical than psychological, at least in terms of traditional positivist, empiricist conceptions of psychology.

These same sorts of observations underlie many classical and contemporary hermeneutic psychologies that aim at determining the meanings of human actions in terms of agents' reasons and purposes, and relating such meanings to particular forms of social life. The social constructionism of Kenneth Gergen (1982, 1985) is a good example of this approach to socially embedded, agential explanation. Of course, others (e.g., Davidson, 1963; Nagel, 1961; Rychlak, 1988) have argued that reasons can and should be treated as legitimate causes, and that conceptions of teleological causation provide more adequate explanations of human actions than do the "reason explanations" and interpretations favored by many analytical philosophers and hermeneutic psychologists.

However, as mentioned earlier, causal theories of human actions and psychological states (at least those that incorporate more traditional conceptions of causality) seem difficult to develop and verify. Nonetheless, the practical success of everyday, folk psychology attests to the fact that such phenomena are not entirely indeterminate. One of the biggest challenges to researchers of psychological practice is to generate and somehow test models and theories of practice phenomena without defining these phenomena in ways that serve to trivialize them or strip them of their essential properties. Eventually, psychologists will be expected to show that their theories are superior, according to some articulated and accepted criteria, to the folk psychologies they attempt to replace (at least for specific scientific purposes).

In considering researchers' accounts of their programs of research, it may be helpful for readers to attempt to determine the ontological and epistemological positions taken with respect to human agency and to link these impressions with the methodologies adopted in the particular research studies described. Specifically, how are explicit concerns for human agency manifested in the method choices and inquiry strategies adopted by the researchers? What kinds of implicit commitments with respect to agency and determinism might be inferred from the accounts of these and other researchers?

Holistic Versus Reductionistic Units of Analysis

The most commonly employed analytical method in psychology has been to reduce phenomena of interest to component parts. The assumptions are that an understanding of components is initially easier to attain and that such component understandings eventually can be aggregated to form an understanding of entire, focal phenomena. Human actions and psychological states of interest to psychologists certainly qualify as complex phenomena, replete with situational, motivational, affective, cognitive, behavioral, and other characteristics. Psychologists using reductionistic analysis attempt to consider these different characteristics as components that can be studied separately from their overall relationships and interactions. Over its history, this penchant for reductionism has led to the creation of subdisciplines and subfields within psychology that are associated primarily with the study of one or a small number of such components (e.g., cognitive psychology, behavioral psychology, social psychology, and so forth). Within these subfields, further reductionistic tendencies are apparent that have served to focus the attention of many psychological specialists on ever smaller units of analysis. For example, in cognitive psychology, currently popular models of human information processing have become concerned with representing the most primitive kinds of informational units possible and modeling ways in which these units are combined into increasingly complex structures to enable complex human abilities in areas such as problem solving and critical thinking.

Reductionism also is apparent in the units of analysis employed in much research on psychological practice. In psychotherapy research, many prominent researchers have advocated fine-grained analyses of therapeutic interactions in terms of the momentary intentions, responses, and reactions of therapists and clients as they engage the therapeutic enterprise (cf. Hill, 1992, for a review of her own and related work of this sort). Work of this kind assumes that it is possible to build useful understandings of therapeutic change from small-gauge analyses of sequences of discrete, but functionally interconnected, therapeutic acts and actions (cf. Martin, Martin, & Slemon, 1989). There is much to recommend reductionistic analyses of research on psychological practice that have led to the construction of compositional models of psychological processes and structures. The complexity of many seemingly simple human capabilities becomes readily apparent from such models. Further, reductionistic methods of psychological practice seem to offer the promise of effective psychological prescriptions for the acquisition of even the most complex human capabilities. For example, numerous training manuals have been developed from reductionistic analyses and research to assist individuals with the acquisition of critical thinking, problem solving, social negotiating, interpersonal empathy, and other "skills." In short, reductionistic analyses in psychology have been perceived as successful to the extent that they seem to provide simpler, partial working models for the complex phenomena of psychology, models that hold promise for practical purposes of facilitating human learning and change in a variety of areas of practice.

Against psychology's penchant for reductionism as a primary analytical mode, are numerous arguments and concerns about the extent to which such analyses distort the very phenomena they are intended to explicate. Humanistic and philosophically minded psychologists have argued that there are severe limits to the extent to which reductionism can function to inform acceptable understanding of human actions and psychological states (cf. Danziger, 1990; Margolis, 1984). Paramount in these arguments is the assertion that most psychological phenomena of interest cannot be subdivided arbitrarily into the artificial divisions created by psychologists' reductionistic tendencies. For example, Harré (1984) considers the reductionism apparent in cognitive, information processing psychology to create all sorts of unnecessary conceptual confusion. In insisting that important human capacities such as empathy or intellectual competence be modeled in terms of computer-style, box diagrams with separate entries for cognitive, emotional, dispositional, and motivational elements, the very nature of such capacities may be distorted. The models that result from reductionistic analysis suggest that it somehow is possible to separate perhaps inseparable, holistic units of human experience and action. What does it really mean to talk about the cognitive elements of empathy if empathy itself is a holistic mode of human understanding and reaction that resists subdivisions of this sort? Further, Harré and others argue that such reductionistic models favor biological, physiological, and mechanistic explanations for psychological phenomena over social, cultural, and ethical explanations. Rather than seeing human development as a result of the internalization of holistic forms of understanding and construing that stem from the linguistic, cultural, and social accomplishments of humankind, reductionists view human development as an individualized adaptation to the physical and social worlds.

Some psychologists, not necessarily opposed to reductionism, nonetheless have been especially concerned about the epistemological status of cognitive variables (e.g., intentions, perceptions, understandings, and private reactions) derived from verbal accounts of private, internal processes provided by participants in psychological research. In particular, commentators such as Nisbett and Wilson (1977) have questioned the veridicality of participants' self-reports of their cognitive processes. In response to such concerns, Ericsson and Simon (1984) have proposed a widely accepted methodology, together with a thoroughgoing theoretical justification, for treating participants' verbal accounts of internal processes and content as valid data in psychological research. Essentially, Ericsson and Simon propose that such accounts may be used as reliable and valid indicators of cognitive variables, especially if there is convincing theoretical reason to suppose that the variables being probed are content resident in participants' long-term memories that can be retrieved consciously. Methods of "process tracing," "think-aloud," and immediate "stimulated recall" have been employed to probe and infer the more ephemeral contents of participants' short-term memories (see research reported by Hill and Martin in Part II of this volume). It may be possible to infer, from such accounts, cognitive operations and their intentional objects that are more or less reliable and accurate, despite being necessarily indirect and incomplete. This latter conclusion is especially true if (1) participants are asked only to describe, not to explain or justify, their internal processes, and (2) the administration of the methodological probes employed is temporally proximate to the contents or processes being probed.

While the work of Ericsson and Simon (1984) has helped to establish the likely reliability and validity of participants' reports of their own inner experiences and processes as data in psychological research on practice, important issues concerning the appropriate units with which to capture such data, and the prescriptive yield from this type of research remain unresolved. As Martin (1991b, 1992) has argued, it is far from clear that the ontological status of proposed cognitive variables, such as intentions and private reactions, is captured appropriately when these variables are considered to reside in distinct, separable units (temporally and spatially) in a manner identical to overt speech and behavior. Further, as mentioned earlier, the indirect observation and inference of sequences of cognitive variables in research on psychological practice may be insufficient to warrant the positing of explicit models of "how to perform" complex intellectual and emotional tasks such as "learning from psychotherapy" (see Martin, 1991b, for an elaboration of this latter point).

In research on therapeutic practice, Greenberg (1986) has suggested different levels of analysis that might be more or less appropriate. While retaining a form of reductionistic analysis at the level of studying speech acts and content in psychotherapy interactions, he has proposed that much valuable understanding of therapeutic change might be generated from a more holistic examination of larger units of psychotherapy interactions. These include those more macroscopic events that researchers, therapists, and clients judge as being of particular importance. In studying such events, researchers like Elliott and Shapiro (1992), Rice and Greenberg (1984), Mahrer and Nadler (1986), and others have de-emphasized microscopic analyses along the lines of classic psychological distinctions among behavior, cognition, and emotion. Instead, they have attempted to explicate (using both quantitative and qualitative methods) more holistic meanings and epistemic transformations resident in such events or "change episodes." Such work illustrates a seemingly functional, progressive use of multiple levels of analysis in an attempt to understand therapeutic change processes in the context of programs of research on psychological practice. (In her chapter in Part II of this book, Friedlander describes an attempt to employ such an approach in her most recent research on psychotherapy.)

One particular way in which researchers' attachments and commitments to different units of analysis is made clear, is in their selection and development of specific measures through which they attempt to capture focal phenomena. Traditionally, the field of psychological measurement has been very concerned with formalized requirements for what constitutes adequate reliability and validity of measures of human abilities and action tendencies. Many researchers of psychotherapy practice have incorporated such concerns into their development of measures of therapist and client in-session responses and experiences. In many instances, the kinds of conceptual and substantive questions asked by researchers become epistemologically and methodologically transformed into questions concerning the degree of association that might be shown to exist between operationalized measures of some of the complex behavioral and experiential phenomena implicated. A frequently voiced criticism of this kind of psychological research is that it somehow never quite succeeds in investigating exactly those matters it claims to study (cf. Brandtstadter, 1987; Smedslund, 1979). The exact nature of this concern is that in devising and employing measures that meet the formal psychometric criteria adopted by psychologists, researchers consequently oversimplify, perhaps even trivialize, the complex phenomena they wish to address. Further, empirical association between such operationalized measures may speak more to psychologists' psychometric preoccupations than to the phenomenal objects purportedly under study.

When reading our researchers' accounts, readers might wish to revisit the foregoing issues with respect to holism and reductionism in the units of analyses used in the different studies that constitute the programs of psychotherapy research. How adequately are focal phenomena captured through the units and measures employed? How are the inevitably complex interactions among various factors involved in psychotherapeutic practice addressed?

Instrumental Versus Conceptual Yield

Interactive with difficulties associated with reductionism versus holism and others discussed previously, is considerable debate over what the yield from research on psychological practice possibly might be. Clearly, a prime motivator behind many psychologists' attempts to employ reductionistic, deterministic, and rigorous verification strategies in research on practice has been the hope that such work will yield tight prescriptions for assisting students, clients, and other recipients of psychological interventions to be better problem solvers, communicators, decision makers, and so forth. If psychological practice can be informed directly and instrumentally from research findings, vastly improved methods for educating clinicians, teachers, parents, managers, and consultants would seem to be forthcoming. More efficient and effective preparation of practitioners is an ever present goal for many researchers of psychological practice. This goal has resulted in an extreme popularity of "what" questions in research on psychological practice. In research on therapeutic practice, researchers have attempted to determine what forms of intervention will work best for what kinds of clients with what types of personal, social, and cultural characteristics, and what types of problems (cf. Garfield & Bergin, 1986).

However, practitioners generally have not found research on practice to be sufficiently useful (Howard, 1985a; Morrow-Bradley & Elliott, 1986). The history of research efforts concerned with the utilization of psychotherapy research by practicing psychotherapists might be summarized succinctly as follows. Researchers of psychotherapeutic practice believe that psychotherapy research should yield information of use to practitioners, and when study after study (cf. Morrow-Bradley & Elliott, 1986, for a review of such work) shows that practitioners do not make much use of such research, psychotherapy researchers take this as a circumstance that requires remediation. [There are some indications (again, cf. Morrow-Bradley & Elliott, 1986) that the theoretical orientations of clinicians, and the amount of time they invest in reading research reports, do predict the extent to which clinicians will make some use of research findings, especially with respect to clinical diagnosis and decision making among possible interventions.]

Several reasons for the underutilization of psychotherapy research by psychotherapists have been posited, including (1) the clinical irrelevance of many research questions, (2) the unrepresentativeness of actual clinical contexts in the treatments, populations, and measures utilized in research, (3) an overemphasis on technical matters (e.g., nuances of statistical analyses) and the outcomes of clinical interventions in research reports, to the neglect of detailed descriptions of the actual clinical practices and experiences under investigation, and (4) too little delineation of possible practical implications of research in published research reports (Barlow, 1981; Elliott, 1983; Hayes & Nelson, 1981; Rice & Greenberg,

1984). However, even when researchers have attempted to provide very specific manuals that detail the precise clinical practices followed in research, practitioners have not been overly receptive. This is perhaps because the primary impetus for such "manualization" has been to safeguard the internal validity and treatment fidelity of research, not to educate and empower practitioners (cf. Dobson & Shaw, 1988). Similarly, many recent attempts to study the process of psychotherapy as conducted by experienced psychotherapists in actual therapy contexts, using more experientially targeted measures (e.g., Hill, 1992), still seem to involve a level of technical precision and complexity that many practitioners find inimical (cf. Martin, 1992).

Despite the accumulation of evidence regarding the historical and contemporary rift between the research and practice of psychotherapy, it is worth noting explicitly that most professional organizations in psychology and psychotherapy continue to advocate various notions of "scientist-practitioner," "research into practice," "applied behavioral scientists," and "the science of practice" (cf. Barlow, Hayes, & Nelson, 1984; Berdie, 1972; Thompson & Super, 1964). Considerable leverage seems to be gained by associating psychological science and practice in matters pertaining to reimbursement for professional services, recognition of the professional status of psychology and psychologists, and the legitimacy of applying psychological knowledge in areas of social problems. The idea that research on psychotherapy practice should inform that practice is not without its sociopolitical context.

It is instructive to turn to various analyses that have been offered as to why the research–practice gap in psychotherapy continues despite the best efforts of a new generation of researchers to adopt alternative, innovative, and more "practice friendly" forms of research on psychotherapy practice. It also is interesting to note the way in which several of these proposed explanations relate to the kinds of issues discussed earlier in this chapter and in the previous two chapters with respect to issues debated frequently in psychotherapy research and to various proposals for the conduct of such research.

Howard (1985a) used Rychlak's (1988) analysis of causal explanations in psychology as a basis for his analysis of the research–practice gap in psychological counseling and therapy. He argued that psychological research, including the majority of research on psychotherapy, has favored explanations that invoke material, efficient, and formal causes as opposed to telic or final causes. The most important way in which telic causes are distinct from the more favored causal explanations in psychology is that telic causality is best understood as "that for the sake of which something occurs" (Howard, 1985a, p. 541). Unlike the efficient, material, and formal causes frequently invoked in natural, physical sciences, telic causality focuses on decidedly human capabilities involving reasons, goals, purposes, and intentions. Howard argued that it is precisely these capabilities with which practitioners of psychotherapy are most concerned. Clients seek psychotherapy for personal reasons related to personal desires and goals. They seek explanations and understandings in these terms, not in the efficient, material, formal causal models of traditional psychological science. Thus, psychotherapists are both constrained and motivated more by the demands of their clients for telic explanations than by the demands of researchers that they employ other, natural scientific systems of understanding and explanation. After all, it is clients, not researchers, with whom practitioners interact on a moment-by-moment, day-to-day basis. In recognition of this reality, Howard calls for researchers of practice to consider the telic dimension in their programs of research.

Taking a slightly different approach, several prominent scholars of psychotherapy have advocated detailed empirical analyses of psychotherapeutic events in the hope of uncovering the psychological processes and change mechanisms at work during significant instances of actual psychotherapeutic practice (e.g., Elliott, 1983; Greenberg & Pinsof, 1986; Mahrer & Nadler, 1986; Rice & Greenberg, 1984). For such individuals, the research–practice gap in psychotherapy is seen to arise from the fact that traditional research practices in psychology do not focus on important complexities of the clinical situation. Traditional canons of experimental psychology such as isolation, simplification, and aggregation serve to detract from the contextualized, complex, and individualized nature of psychotherapeutic practice. An alternative strategy favored by this group of researchers consists of (1) a multistage, rational-empirical analysis of specific, significant therapeutic tasks through which client change is achieved, and (2) the formation of elaborated micro theories of the change processes and mechanisms involved.

A major difficulty associated with any psychological research agenda that becomes dominated by questions of prescription (e.g., "What works under what conditions and for whom?") is that it seems impossible to conduct experiments large or numerous enough to instantiate all possible combinations that arise when relevant individual, temporal, and contextual factors interact with particular treatment factors and levels (cf. Cronbach, 1975). This difficulty may be especially troublesome for researchers or for phases of research programs that are devoid of at least some *a priori* theorizing or hypothesizing (Martin, 1991a). Humans and the contexts in which we reside may be too varied to permit tightly prescriptive applications of the findings generated by research on practice.

In recognition of the potential difficulties of generating, verifying, and applying results of research on psychological practice in highly prescriptive manners, many psychologists have suggested that research on psychological practice adjust its sights from a focus on prescriptive yield to a more modest, conceptual yield. Under such proposals, research on practice might succeed in enhancing a general understanding of how a particular form of psychological intervention might work, together with documenting a few specific examples of effective uses of the intervention. However, no attempt would be made to offer practitioners specific, step-by-step prescriptions of exactly what to do in their own practice settings. Rather, it would be up to practitioners to take the general understandings of principles of human learning and change that research might supply, and to work out for themselves how best to utilize these conceptual understandings in the context of their own practice.

Martin (1991a, 1992) pointed out that in the absence of theoretical frameworks that can be developed and communicated between researchers and practitioners, the results of psychotherapeutic research cannot be integrated into forms conducive to the conceptualization of practice. Because much research on psychotherapeutic practice is atheoretical or does not have significant theoretical contributions and linkages, it offers little in the way of integrative frameworks that might be useful to practitioners. While sharing Martin's concern for theory in psychotherapy research, Polkinghorne (1991) and Strong (1991, 1992) seemed generally less concerned with the existence of the research–practice gap in psychotherapy, regarding it as a perhaps necessary reflection of real and legitimate differences in the nature of psychological research and practice. Polkinghorne, like Cohen, Sargent, and Sechrest (1986), stressed the conceptual nature of the yield that might be expected from psychological research on therapeutic practice. Like Schön (1983), he believed that the judgments of practitioners do not consist of simple applications of research findings, but reflect their background knowledge and experiences, and awareness of a multitude of current situational factors with respect to individual clients and therapeutic contexts. Thus, he concluded that the research–practice gap in counseling and therapeutic psychology has perhaps been overstated as a problem that should be remedied. While advocating increased methodological pluralism in research on psychotherapy, Polkinghorne (1991) did not believe that research will or should be the only (or even major) source of information for practitioners. Rather, his advocacy of both alternative and traditional methodologies in psychotherapy research is related to the extent to which a plurality of research methods might better parallel the repertoire of information-gathering and analyzing methods used by practitioners in their work with clients. Thus,

Polkinghorne seemed to argue for a conceptual yield from psychotherapy research in terms of possible processes and methods of conceptualizing clients and their problems, rather than any sort of compendium of rules such as "what to do with client X with concern Y" (also see Martin, 1988).

Strong (1991, 1992) also believed that the context of psychological research and the context of psychotherapy practice are distinctive, yet with the potential to inform mutually. The basis for Strong's analysis of differences between research and practice is his view that the purpose of research is to enable the researcher to test theories, whereas the purpose of practice is to enable the practitioner to prove theories. He argued that researchers must be fundamentally skeptical of their theories, while such skepticism is anathema to practitioners who require faith in the therapeutic value of their theories. Even though the underlying motive for researchers and practitioners may be to prove the validity of their theories, the manner in which the research and practice communities condone and promote this activity is very different. Research demands tentativeness; practice demands much more certitude. Strong seemed to believe that encouraging methodological diversity in psychological research for practice may be valuable in providing more means of testing and verifying theories for both researchers and practitioners, but cannot be expected to bridge the fundamental differences in purpose that attach to these different communities.

Reconceptualizing the yield from research on psychological practice from an instrumental, prescriptive perspective to envision a more impressionistic, conceptual use of such research and its findings might go a long way toward alleviating the sorts of pragmatic difficulties engendered by vast and numerous differences across psychological practitioners, clients, and practice contexts. Nonetheless, such a conceptual yield, while perhaps more feasible, may not satisfy the ambitions of many researchers of practice to provide a more directly helpful hand to practitioners and their clients. In our pragmatist framework, the kind of conceptual yield discussed here probably is a reasonable expectation from research on therapeutic practice. Just as researchers need to solve particular methodological, theoretical, and empirical problems as these are manifest in their ongoing programs of research, so too do practitioners need to solve particular therapeutic, procedural, interpersonal, and other problems as these arise in the context of their therapeutic practice. Conceptual, theoretical understandings bolstered by empirical findings from research on psychotherapeutic practice hopefully can help therapeutic practitioners engage in such problem solving in more comprehensive and fruitful ways. However, it probably must be left to the informed artistry and craft of the practitioner to determine which interventions and manners to employ with which clients in particular cases of psychotherapy practice.

Once again, we want to encourage readers to make their own judgments concerning the kinds of yield (instrumental, conceptual, or other) that they believe issue from the programs of research discussed herein. What kinds of yield do our researchers seem to be seeking? To what extent does their work seem to be furnishing such outcomes? Perhaps, most important, how might the kinds of yield sought by different researchers influence the kinds of research questions and methods they adopt? We have committed ourselves to a pragmatist account, but we wish to remain open to other possibilities in understanding researchers' stories. Hopefully, some of our readers will supply alternative interpretations that might be set against those we provide.

SOME BASIC ONTOLOGICAL AND EPISTEMOLOGICAL ISSUES REVISITED

At this point in our consideration of difficulties and other issues encountered in conducting research on psychological practice, it seems appropriate to consider more explicitly how questions about the nature or ontology of psychological phenomena find their way into research on practice. Further, we must revisit such fundamental ontological questions in relation to epistemological problems that are entailed in many of the issues discussed thus far in this chapter. We believe that epistemological issues in psychological research can arise from the unique ontological status of psychological phenomena granted in our conceptualization of them. Reciprocally, our epistemological approach can fashion the ontological nature of those human actions and psychological states that we take to constitute the subject matter of research on psychological practice. Method and content are interrelated in research, philosophically and realistically.

We stated that human actions and psychological states are both socially located and intentionally represented. Unlike the phenomena of natural, physical sciences, the phenomena of psychological science cannot be preserved if they are isolated from the social-cultural contexts in which they occur or from the individual and collective representations (construals or understandings of intentions and meanings) within which they reside. The phenomena of research on therapeutic practice are not constituted atomistically or essentially. There are no essential defining features of phenomena such as empathy or insight that reside inside of these entities themselves. Phenomena such as empathy or insight cannot be removed from the therapeutic contexts in which they occur, divided into component parts or materials, and understood. There is nothing like "chemical profiling" or "force vectoring" in psychological science. Phenomena like empathy reside in the social interactions between therapists and clients, set against a social-cultural background of psychological helping and healing. Within this context, empathy resides in the intentions of therapists to attempt to understand clients' stories and problems, knowing full well that complete understanding of the clients' perspectives is ultimately elusive. Empathy also consists of clients' recognition and appreciation of therapists' attempts to enter their phenomenal worlds in ways intended to be helpful. The phenomena of psychological, therapeutic science take their meaning from their relevant social locations and from their representations in the minds of interacting participants in these contexts (cf. Bhaskar, 1989; Greenwood, 1991). To ignore or fail to appreciate this basic ontological status of psychological phenomena is to court both scientific and practical irrelevance. An important implication of the social location and meaningful, intentional representation of psychological phenomena (i.e., human actions and psychological states) is that they may be extremely difficult to determine from the verbal, experiential reports of participants in psychological research alone. Ericsson and Simon (1984) acknowledge the necessary incompleteness of participants' verbal reports of internal processes and content. However, the reasons for their caution reside primarily in the difficulty of attaining conscious awareness of many "automatized" cognitive functions and in recapturing content in short-term memory. Ericsson and Simon do not address explicitly the likelihood that many important determinants of humans' psychological experience reside in the socially and culturally embedded conversations in which they participate (cf. Williams, 1992). When this larger, dialogical context is recognized, the ability of microscopic, cognitive units of analysis to capture individuals' private, yet conversationally embedded, experiences may be problematic in a more fundamental, ontological way.

A second important implication of the social location and intentional representation (individually and collectively) of psychological phenomena is that they may be affected by causal forces other than those typically considered in physical sciences. Rychlak (1988), roughly following distinctions in ways of knowing that were initially drawn by Aristotle, categorized the types of causes considered in physical science (and in much extant psychological science) to be material, efficient, or formal. Material causes arise from the substances of which entities are composed. For example, glass breaks against cement due to brittleness arising from the molecular structure of its materials. Efficient causes are forces behind events, such as the striking of a billiard ball with a cue stick that sets the ball in motion. Formal causes are more germane to psychological phenomena as construed herein, given that they consist of influences occasioned by anticipated patterns of action, such as problem-solving strategies in games like chess. However, most germane to psychological phenomena, understood as socially located and intentionally, meaningfully represented, is a fourth type of causation, telic or final causation.

Telic causation is that for which something occurs. It encompasses reasons, goals, purposes, and intentions that influence human actions. Much classical philosophy has differentiated between causes and reasons, in recognition of the difficulties of obtaining access to, and verifying the causal influence of, human intentions and reasons. Nonetheless, it seems difficult to deny their influence in the domain of psychological practice. If psychological states and human actions are represented in the minds of individuals and groups of individuals, as well as embedded in describable social locations, it seems mistaken to deny potential causal influences that might arise from reasons derivative from such representations. Such is the relevance of human agency. If human intentions and reasons are part of the ontology of psychological phenomena, just as the molecular structure of glass is part of its ontological makeup, they presumably must be granted at least the possibility of causal force.

When the epistemological implications of the foregoing ontological analysis are examined, the enormous challenge of conducting psychological research in areas such as psychotherapeutic practice becomes clear. Foremost among these epistemological problems is an absence of satisfactory methodologies for verifying causal claims of a possibly telic nature in real-world, open systems. We simply do not know how to do this. Researchers in the physical sciences may have succeeded in ascertaining material and efficient causes, to the extent that they have, because (as noted previously) they have been able to adopt a general methodology of isolating focal phenomena in idealized, decidedly "unnatural" contexts, thus removing them from "causally noisy," open, real-world contexts. Clearly, when psychological phenomena are understood as arising from their social and representational contexts, such a methodology cannot be employed in psychological science without altering focal phenomena, phenomena that (unlike many of the phenomena of natural science) are not constituted atomistically. To compound this difficulty, when causal forms themselves are embedded only within real-world, open systems (as seems to be the case with telic causes), it seems difficult to generate and verify causal claims (let alone theories) that might have any generality beyond the specific, temporary, real-world contexts in which they are embedded.

Recognition of the foregoing epistemological difficulties in social and psychological science has led to a variety of relatively recent reconceptualizations of psychological science. Some prominent scholars of psychological research (e.g., Campbell, 1978; Cronbach, 1975) have become highly skeptical about the possibility of verifying any sort of causal claims in psychological science that possess any type of generalizability beyond highly local and temporally bound contexts. In a related vein, others (e.g., Rorty, 1980, 1983) have suggested that any notions of generalizable causal theory in psychological science be given up in favor of a more modest attempt to determine pragmatically useful understandings given particular purposes of human actors and researchers. Still others (e.g., Gadamer, 1977; Gergen, 1982; Polkinghorne, 1988) have suggested an approach to psychological science that may have more in common with studies in the humanities that depend on the interpretive methods of narratology and hermeneutics, rather than on methods of verifying generalizable, causal theories used in natural, physical science. Rather than aiming at explanations of human action and experience that are at least partially predictive, these approaches aim at understandings of human action and experience that are mostly postdictive.

Various calls for a broadening of psychological research strategies with the use of alternative paradigms and a pluralistic approach to research methods, summarized in Chapter 1, may be seen as suggestions for coping with the ontologically entailed, epistemological difficulties encountered when researching psychological phenomena. That these and other proposals for the conduct of social psychological inquiry are motivated by serious reflection on the sorts of ontological and epistemological matters raised briefly herein cannot be doubted. However, what is much less clear is whether such alternative epistemological and methodological stances and suggestions can result in progress in psychological practice and our knowledge about it.

NON-METHODOLOGICAL, NON-EPISTEMIC CONSIDERATIONS

Our discussion of issues encountered in the conduct of research on psychological practice must include a consideration of non-epistemic matters, matters that seem to be more ethical than methodological, more axiological (perhaps even ideological) than epistemological. Such factors are influential with respect to method choice and inquiry process in any psychological study of psychotherapeutic practice, where subjective and moral considerations abound. Howard (1985b) drew a distinction between epistemic values that guide the judgments, decisions, preferences, and orientations of psychologists in determining the relative merits of competing theoretical, empirical accounts, and non-epistemic values underlying those moral, ethical, and ideological positions that psychologists bring to bear on their work, explicitly or implicitly. Of perhaps unique importance, among these latter values, are the moral values that researchers place on the possibilities they imagine for individual humans and for humankind. Such values take on particular significance in what many commentators on contemporary society and social science have come to call the postmodern experience (cf. Best & Kellner, 1991; Taylor, 1989). For, if we increasingly see ourselves without the benefit of any firm foundation for the knowledge we seek and create, on what basis do we promote what we take to be knowledge that we hold as appropriate, worthwhile, or valuable?

Clearly, non-epistemic valuing of imagined possibilities for humans and humankind looms large on the postmodern horizon. However, even if one chooses not to enter any of the various postmodern ethics, it can be argued convincingly that all research on psychological practice carries with it some overriding sense of what human capacities and capabilities should be promoted through such practice and through enhancements to this practice potentially enabled by research. Consequently, it is crucial when considering the various accounts of programmatic research contained in this book, to attempt to infer the kinds of visions for psychotherapeutic practice that might lie behind, and motivate, the conceptual and empirical work reported. For example, is there an implicit sense of empowering clients who may simultaneously serve as subjects of a study on therapeutic practice? Is there a moral tone that implicitly charges psychotherapists with utilizing knowledge derivative from such programs of research in a way that promotes certain collective, cooperative goals for professional psychology or for society as a whole? Are there intimations of social progress and equity, individual rights, or some other personal, social, cultural ends? What are the ethics of researching the intentions, actions, and phenomenologies constituting therapeutic practice? What visions of human possibility influence the kind of questions, methods, warrants, and manner of the work reported?

In briefly raising such non-epistemic considerations, we are recognizing explicitly that all research, and especially psychological research, has important moral, ethical dimensions. Psychotherapy, in particular, may be seen as much as a moral engagement predicated on what Aristotle referred to as "the moral virtues" as it is an intellectual-emotional engagement requiring strong feelings and powerful ideas. It may be that non-epistemic issues and moral questions have not received an appropriately prominent place in psychotherapy research. On the other hand, it may be that such considerations permeate work that has been done in this area, requiring only a focused spotlight to bring them out. The relation between cultural and personal, and rational and non-rational, factors in the development of psychological science was a major theme in Boring's (1954) historical analysis of psychology. In addition, classic histories of science by Polanyi (1966) and Feyerabend (1975) have emphasized the impossibility of determining strict rules for establishing knowledge, and the role of unconscious factors in the evolution of research programs. We want to encourage readers to consider what kinds of non-epistemic, ideological, and other personal commitments might interact with various aspects of the research reported by the researchers whose accounts appear in Part II of this book.

THE PRESENT PROJECT

All of the dimensions and issues previously discussed converge in our conception of the present project. Various proposals for reconceptualizing psychological research contain competing suggestions concerning appropriate epistemologies and methodologies. In an attempt to move beyond those current debates, our purpose here is to undertake a more empirically oriented approach to developing a naturalized or applied epistemology for research on psychotherapeutic practice. We believe that research on psychotherapeutic practice requires a working theory of knowledge, even if it is only contingent and evolving. Further, as argued in Chapter 2, we believe that such an epistemology (or perhaps a set of epistemologies and associated methodologies, grouped under an overarching meta-methodological framework) might be supported on pragmatic grounds (cf. Heidegger, 1962; Margolis, 1986; Rorty, 1991; Toulmin, 1972, 1983).

In Part II of this book, a number of experienced researchers of psychotherapeutic practice write in detail about their own processes of inquiry and method choices as they have gone about their programs of research. In addition, in the hope of illuminating the nature of their knowledge goals and interests, we have encouraged contributors to reflect on their own cognitive values and social interests in relation to their selection of problems and methods, as well as their implicit and explicit criteria for progress. As we shall see from their accounts of their inquiries, these researchers have not avoided addressing critical issues relating to human agency and intentionality, explanation/understanding (both causal and interpretive), and theory/model-building. While not all these programs of inquiry share the same emphases on these topics, all inevitably have something to say concerning the kind of knowledge about psychotherapeutic practice that might be generated from sustained programmatic inquiry in this genre. We hope that our interpretations of the autobiographical, reflective accounts in Part II of this volume will enable us to revisit (in Part III) these and the other issues, difficulties, and debates discussed throughout this book. To this end, clusters of questions summarized at the end of Chapter 2 and in the previous sections of this chapter will guide our interpretive analyses (reported in the third and final part of this volume) of these researchers' accounts of their inquiry processes and method choices. Through these analyses, we hope to sketch the beginnings of a contingent theory of the knowledge practices of researchers in the therapeutic domain and, possibly, other areas of psychological practice.

REFERENCES

Allport, G. W. (1962). The general and the unique in psychological science. *Journal of Personality, 30,* 405–422.

Aristotle. (1987). *The Nicomachean ethics* (J. E. C. Welldon, Trans.). Buffalo, NY: Prometheus Books.

Banaji, M. R., & Crowder, R. G. (1989). The bankruptcy of everyday memory. *American Psychologist, 44,* 1185–1193.

Bandura, A. (1989). Human agency in social cognitive theory. *American Psychologist, 44,* 1175–1184.

Barlow, D. (1981). On the relation of clinical research to clinical practice: Current issues. *Journal of Consulting and Clinical Psychology, 49,* 147–155.

Barlow, D., Hayes, S., & Nelson, R. (1984). *The scientist-practitioner: Research and accountability in clinical and educational settings.* New York: Pergamon.

Berdie, R. (1972). The 1980 counselor: Applied behavioral scientist. *Personnel and Guidance Journal, 50,* 451–456.

Bernstein, R. J. (1983). *Beyond objectivism and relativism: Science, hermeneutics, and praxis.* Philadelphia: University of Pennsylvania Press.

Best, S., & Kellner, D. (1991). *Postmodern theory: Critical interrogations?* New York: Guilford.

Bhaskar, R. (1989). *Reclaiming reality: A critical introduction to contemporary philosophy.* London: Verso.

Boring, E. G. (1954). Psychological factors in scientific progress. *American Scientist, 42,* 639–645.

Brandtstadter, J. (1987). On certainty and universality in human development: Developmental psychology between apriorism and empiricism. In M. Chapman & R. A. Dixon (Eds.), *Meaning and the growth of understanding: Wittgenstein's significance for developmental psychology* (pp. 69–84). New York: Springer-Verlag.

Campbell, D. (1978). Qualitative knowing in action research. In M. Brenner et al. (Eds.), *The social context of method* (pp. 187–212). New York: St. Martin's.

Cohen, L. H., Sargent, M. M., & Sechrest, L. B. (1986). Use of psychotherapy research by professional psychologists. *American Psychologist, 41,* 198–206.

Cornfield, J., & Tukey, J. W. (1956). Average values of mean squares in factorials. *Annals of Mathematical Statistics, 27,* 907–959.

Cronbach, L. J. (1975). Beyond the two disciplines of scientific psychology. *American Psychologist, 30,* 116–127.

Cronbach, L. J. (1984). *Essentials of psychological testing* (4th ed.). New York: Harper & Row.

Cronbach, L. J. (1988). Five perspectives on validity argument. In W. Wainer & H. I. Braun (Eds.), *Test validity* (pp. 3–17). Hillsdale, NJ: Lawrence Erlbaum.

Cronbach, L. J., & Meehl, P. E. (1955). Construct validity in psychological tests. *Psychological Bulletin, 52,* 281–302.

Danziger, K. (1990). *Constructing the subject: Historical origins of psychological research.* Cambridge: Cambridge University Press.

Davidson, D. (1963). Actions, reasons and causes. *Journal of Philosophy, 60,* 685–700.

Dilthey, W. (1989). *Explanation and experiment in social psychological science* (J. D. Greenwood, Trans.). New York: Springer-Verlag. (Original work published 1937)

Dobson, K. S., & Shaw, B. F. (1988). The use of treatment manuals in cognitive therapy: Experience and issues. *Journal of Consulting and Clinical Psychology, 56,* 673–680.

Elliott, R. (1983). Fitting process research to the practicing psychotherapist. *Psychotherapy: Theory, Research, and Practice, 20,* 47–55.

Elliott, R., & Shapiro, D. A. (1992). Client and therapist as analysts of significant events. In S. G. Toukmanian & D. L. Rennie (Eds.), *Psychotherapy process research: Paradigmatic and narrative approaches* (pp. 163–186). Newbury Park, CA: Sage.

Ericsson, K. A., & Simon, H. A. (1984). *Protocol analysis: Verbal accounts as data.* Cambridge, MA: MIT Press.

Feyerabend, P. K. (1975). *Against method: An outline of an anarchistic theory of knowledge.* London: New Left Books.

Gadamer, H. G. (1975). *Truth and method.* New York: Seabury. (Original work published 1960)

Gadamer, H. G. (1977). *Philosophical hermeneutics.* Berkeley: University of California Press.

Garfield, S. L., & Bergin, A. E. (Eds.). (1986). *Handbook of psychotherapy and behavior change* (3rd ed.). New York: Wiley.

Gergen, K. J. (1982). *Toward transformation in social knowledge.* New York: Springer-Verlag.

Gergen, K. J. (1985). The social constructionist movement in modern psychology. *American Psychologist, 40,* 266–275.

Greenberg, L. S. (1986). Research strategies. In L. S. Greenberg & W. M. Pinsof

(Eds.), *The psychotherapeutic process: A research handbook* (pp. 707–734). New York: Guilford.
Greenberg, L. S., & Pinsof, W. M. (Eds.). (1986). *The psychotherapeutic process: A research handbook.* New York: Guilford.
Greenwood, J. D. (1991). *Relations and representations: An introduction to the philosophy of social psychological science.* New York: Routledge.
Gutting, G. (1980). The logic of invention. In T. Nickles (Ed.), *Scientific discovery, logic, and rationality* (pp. 221–234). London: D. Reidel.
Harré, R. (1984). *Personal being: A theory for individual psychology.* Cambridge, MA: Harvard University Press.
Hayes, S. C., & Nelson, R. O. (1981). Clinically relevant research: Requirements, problems, and solutions. *Behavioral Assessment, 3,* 209–215.
Heidegger, M. (1962). *Being and time.* New York: Harper & Row.
Hermans, J. M., Kempen, H. J. G., & van Loon, R. J. P. (1992). The dialogical self: Beyond individualism and rationalism. *American Psychologist, 47,* 23–33.
Hill, C. E. (1992). An overview of four measures developed to test the Hill process model: Therapist intentions, therapist response modes, client reactions, and client behaviors. *Journal of Counseling and Development, 70,* 728–739.
Hoshmand, L. T., & Polkinghorne, D. E. (1992). Redefining the science–practice relationship and professional training. *American Psychologist, 47,* 55–66.
Howard, G. S. (1985a). Can research in the human sciences become more relevant to practice? *Journal of Counseling and Development, 63,* 539–544.
Howard, G. S. (1985b). The role of values in the science of psychology. *American Psychologist, 40,* 255–265.
Howard, G. S., & Conway, C. G. (1986). Can there be an empirical science of volitional action? *American Psychologist, 41,* 1241–1251.
James, W. (1907). *Pragmatism.* New York: Longmans.
Lefcourt, H. M. (1973). The function of the illusions of control and freedom. *American Psychologist, 47,* 417–425.
Mahrer, A. R. (1988). Discovery-oriented psychotherapy research: Rationale, aims, and methods. *American Psychologist, 43,* 694–702.
Mahrer, A. R., & Nadler, W. P. (1986). Good moments in psychotherapy: A preliminary review, a list, and some promising research avenues. *Journal of Consulting and Clinical Psychology, 54,* 10–15.
Margolis, J. (1984). *Philosophy of psychology.* Englewood Cliffs, NJ: Prentice-Hall.
Margolis, J. (1986). *Pragmatism without foundations: Reconciling realism and relativism.* New York: Basil Blackwell.
Martin, J. (1988). A proposal for researching possible relationships between scientific theories and the personal theories of counselors and clients. *Journal of Counseling and Development, 66,* 261–265.
Martin, J. (1991a). To hypothesize or not to hypothesize? *American Psychologist, 46,* 651–652.
Martin, J. (1991b). The perils of "process talk" in counseling and counselor education. *The Counseling Psychologist, 19,* 260–272.
Martin, J. (1992). Intentions, responses, and private reactions: Methodological,

ontological, and epistemological reflections on process research. *Journal of Counseling and Development, 70,* 742–743.
Martin, J., Martin, W., & Slemon, A. G. (1989). Cognitive-mediational models of action-act sequences in counseling. *Journal of Counseling Psychology, 36,* 8–16.
Messick, S. (1989). Validity. In R. L. Linn (Ed.), *Educational measurement* (3rd ed., pp. 13–103). New York: Macmillan.
Morrow-Bradley, C., & Elliott, R. (1986). Utilization of psychotherapy research by practicing psychotherapists. *American Psychologist, 41,* 188–197.
Nagel, E. (1961). *The structure of science.* London: Routledge and Kegan Paul.
Neisser, U. (1978). Memory: What are the important questions? In M. M. Gruneberg, P. E. Morris, & R. N. Sykes (Eds.), *Practical aspects of memory* (pp. 3–24). London: Academic Press.
Nickles, T. (Ed.). (1980). *Scientific discovery, logic, and rationality.* London: D. Reidel.
Nisbett, R. E., & Wilson, T. D. (1977). Telling more than we know: Verbal reports on mental processes. *Psychological Review, 84,* 231–259.
Peters, R. S. (1958). *The concept of motivation.* London: Routledge and Kegan Paul.
Phillips, D. C. (1987). *Philosophy, science, and social inquiry.* New York: Pergamon.
Polanyi, M. (1966). *The tacit dimension.* London: Routledge and Kegan Paul.
Polkinghorne, D. E. (1988). *Narrative knowing and the human sciences: Systems of inquiry.* Albany: State University of New York Press.
Polkinghorne, D. E. (1991). Two conflicting calls for methodological reform. *The Counseling Psychologist, 19,* 103–114.
Reichenbach, H. (1938). *Experience and prediction.* Chicago: University of Chicago Press.
Rennie, D. L., & Toukmanian, S. G. (1992). Explanations in psychotherapy process research. In S. G. Toukmanian & D. L. Rennie (Eds.), *Psychotherapy process research: Paradigmatic and narrative approaches* (pp. 234–251). Newbury Park, CA: Sage.
Rice, L. N., & Greenberg, L. S. (Eds.). (1984). *Patterns of change: Intensive analysis of psychotherapy process.* New York: Guilford.
Rorty, R. (1980). *Philosophy and the mirror of nature.* Princeton, NJ: Princeton University Press.
Rorty, R. (1983). *Consequences of pragmatism.* Minneapolis: University of Minnesota Press.
Rorty, R. (1991). *Objectivity, relativism, and truth: Philosophical papers* (Vol. 1). Cambridge: Cambridge University Press.
Rychlak, J. F. (1988). *The psychology of rigorous humanism* (2nd ed.). New York: New York University Press.
Schön, D. (1983). *The reflective practitioner: How professionals think in action.* New York: Basic Books.
Smedslund, J. (1979). Between the analytic and the arbitrary: A case study of psychological research. *Scandinavian Journal of Psychology, 20,* 129–140.
Strong, S. (1991). Theory-driven science and naive empiricism in counseling psychology. *Journal of Counseling Psychology, 38,* 204–210.

Strong, S. (1992, August). *Theory: The integrator of science and practice.* Paper presented at the annual meeting of the American Psychological Association, Washington, DC.
Taylor, C. (1989). *Sources of the self: The making of modern identity.* Cambridge, MA: Harvard University Press.
Thompson, A. S., & Super, D. E. (Eds.). (1964). *The professional preparation of counseling psychologists.* New York: Teachers College Press.
Toulmin, S. (1972). *Human understanding: The collective use and evolution of concepts.* Princeton, NJ: Princeton University Press.
Toulmin, S. (1983). The construal of reality: Criticism in modern and post modern science. In W. J. T. Mitchell (Ed.), *The politics of interpretation* (pp. 99–117). Chicago: University of Chicago Press.
Wartofsky, M. W. (1980). Scientific judgment: Creativity and discovery in scientific thought. In T. Nickles (Ed.), *Scientific discovery: Case studies* (pp. 1–20). Dordrecht, N. Holland: Reidel.
Westcott, M. (1988). *The psychology of human freedom: A human science perspective and critique.* New York: Springer-Verlag.
Wexler, D. A., & Rice, L. N. (Eds.). (1974). *Innovations in client-centered therapy.* New York: Wiley.
Williams, R. N. (1992). The human context of agency. *American Psychologist, 47,* 752–760.
Winch, P. (1958). *The idea of social science and its relation to philosophy.* London: Routledge and Kegan Paul.

PART II

Reflective Accounts of Research Programs in Therapeutic Practice

CHAPTER 4

Musings About How to Study Therapist Techniques

CLARA E. HILL

In 1984, I wrote about my journey in becoming a psychotherapy process researcher. I discussed some of the doubts I had about the utility of our research paradigms for allowing us to answer questions about therapy. I talked about my disillusionment with traditional research methods and our need to discover new methods. I also discussed how decisions in my personal and family life influenced my research career. I do not want to repeat the same material in this chapter, even though many students have commented on the utility of that paper in encouraging them to develop their own research careers. Instead, I want to take the opportunity here to focus more on a substantive topic with which that I have been struggling, namely, how to study therapist techniques.

First, let me give a definition of techniques. Techniques are tools or methods that therapists use to facilitate effective therapy or positive client behavior change (Harper & Bruce-Sanford, 1981). Therapist techniques are what therapists *do* (or don't do) to help clients during sessions. Therapist techniques are important because they represent how therapists construct their knowledge of client dynamics and the immediate situation to determine how to intervene to have the greatest impact on clients.

I became interested in studying therapist techniques during my graduate training at Southern Illinois University with Bill Anthony, who taught me the Carkhuff (1969) model of counselor skill training. We were taught specifically that it was what the therapist did that led to client change. Clients could only rise to the level of their therapists. Minimal attention was given to client dynamics. Fortunately, therapists could learn the skills of helping, although they did not always learn them in traditional graduate training. This thinking appealed to me as a graduate student because I was eager to do the right things to become a good therapist.

As I switched from the student to the professor role and began teaching helping skills to undergraduate and graduate students, I tempered my views. Many of my students challenged me about the idea that a certain set of skills works for all clients at all times. Further, doing process research has challenged my thinking as I have struggled to understand therapist techniques. I remain convinced that therapist techniques are important, although they interact with other key variables such as client and therapist personality variables and the therapeutic relationship.

Most therapists, theoreticians, and researchers would probably agree that techniques are important. They disagree, however, as to the relative importance of techniques compared with other variables such as the therapeutic relationship and therapist and client characteristics. For example, Bergin and Lambert (1978) stated that techniques are less important than client and therapist factors. They believed that techniques were crucial only in providing a credible rationale to clients about how change occurred. Orlinsky and Howard (1978) concluded that techniques in and of themselves have not yet been shown to yield a consistently powerful differential effect on therapeutic outcome, but that without some technique that feels right, therapists cannot participate confidently in treatment.

I assert that techniques are even more important than has been suggested previously. Demonstrating their effectiveness, however, has been difficult because of our lack of understanding about how to measure and study them. In this chapter, I will discuss several methods that I have explored for defining and studying therapist techniques: (1) empathy scales, (2) verbal response modes, (3) verbal response modes in the context of a process model, (4) global scales, and (5) open-ended methods of defining techniques.

EMPATHY SCALES

In the Rogerian tradition, empathy was thought to be the ultimate therapist quality (see Hill & Corbett, 1993). Rogers (1957) described empathy as an *attitude or belief* about the capacity of the individual to manage his or her psychological situation. Although Rogers strongly believed that the facilitative conditions were constituted by attitudes, he and his colleagues developed unidimensional Likert-type scales to measure empathic behaviors of therapists in sessions (Carkhuff, 1969; Truax & Carkhuff, 1967). To enhance interrater reliability and to reflect the skills-training programs that were developed to teach facilitative conditions, researchers began to assign different therapist behaviors to points on the scale. For example, reflection and interpretation would receive higher ratings than questions and advice. In our research, we measured the effects of training students in the skills model (Anthony & Hill, 1976; Gormally, Hill, Gulanik, & McGovern, 1975; Schroeder, Hill, Gormally, & Anthony, 1973) and generally found skills training to be effective and to persist over time.

The advantages of using the empathy scales as measures of techniques are that they are simple to conceptualize and teach raters to use and they provide interval data that are easy to analyze. However, several problems emerge in using the empathy scales. First, they assess therapist manner rather than techniques. Second, they are unidimensional, which assumes *a priori* that some therapist behaviors are better or worse than others. Third, the use of a single number to describe therapist behavior is not very descriptive of the behavior. Because I was more interested in the separate therapist skills rather than empathy, the empathy scales appeared inadequate for my purposes.

VERBAL RESPONSE MODES (VRMs)

Preliminary Development of a Category System

Because of my dissatisfaction with the empathy scales as a method for describing therapist techniques, I decided that it would be more appropriate to put each technique into a separate category with no assumptions about which categories were better. For my dissertation (Hill, 1975), I made up a preliminary category system of therapist verbal response modes, or VRMs (e.g., open question, reflection, interpretation), that fit the Carkhuff (1969) skills training model. The purpose of my dissertation was to examine whether male and female therapists of different experience levels used different VRMs with male and female clients in a second session of naturally occurring therapy. The results of this study indicated that therapists did act differently with different clients.

Analogue Research

I felt uneasy with the naturalistic methodology in my dissertation because I was not able to make any claims about the effects that therapist techniques had on clients. Furthermore, the techniques as they naturally occurred in the counseling session did not always fit nicely within my categories. The methodological answer seemed to lie in gaining more control over the situation. I reasoned that if we carefully defined therapist techniques and controlled extraneous variables, we would have more certainty that particular therapist behaviors were responsible for subsequent client behaviors.

In Hill and Gormally (1977), we designed a study to test the differential effects of three well-defined verbal interventions (reflection, restatement, and probe) and two nonverbal conditions (presence or absence of facilitating nonverbal behaviors). We used an ABAB design (baseline of no or minimal intervention, implementation of one of the six treatment conditions when cued by flashing lights, return to baseline, return to intervention) to determine the effects of the therapist interventions on client's affective self-referents. The results from this study were disappointing, primarily because the methodology seemed inadequate for assessing the effects of therapist behavior in counseling. Problems with the method included the artificiality of the setting, the difficulty that counselors had with forcing their interventions into the requisite categories, the lack of a fit of the designated intervention for the needs of the client at a particular moment, the anxiety that some clients experienced with the minimal intervention period, and the confounding of other uncontrolled variables (e.g., eye contact, content of interventions). Furthermore, despite our efforts to define the three types of techniques carefully and narrowly, the interventions that were delivered within each category were quite diverse because therapists tried to adapt their responses to the situation.

Refinement of the Category System

Given my disenchantment with analogue research for studying therapist techniques, I returned to the idea of developing a category system of therapist skills to use in a more naturalistic setting. I relied heavily on Snyder's (1945) and Strupp's (1955, 1957) classification systems in developing the Hill Counselor Verbal Response Category System (HCVRCS; Hill, 1978) but tried to make it a system that would apply to all theoretical approaches. I struggled with how to get validity and reliability for the system and revised the system five or six times based on feedback from many colleagues.

Interestingly, at the time I developed my system, a number of other VRM systems were also appearing (e.g., Elliott, Barker, Caskey, & Pistrang, 1982; Goodman & Dooley, 1976; Stiles, 1979). Thus, after a hiatus when researchers turned away from response modes to embracing empathy scales, researchers returned to viewing techniques through a VRM paradigm. In fact, new VRM systems continue to be developed (e.g., Lonberg, Daniels, Hammond, Houghton-Wenger, & Brace, 1991), indicating that some researchers see inherent value in defining therapist techniques as response modes.

Let me define what VRMs are and how they fit into the structure of therapy. VRMs fit into what Russell and Stiles (1979) called an intersubjective category (as opposed to a content or extralinguistic category) of language analysis systems because they focus on the grammatical structure of language and reflect an interaction between individuals. VRMs also can be viewed as fitting within Elliott and co-authors' (1987) action domain (what is done) rather than in content (what is said), style (how it is done), or quality (how well it is carried out). VRMs are nominal, so that judgments are made of just the presence or absence of each category. No ratings of quality are made, nor are any response modes assumed to be better than any others. The categories are mutually exclusive, so that each sentence gets classified into a single VRM category. The definitions of the categories specify observable behavior as criteria, although some inference is required. The categories are meant to be representative of the whole range of possible behaviors at this level of analysis and to cover behaviors observed in all theoretical orientations (i.e., they are pantheoretical).

Response modes are coded by three or four trained observers for each response unit (essentially a grammatical sentence), although recently we have developed a method for determining predominant response modes within speaking turns (Heaton, Hill, & Edwards, in press). Using a verbatim transcript, judges read everything that occurred in the session prior to coding the designated unit. Additionally, using videotapes in conjunction with transcripts is advised because of the additional non-verbal information about what was occurring in a session, which enhances the validity of judgments.

After a number of revisions and considerable research using the HCVRCS, we have demonstrated face, content, and construct validity as well as adequate interrater reliability (see Hill, 1992, for details). Additionally, we found concurrent validity in that the HCVRCS was correlated with five other VRM systems (Elliott et al., 1987).

Case Study Research

I got quite excited about the idea of case study research because I thought that using a case study method would allow researchers to understand the phenomenon of interest within the context of the complexity of the individual case. When I started working on my first case study (Hill, Carter, & O'Farrell, 1983), I wanted to remain open to allowing the data to "speak for themselves." I sat down after every session and wrote copious notes about what happened. The client kept a diary about her experiences as well. I was faced with a mountain of data but no guidelines for what to do with it. If I had been more familiar with qualitative research paradigms, I might have pursued that approach, but instead I decided to return to the methods that my colleagues and I had developed for having judges code therapist and client behavior. We then used sequential analysis to assess whether therapist behaviors were reliably associated with the immediate client behaviors (e.g., whether therapist interpretation precedes client insight). The case study and sequential analysis approach did seem to get us one step closer to what we were looking for in that it enabled us to examine one case in its entirety and search for connections between therapist and immediate client behavior.

We did another case study (O'Farrell, Hill, & Patton, 1986), using a client similar to the one in the previous study and myself as therapist again, to determine if we could replicate the findings of the first case study when therapist and client variables were controlled. Across both cases, interpretation and exploration of feelings were useful. Other interventions (e.g., direct feedback about behavior, gestalt exercises, discussion of the therapy relationship, confrontation, permission to the client to be herself, analogies, and direct guidance) were helpful in one case but not the other. Clearly, different techniques were effective with similar clients, even when used by the same therapist. Some differences between the cases that might have led to the differential helpfulness of techniques were length of treatment (12 versus 20 sessions), client capacity for therapy (e.g., experiencing levels, interpersonal skills, and ability to profit from interventions), and client social support outside of treatment.

An interesting methodological aspect of the two cases (Hill et al., 1983; O'Farrell et al., 1986) is that I was the therapist in both cases. Although often advised against, it was useful to serve as therapist because it made me sensitive to the demands put on therapists in this type of research. Additionally, because I was involved in the cases, I had an inside perspective on what happened. Of course, my biases had to be balanced by other people who were willing to challenge my interpretation of events. We accomplished this by having other people watch sessions and comment on the proceedings, categorize the data, and question the interpretation of the results.

Although the wealth of data from a single case study provides much food for thought and clinical speculation, the ability to make general statements about the therapy process is limited to the specific dyad. One solution to this dilemma is to do multiple case studies (thus preserving individual change patterns) and determine whether the results generalize

(Hayes, 1981; Kazdin, 1981). With similarity of results across a number of cases, one can be more confident of findings.

Therefore, using the two previous case studies as models, we did a series of eight cases with a new set of experienced therapists and anxious/depressed female clients (Hill et al., 1988). To retain the inside flavor that I had been able to provide as the therapist in the earlier cases, we interviewed therapists after each session and interviewed both clients and therapists after the termination of therapy to obtain their perspective on what had happened. We first analyzed the data for consistencies across the entire group (controlling for the individual cases) and found that interpretation, self-disclosure, paraphrase, and approval were viewed as particularly helpful. But VRMs alone accounted for only a small proportion (1%) of the variance of perceived helpfulness of interventions.

The marked differences between cases in therapist use of response modes and client receptiveness to them led me to do an individual analysis on each case to determine the reasons for such variability (Hill, 1989). When we studied both the quantitative and qualitative data derived from interviews, we found that only interpretation and approval were helpful in every case. Additionally, we found a wealth of information about how techniques were used in individual cases, and we used this information to understand the change process in each case.

Although I liked aspects of the case study method, I came out of the experience not convinced that the way I had tackled case studies was the approach to take. Perhaps I had gone into the case study approach with too few specific hypotheses. Asking about the overall effectiveness of therapist techniques may be doomed to failure as a research question; perhaps we need to ask more specific questions.

The advantages of using VRMs to assess therapist techniques are: (1) VRMs fit with specific skills that are taught in skills-training programs; (2) VRMs are useful for objectively describing what therapists do from different orientations or from different types of treatments; and (3) VRMs are relatively easy to judge and to use in sequential analyses for studying what client behaviors follow therapist interventions. The disadvantages are: (1) VRMs miss important elements of techniques, such as nonverbal behavior, style or manner, quality or competence, and the subjective experience of clients and therapists; (2) VRMs do not encompass techniques that are not defined by grammatical structures (e.g., analysis of transference, empathy, assignment of homework); (3) VRMs are expensive to obtain because transcripts are required for accuracy and three or four well-trained judges are needed to reach reliability; (4) studying the interaction between techniques and other variables such as the therapeutic relationship, client and therapist variables, and long-term outcome is difficult because VRMs are measured on a molecular basis; and (5) VRMs explain only a small amount of the variance even in immediate client behavior. Thus, although useful from a descriptive perspective, VRMs are problematic as measures of therapist techniques, especially when studied in isolation from other process variables.

VRMs WITHIN THE CONTEXT OF OTHER PROCESS VARIABLES

I began to speculate that VRMs are inadequate because they do not capture other aspects of the moment-by-moment process. Therapists might make the same intervention for various reasons. For example, a therapist might ask a closed question either to gather information or to challenge the client. Although the grammatical structure of the two interventions might be the same, the impact on the client probably would be quite different. Thus, I argued that we would get a more adequate description of therapist techniques by adding intentions to VRMs. Additionally, I felt that we needed to capture the context of what the client was doing prior to the therapist intervention. Rather than giving interventions at random, therapists undoubtedly respond to what clients are expressing at a given moment.

We developed a process model that describes the interaction between overt and covert behaviors of therapists and clients on a moment-by-moment basis in therapy (Hill & O'Grady, 1985). Pre-existing client and therapist variables and contextual variables within the therapy process set the stage for what occurs at a given moment within treatment. The therapist draws from theory, diagnostic formulations, and clinical observations of the client to develop an *intention* for the impact he or she wants to have on the client. To implement the intention, the therapist decides to use specific *verbal response modes* (e.g., to intensify feelings, the therapist may use a paraphrase or an open question). The client's *reactions* to the therapist's interventions determine how he or she *behaves* or responds to the therapist (e.g., if the client feels supported, he or she may choose to reveal more to the therapist). On the basis of his or her perceptions of the client's response, the therapist formulates his or her next intentions and response modes to meet the altered needs of the client, yielding a continually evolving process. Martin (1984) described a similar model relating client change to a continuous cycle of counselor intention, counselor behavior, client perception, client cognitive processing, and client behavior.

When we first tried to figure out how to measure intentions, we were not aware of any methodologies that we could use to guide us. The empiricist tradition held that only observable behaviors were worthy of measurement. To try to assess therapist intentions, we had several therapists review their videotapes immediately after sessions and tell us why they did what they did, using a method similar to Interpersonal Process Recall (Kagan, 1975). After listening to several reviews, we began to get some sense of consistency among the responses. On the basis of these responses, we developed a list of therapist intentions and eventually reduced it to 19 categories (Hill & O'Grady, 1985).

Several methodological problems arose in trying to measure intentions. How do you measure thoughts when they are not necessarily manifested in overt behaviors? Should there be reliability? After all, thoughts change over time. After therapists reflect on their intentions, they might be able to rationalize or intellectualize what they did at the time.

Another issue that we struggled with is who should judge the intentions. We first used observers to judge the intentions on the basis of reading the transcript or viewing the overt behaviors (Hill et al., 1983). We came to realize, however, that the intentions may be covert and observers might not be able to detect them, so we felt that only therapists could be accurate reporters of their intentions. Hence, we developed a structured recall method in which therapists watched and listened to the videotape of the session, stopped the tape after each therapist speaking turn, and, for each intervention, wrote down the numbers of up to three intentions from the Intentions List (Hill & O'Grady, 1985). An additional issue is that some therapists complain that the intentions do not exactly fit their experience; they want to modify the Intentions List to fit their own style. I agree that when you segment experience into a certain number of categories, the Intentions List does not fit any given person's experience exactly. The inability to describe a given person's experience is a drawback to any standardized measure.

Another issue that Stiles (1987) has raised is that there are different levels of intentions. Some intentions are public or on record and can be determined by observers listening to the communication. Others are private and knowable most directly by report of the person (Stiles refers to these as purposes). Our understanding is that intentions are what therapists privately want to accomplish in their interventions, whether or not communicated, which is someplace between intentions and purposes as defined by Stiles.

Martin (1992) has proposed another method of assessing intentions. First, therapists talk in an open-ended manner to a researcher about their intentions for each intervention. Then, judges, who are trained in what the intention categories mean, place the open-ended material into the categories. He argues that this leads to more precision in arriving at the accurate intentions. This method assumes that judges have no biases and are better at categorizing intentions than are therapists. I prefer having therapists do the categorizing because they are the ones who are most aware of their intentions.

Some have questioned whether the videotape-assisted review process yields data that validly reflect therapists' experiences during sessions (Friedlander, 1992). Furthermore, reviewers of our first article on intentions (Hill & O'Grady, 1985) questioned why we did not include data on stability. In a study that we have completed recently (Hill et al., 1994), we examined both of these issues. Using three sessions of therapy with anxious clients, therapists were interrupted during sessions and asked to indicate their intentions. Immediately following the session, they went through a videotape-assisted review and again identified their intentions for the same interventions. Two weeks later they did a videotape-assisted review of the second session once again and identified their intentions. Similar therapist intentions were reported both during and after sessions, indicating that videotape-assisted reviews yield valid data. Furthermore, we found evidence for the stability of therapist intentions across 2 weeks.

Our major test of the efficacy of adding therapist intentions and previous client behavior to VRMs was published in Hill and co-authors (1988). We found that the combination of intentions and response modes provided the best description of therapist behavior in predicting client behavior. Furthermore, we found that the level of client experiencing in the turn prior to the therapist intervention made a difference in the perceived effectiveness of the intervention, indicating the importance of the immediate context for therapist techniques and providing support for the process model described earlier. Rather than accounting for only about 1% of the variance, we could now account for about 2–7% of the variance, still not a huge amount.

Martin and colleagues (Martin, Martin, Meyer, & Slemon, 1986; Martin, Martin, & Slemon, 1987, 1989) have shown that ratings of session effectiveness are related to consistency in the various parts of the chain of their similar cognitive-mediational model. Thus, some evidence has been found across two research teams for moment-by-moment process models.

In summary, adding therapist cognitions and previous client behavior to VRMs seems to be an improvement over just examining VRMs. Therapist techniques are described more adequately, and more of the immediate context is accounted for. However, the larger context is still not accounted for in that variables such as individual differences in clients and in therapists, the therapeutic relationship, stage of treatment, or process within the session are not considered. Additionally, one could question whether the gain in explained variance is worth the burden on therapists of doing a videotape-assisted review to assess intentions and on researchers of collecting another set of observer ratings for client behavior.

GLOBAL MEASURES OF THERAPIST TECHNIQUES

A contrasting method to VRMs for classifying therapist techniques is a global method (Kiesler, 1973), in which therapist behavior is judged across an entire session. Observers listen to an entire session (or large segment thereof) and indicate how much each type of behavior occurred. Observers are required to use their clinical judgment to determine how to aggregate the behaviors to arrive at their judgments about the intensity of their ratings.

In Hill, O'Grady, and Elkin (1992), we used the Collaborative Study Psychotherapy Rating Scale (CSPRS; Hollon et al., 1988) to judge whether therapists adhered to the behaviors required of them in cognitive-behavior therapy, interpersonal therapy, or clinical management. The CSPRS has scales that assess behaviors relevant to each of the three treatment modalities as well as some items that are non-modality specific behaviors (e.g., facilitative conditions and explicit directiveness). After listening to an entire therapy session, two judges rate therapists for how much they engaged in each of the 96 behaviors on the CSPRS. Results indicated that therapists exhibited more behaviors appropriate to their respective treatment modality than to the other treatment approaches. The treatments could be discriminated almost perfectly using the modality-specific scales of the CSPRS.

In Heaton, Hill, and Edwards (in press), we compared two global measures with the HCVRCS (our molecular measure of VRMs). The two global measures were the Psychotherapy Q-Set (PQS; Jones, Cumming, & Horowitz, 1988) and the Therapeutic Interventions Scale of the Therapeutic Procedures Inventory–Revised (TPI-R; McNeilly & Howard, 1991). All three measures were judged by different teams of undergraduate observers to control for perspective and levels of training of judges, with judges using either the speaking turn (for the HCVRCS) or the entire session (for the PQS and TPI-R) as the unit that was categorized. To make the comparison fair, items were chosen from the PQS and TPI-R that directly corresponded to the HCVRCS response mode clusters. For example a PQS item for paraphrase was "Therapist clarifies, restates, or paraphrases patient's communication," whereas the TPI-R item was "Tries to reflect patient's feelings." Results indicated that the directives, paraphrase, and interpretation items on the PQS were related to the corresponding items on the TPI-R, but that none of the PQS or TPI-R clusters were related to the corresponding HCVRCS clusters. Thus, there was no correspondence between the global method (PQS, TPI-R) and the molecular method (HCVRCS), which raises concerns about the validity of both types of measures.

Advantages of global measures are: (1) they are not confined by grammatical structures (as are VRMs), but can include items that are more descriptive of many types of therapist behavior; (2) many systems provide a comprehensive list of therapist behaviors that can be modality-specific as well as general across treatment approaches; and (3) global measures can assess techniques that do not occur within discrete segments of sessions (e.g., speaking turns) but occur throughout sessions (e.g., analysis of transference, support). Disadvantages are: (1) the criteria judges use to determine whether a specific technique occurred are unclear given that global measures are applied to whole sessions; (2) because measures do not require identification of specific behaviors within sessions, the immediate in-session effects of the technique cannot be examined, and (3) it is often unclear whether raters base their judgments on frequency of behavior or the quality of the delivery. But perhaps most problematic is the lack of relationship between molecular and global measures. Thus, the global measures do not seem to provide any magical answers to the dilemma of how to measure techniques.

OPEN-ENDED METHODS OF DEFINING TECHNIQUES

An overriding problem with the empathy scales, VRMs, and global measures is that all were developed to be used by trained judges. Yet a repeated problem discovered in the empirical literature is the lack of relationship between therapist, client, and observer perspectives (see Lambert & Hill, 1994, for review). Thus, we need to try methods for assessing therapist techniques that assess both client and therapist experiences. Recently, to try to get around some of the problems involved in using judges, we have employed an exploratory (see Hill, 1990), discovery-oriented (Elliott, 1984; Mahrer, 1988), or qualitative strategy (Strauss & Corbin, 1990) of trying to stay close to the data to allow the data to "speak for themselves."

Following each session as well as following the entire therapy, for eight cases (Hill, 1989), we asked therapists and clients to tell us what the most helpful and hindering events were within the sessions. We used this open-ended format so that we would not be constrained by previous expectations about what the important events were within the session. We analyzed the data in two ways. First, we asked judges to develop categories by examining the open-ended responses. From the data, five clusters emerged: therapist techniques, therapist manner, client tasks, client manner, and working alliance. Across cases, the most helpful events were in the category of therapist techniques, supporting the belief about the efficacy of techniques. Second, we studied the data from a qualitative perspective in each case to see what it added to our knowledge. Often, highly individualized salient events from sessions were discovered in these analyses. Other researchers also have studied helpful and hindering events using similar methods (e.g., Llewelyn, Elliott, Shapiro, Hardy, & Firth-Cozens, 1988; Martin & Stelmaczonek, 1988).

In Thompson and Hill (1993), we examined client perceptions of therapist competence and how these evaluations of competence were related to session outcome, treatment outcome, and client satisfaction. Clients were interviewed about their perceptions of therapist competence after the third of six sessions. Categories were developed through examination of the open-ended responses. These open-ended responses were then classified by judges into 27 categories, which were grouped into seven supercategories: Facilitating Style, Facilitating Intervention, Facilitating Effect, Detracting Style, Detracting Intervention, Detracting Effect, and Client Minimization. Therapist competence was more often attributed to Facilitating Style than to Facilitating Intervention. When clients perceived their therapists as facilitative, they rated session outcome and satisfaction positively.

In Rhodes, Hill, Thompson, and Elliott (1994), we explored clients' retrospective accounts of misunderstanding events in psychotherapy. We asked clients what happened when they felt misunderstood in therapy. We analyzed the data using a qualitative methodology to see if there were consistencies in the process of resolved and unresolved misunderstanding events. In an initial examination, we noted that clients reported a variety of therapist behaviors as leading to misunderstanding events, ranging from inappropriate advice to knitting within sessions. How the misunderstanding event was processed in therapy as well as the context within which the event occurred seemed more important than whether a misunderstanding event occurred, leading to the conclusion that a repair of a rupture can strengthen therapy.

An advantage of using these more open-ended methods for defining therapist techniques is that we assess the participants' experiences of events, but then use trained judges to categorize the experiences so that events can be compared across cases. A disadvantage is that because we rely on the participants' reports, we might not always know where the events occurred in the objective record of the session, making it difficult to describe what actually happened and relate it to outcome. However, in general this more exploratory qualitative strategy seems promising as a method for learning about participants' experiences of therapist techniques.

ISSUES TO CONSIDER IN MEASURING THERAPIST TECHNIQUES

Although over the past 24 years I have tried a number of different methods for studying therapist techniques, I have not found any one method to be completely satisfactory in reflecting the richness of what therapists do in sessions. Indeed, all of the methods seem to be missing fundamental aspects. Clearly, we need new measures and new methods of analyzing the data derived from existing measures. Some issues to consider in measuring therapist techniques are complexity, the need to study discrete events, and perspective.

Complexity

Measures need to reflect the complexity and richness of what therapists do to intervene with clients. At least four dimensions (see also Elliott et al., 1987; Schaffer, 1982) are important. First, *type* of intervention has been studied most often using response modes, but it should be noted that there are an endless number of techniques. Many have been better specified in the global measures, but work needs to be done to define where they occur in actual sessions. Second, we need to know not only what was done but how well it was done. The *quality* of intervention may be more important than type of intervention. Quality includes such aspects as timing and appropriateness, which are very subjective judgments and often are biased by theoretical orientation. Third, *manner* refers to the style in which the intervention is made and involves such variables as empathy, warmth, genuineness, expertness, attractiveness, and trustworthiness. Finally, *content* refers to what is being discussed (e.g., family issues, vocational issues, interpersonal issues). Although content usually is not measured, it could be quite important.

We also must remember that techniques are not just made up of overt verbal behaviors. Therapists often use nonverbal behaviors (e.g., a shrug or a raised eyebrow) to communicate the entire meaning of an intervention or use nonverbal behaviors (e.g., hand gestures) to modify or enhance their communication (see Harper, Wiens, & Matarazzo, 1978). Additionally, therapists have covert behavior that is not obvious from viewing their overt behavior, such as intentions for their interventions and private reactions to client behaviors. Covert events modify overt behaviors and provide a more comprehensive picture of interventions.

Discrete Events

To make them useful, techniques should be identifiable as discrete events in sessions. Each event does not need to be comparable in length, but to examine the effects of the techniques, we need to be able to identify where techniques occur and what they are composed of. Thus, the global method of identifying how often particular techniques occurred in each session is valuable only as a first step. Once a technique has been identified as occurring within the session, researchers need to go back and find out where it occurred so that we can begin to determine what makes up the event.

Perspective

Although researchers who study therapist techniques have been enamored with observable behaviors, we may need to consider, as with empathy (see Gurman, 1977), that the client's experience of what the therapist does is more important than the actual therapist behavior. For example, a judge may perceive a therapist technique to be very confrontive, but the client's perception of it as supportive is probably what leads the client to respond in a particular way. Clients may not be able to give the technical terms (e.g., analysis of defenses), but they could describe what they thought therapists were doing, and judges could classify these into categories. Of course, problems arise with interventions that are supposed to work at an indirect or less conscious level, such as paradoxical interventions. In these cases, clients might react in the intended manner but might not be able to describe what the therapist did.

Perhaps again using the example of empathy (Barrett-Lennard, 1981), we might conceive of techniques as following a three-stage model. First, the therapist intends to be delivering a particular intervention, which could be determined only by direct therapist report. Second, there is an observable intervention that would include all the factors above (type, quality, manner, content; verbal and nonverbal) and could be judged by trained judges. Third, there is the client experience of what the therapist did. For example, the therapist might intend to get more information because he or she did not quite understand what the client was talking about. Objective judges might view the intervention as a confrontation because it was delivered in a challenging manner. The client, on the other hand, might not even hear the intervention because he or she was thinking about something else. If we are interested in studying the immediate reaction of the intervention on the client, the client's experience is the only relevant data. If we are interested in studying the therapist's choice of subsequent intervention, the relevant data are the therapist intentions as well as his or her perception of the client reaction. If we are interested in teaching students how to do therapy, we would want to have actual examples of what therapists did overtly as well as what they intended to do.

VARIABLES TO CONSIDER WHEN TESTING THE EFFICACY OF TECHNIQUES

Several variables that need to be considered when studying techniques are the stage of treatment, individual client needs, belief in the techniques, and general vs. specific questions about techniques.

Stage of Treatment

Several stage models of treatment have been proposed (e.g., Egan, 1986; Mann, 1973). The first stage usually is involved with establishing the relationship, assessing client needs, and setting goals. The second stage typically consists of working on the identified problems, usually in a recycling process where the client hopefully learns more about him- or herself through the process of working on each identified problem. This process often consists of therapists helping clients attain insight, overcome resistances, and implement and assess new behaviors or attitudes. Sometimes the therapy relationship becomes a focus during this stage, particularly with anger at and disappointment with the therapist coming to the foreground. The third or final stage usually consists of termination and summing up what has been learned during treatment. I hypothesize that techniques operate differently within each of the three stages.

Individual Client Needs

Even within stages, which techniques are the most potent and useful probably depends on the type of client. Establishing the relationship with a well-functioning client may require a different set of techniques than establishing the relationship with a borderline patient. Direct support and moving quickly to interpretation might help well-functioning clients feel that therapists have something to offer, whereas borderline clients may need more distance and authoritarianism from therapists.

Stiles (1988) cited client needs as a reason for the typical lack of relationship between frequency of process variables and session or treatment outcome. One client may need to be given several interpretations before hearing the message, whereas another needs a single interpretation. The differential responsiveness of individual clients will probably prevent us from ever making more than very general statements about the effectiveness of techniques, although we may be able to identify how specific personality types react to different types of techniques. For example, researchers have found that reactant clients respond better to indirect or paradoxical techniques, whereas nonreactant clients respond better to direct techniques (Shoham-Salomon, Avner, & Neeman, 1989; Shoham-Salomon & Rosenthal, 1987).

Belief in the Techniques

As Frank and Frank (1991) noted, clients' and therapists' beliefs in the particular technique might be a crucial factor in their evaluation of the efficacy of that technique. Consider the client who goes a long distance to consult with a world-renowned therapist for hypnosis. Both client and therapist begin with an expectation that this treatment will be effective. This expectation undoubtedly plays a part in the effectiveness of the intervention, although it could backfire with some clients who have a need to undermine therapists.

General vs. Specific Questions About Techniques

Asking the question about what techniques are the most effective in general is probably fruitless. Asking the more differentiated question of what technique has what effect at what time with what type of client by what type of therapist is more appropriate (e.g., Krumboltz, 1966; Paul, 1967). But even at that, we need to be aware that there is probably a range of techniques that could be effective at any given time and a range that would not. An events approach, where researchers examine specific types of events such as misunderstanding events, may be a more productive approach to studying therapist techniques than the more general approach of asking if therapist techniques work.

TESTING THE EFFICACY OF TECHNIQUES

Two statistical methods have been used frequently to connect therapist techniques to outcome. Correlational analyses have been used for connecting the frequency of use of techniques with session or treatment outcome, but these have been roundly criticized as inappropriate because they do not account for timing, quality, or client needs (see review in Lambert & Hill, 1994). Sequential analyses have been used to examine the immediate effects of therapist techniques as defined by molecular measures (e.g., Hill et al., 1988), but cannot be used for techniques as defined by global methods because these methods do not identify discrete events within sessions. Furthermore, sequential analysis is not appropriate for assessing effects that occur at variable intervals rather than immediately following the therapist intervention, nor is it appropriate for assessing longer-term effects. Thus, at present we need new methods for determining the effects of therapist techniques. These methods will have to take into account all the variables mentioned above, for example, complexity in the measure, interaction with the therapy relationship, stage of treatment, and client needs. New methods such as task analysis (Greenberg, 1984, 1986, 1991) and qualitative methods (e.g., Strauss & Corbin, 1990) may be useful next steps for studying the sequence of events of therapist techniques and client behaviors.

CONCLUSIONS

Where am I presently in the journey of studying therapist techniques? I have given up on empathy scales as good measures of techniques. I believe that VRMs and global scales are useful for describing what occurs in sessions but are limited in terms of testing patterns of change within therapy. My disillusionment with VRMs is difficult because I have invested so much of my research career in studying them. VRMs seem to capture some aspects of the process, so I am not willing to drop them completely, but at best they probably can only serve as part of an overall measure of techniques.

I like the idea of using more exploratory and qualitative approaches, at least initially, to begin to include all the complexity of the context that surrounds therapist techniques, but I am just now trying to understand how to apply these approaches. I am confident in our ultimate ability to answer questions through research once we develop the appropriate paradigms.

I am sure that our questions need to become more sophisticated. The question, "What is the overall impact of therapist techniques?" is too simplistic. Perhaps we need to adopt an events approach in which we try to specify particular events quite narrowly for specific types of clients and then examine the range of therapist techniques that is useful from different perspectives. For example, perhaps we need to study the range of therapist techniques that work for anxious, insight-oriented clients when they present with a problematic reaction to a recent event during the middle phase of therapy within a good therapeutic relationship. Contemplating the variety of approaches that will begin to help us figure out how change occurs in therapy, and where therapist techniques fit into the picture, is exciting. The arena is certainly wide open for lots of innovative researchers to make contributions.

Author's Note: I wish to express my appreciation to Kristin Heaton, Annie Judge, Jim Mahalik, and Elizabeth Nutt for reading drafts of this chapter.

REFERENCES

Anthony, W. A., & Hill, C. E. (1976). A student evaluation of systematic human relations training. *Counselor Education and Supervision, 15,* 305–309.

Barrett-Lennard, G. T. (1981). The empathy cycle: Refinement of a nuclear concept. *Journal of Counseling Psychology, 28,* 91–100.

Bergin, A. E., & Lambert, M. J. (1978). The evaluation of therapeutic outcome. In S. L. Garfield & A. E. Bergin (Eds.), *Handbook of psychotherapy and behavior change* (2nd ed., pp. 139–190). New York: Wiley.

Carkhuff, R. R. (1969). *Human and helping relations* (Vols. 1 & 2). New York: Holt, Rinehart & Winston.

Egan, G. (1986). *The skilled helper* (3rd ed.). Monterey, CA: Brooks/Cole.

Elliott, R. (1984). A discovery-oriented approach to significant change events in psychotherapy: Interpersonal process recall and comprehensive process analysis. In L. N. Rice & L. S. Greenberg (Eds.), *Patterns of change: Intensive analysis of psychotherapy process* (pp. 249–286). New York: Guilford.

Elliott, R., Barker, C. B., Caskey, N., & Pistrang, N. (1982). Differential helpfulness of counselor verbal response modes. *Journal of Counseling Psychology, 29,* 354–361.

Elliott, R., Hill, C. E., Stiles, W. B., Friedlander, M. L., Mahrer, A. R., & Margison, F. R. (1987). Primary therapist response modes: Comparison of six rating systems. *Journal of Consulting and Clinical Psychology, 55,* 218–223.

Frank, J. D., & Frank, J. B. (1991). *Persuasion and healing* (3rd ed.). Baltimore: Johns Hopkins University Press.

Friedlander, M. L. (1992). Psychotherapeutic process: About the art, about the science. *Journal of Counseling and Development, 70,* 740–741.

Goodman, G., & Dooley, D. A. (1976). A framework for help-intended communication. *Psychotherapy: Theory, Research, and Practice, 13,* 106–117.

Gormally, J., Hill, C. E., Gulanik, N., & McGovern, T. (1975). The persistence of communication skills for undergraduate trainees. *Journal of Clinical Psychology, 31,* 369–372.

Greenberg, L. S. (1984). Task analysis: The general approach. In L. N. Rice & L. S. Greenberg (Eds.), *Patterns of change: Intensive analysis of psychotherapy process* (pp. 124–148). New York: Guilford.
Greenberg, L. S. (1986). Change process research. *Journal of Consulting and Clinical Psychology, 54,* 4–9.
Greenberg, L. S. (1991). Research on the process of change. *Psychotherapy Research, 1,* 3–16.
Gurman, A. S. (1977). The patient's perception of the therapeutic relationship. In A. S. Gurman & A. M. Razin (Eds.), *Effective psychotherapy: A handbook of research* (pp. 503–543). Elmsford, NY: Pergamon.
Harper, F. D., & Bruce-Sanford, G. C. (1981). *Counseling techniques: An outline and overview.* Alexandria, VA: Douglass Press.
Harper, R. G., Wiens, A. N., & Matarazzo, J. D. (1978). *Nonverbal communication: The state of the art.* New York: Wiley.
Hayes, S. C. (1981). Single case experimental design in empirical and clinical practice. *Journal of Consulting and Clinical Psychology, 49,* 193–211.
Heaton, K., Hill, C. E., & Edwards, L. (in press). A comparison of molecular and molar methods of judging therapist techniques. *Psychotherapy Research.*
Hill, C. E. (1975). Sex of client and sex and experience level of counselor. *Journal of Counseling Psychology, 22,* 6–11.
Hill, C. E. (1978). Development of a counselor verbal response category system. *Journal of Counseling Psychology, 25,* 461–468.
Hill, C. E. (1984). A personal account of the process of becoming a counseling process researcher. *The Counseling Psychologist, 12*(3), 99–109.
Hill, C. E. (1989). *Therapist techniques and client outcomes: Eight cases of brief psychotherapy.* Newbury Park, CA: Sage.
Hill, C. E. (1990). A review of exploratory in-session process research. *Journal of Consulting and Clinical Psychology, 58,* 288–294.
Hill, C. E. (1992). An overview of four measures developed to test the Hill process model: Therapist intentions, therapist response modes, client reactions, and client behaviors. *Journal of Counseling and Development, 70,* 728–739.
Hill, C. E., Carter, J. A., & O'Farrell, M. K. (1983). A case study of the process and outcome of time-limited counseling. *Journal of Counseling Psychology, 30,* 3–18.
Hill, C. E., & Corbett, M. M. (1993). A perspective on the history of process and outcome research in counseling psychology. *Journal of Counseling Psychology, 40,* 3–25.
Hill, C. E., & Gormally, J. (1977). Effect of reflection, restatement, probe, and nonverbal behaviors on client affect. *Journal of Counseling Psychology, 24,* 92–97.
Hill, C. E., Helms, J. E., Tichenor, V., Spiegel, S. B., O'Grady, K. E., & Perry, E. (1988). The effects of therapist response modes in brief psychotherapy. *Journal of Counseling Psychology, 35,* 222–233.
Hill, C. E., & O'Grady, K. E. (1985). List of therapist intentions illustrated in a case study and with therapists of varying theoretical orientations. *Journal of Counseling Psychology, 32,* 3–22.
Hill, C. E., O'Grady, K. E., Balenger, V., Busse, W., Falk, D. R., Hill, M., Rios, P., & Taffe, R. (1994). A methodological examination of videotape-assisted reviews

in brief therapy: Helpfulness ratings, therapist intentions, client reactions, mood, and session evaluation. *Journal of Counseling Psychology, 41,* 236–247.

Hill, C. E., O'Grady, K. E., & Elkin, I. E. (1992). Applying the Collaborative Study Psychotherapy Rating Scale to rate therapist adherence in cognitive-behavior therapy, interpersonal therapy, and clinical management. *Journal of Consulting and Clinical Psychology, 60,* 73–79.

Hollon, S. D., Evans, M. D., Auerbach, A., DeRubeis, R. J., Elkin, I., Lowery, A., Kriss, M., Grove, W., Tuason, V. B., & Piasecki, J. (1988, June). *Development of a system for rating therapies for depression: Differentiating cognitive therapy, interpersonal psychotherapy, and clinical management pharmacotherapy.* Paper presented at the meeting of the Society for Psychotherapy Research, Santa Fe, NM.

Jones, E. E., Cumming, J. D., & Horowitz, M. J. (1988). Another look at the nonspecific hypothesis of therapeutic effectiveness. *Journal of Consulting and Clinical Psychology, 56,* 48–55.

Kagan, N. (1975). *Interpersonal process recall: A method of influencing human interaction.* East Lansing: Michigan State University.

Kazdin, A. E. (1981). Drawing valid inferences from case studies. *Journal of Consulting and Clinical Psychology, 49,* 183–192.

Kiesler, D. J. (1973). *The process of psychotherapy.* Chicago: Aldine.

Krumboltz, J. D. (1966). *Revolution in counseling: Implications of behavioral science.* Boston: Houghton Mifflin.

Lambert, M. J., & Hill, C. E. (1994). Methodological issues in studying psychotherapy process and outcome. In A. E. Bergin & S. L. Garfield (Eds.), *Handbook of psychotherapy and behavior change* (4th ed., pp. 772–113). New York: Wiley.

Llewelyn, S. P., Elliott, R., Shapiro, D. A., Hardy, G., & Firth-Cozens, J. (1988). Client perceptions of significant events in prescriptive and exploratory periods of individual therapy. *British Journal of Clinical Psychology, 27,* 105–114.

Lonberg, S. D., Daniels, J. A., Hammond, S. G., Houghton-Wenger, B., & Brace, L. J. (1991). Counselor and client verbal response mode changes during initial counseling sessions. *Journal of Counseling Psychology, 38,* 394–400.

Mahrer, A. R. (1988). Discovery-oriented psychotherapy research: Rationale, aims, and methods. *American Psychologist, 43,* 694–702.

Mann, J. (1973). *Time-limited psychotherapy.* Cambridge, MA: Harvard University Press.

Martin, J. (1984). The cognitive mediational paradigm for research on counseling. *Journal of Counseling Psychology, 31,* 559–572.

Martin, J. (1992). Intentions, responses, and private reactions: Methodological, ontological, and epistemological reflections on process research. *Journal of Counseling and Development, 70,* 742–743.

Martin, J., Martin, W., Meyer, M., & Slemon, A. G. (1986). An empirical investigation of the cognitive mediational paradigm for research on counseling. *Journal of Counseling Psychology, 33,* 115–123.

Martin, J., Martin, W., & Slemon, A. G. (1987). Cognitive mediation in person-centered and rational-emotive therapy. *Journal of Counseling Psychology, 34,* 251–260.

Martin, J., Martin, W., & Slemon, A. G. (1989). Cognitive-mediational models of action-act sequences in counseling. *Journal of Counseling Psychology, 36,* 8–16.

Martin, J., & Stelmaczonek, K. (1988). Participants' identification and recall of important events in counseling. *Journal of Counseling Psychology, 35,* 385–390.

McNeilly, C. L., & Howard, K. I. (1991). The Therapeutic Procedures Inventory: Psychometric properties and relationship to phase of treatment. *Journal of Psychotherapy Integration, 1,* 223–234.

O'Farrell, M. K., Hill, C. E., & Patton, S. (1986). Comparison of two cases of counseling with the same counselor. *Journal of Counseling and Development, 65,* 141–145.

Orlinsky, D. E., & Howard, K. I. (1978). The relation of process to outcome in psychotherapy. In S. L. Garfield & A. E. Bergin (Eds.), *Handbook of psychotherapy and behavior change* (2nd ed., pp. 283–330). New York: Wiley.

Paul, G. (1967). Strategy in outcome research in psychotherapy. *Journal of Consulting Psychology, 31,* 109–118.

Rhodes, R., Hill, C. E., Thompson, B. J., & Elliott, R. (1994). Client retrospective recall of resolved and unresolved misunderstanding events. *Journal of Counseling Psychology.*

Rogers, C. R. (1957). The necessary and sufficient conditions of therapeutic personality change. *Journal of Consulting Psychology, 21,* 95–103.

Russell, R. L., & Stiles, W. B. (1979). Categories for classifying language in psychotherapy. *Psychological Bulletin, 86,* 404–419.

Schaffer, N. D. (1982). Multidimensional measures of therapist behaviors as predictors of outcome. *Psychological Bulletin, 92,* 670–681.

Schroeder, K., Hill, C. E., Gormally, J., & Anthony, W. A. (1973). Systematic human relations training for resident assistants. *Journal of College Student Personnel, 52,* 313–316.

Shoham-Salomon, V., Avner, R., & Neeman, R. (1989). You're changed if you do and changed if you don't: Mechanisms underlying paradoxical interventions. *Journal of Consulting and Clinical Psychology, 75,* 590–598.

Shoham-Salomon, V., & Rosenthal, R. (1987). Paradoxical interventions: A meta-analysis. *Journal of Consulting and Clinical Psychology, 55,* 22–28.

Snyder, W. U. (1945). An investigation of the nature of nondirective psychotherapy. *Journal of General Psychology, 33,* 193–223.

Stiles, W. B. (1979). Verbal response modes and psychotherapeutic technique. *Psychiatry, 42,* 49–62.

Stiles, W. B. (1987). Some intentions are observable. *Journal of Counseling Psychology, 34,* 236–239.

Stiles, W. B. (1988). Psychotherapy process–outcome correlations may be misleading. *Psychotherapy, 25,* 27–35.

Strauss, A., & Corbin, J. (1990). *Basics of qualitative research.* Newbury Park, CA: Sage.

Strupp, H. H. (1955). An objective comparison of Rogerian and psychoanalytic techniques. *Journal of Consulting Psychology, 19,* 1–7.

Strupp, H. H. (1957). A multidimensional analysis of therapist activity in analytic and client-centered therapy. *Journal of Consulting Psychology, 21,* 301–308.

Thompson, B. J., & Hill, C. E. (1993). Client perceptions of therapist competence. *Psychotherapy Research, 3,* 124–130.
Truax, C. B., & Carkhuff, R. R. (1967). *Toward effective counseling and psychotherapy: Training and practice.* Chicago: Aldine.

CHAPTER 5

How Does Psychotherapy Work?
A Personal Account of Model Building

JACK MARTIN

My doctoral thesis, written at the University of Alberta, described a series of functional analyses of verbal behavior in small learning groups and psychotherapy groups. As this project progressed, my advisor (Professor John McLeish) and I became increasingly aware of the inevitable uncertainties that attended our attempts as social scientists to interpret the functions of verbal behavior in natural settings without knowledge of the motives, perceptions, and understandings of those participants (subjects) whose behavior we studied. Consistent with the prevailing zeitgeist of those times (at least at Alberta), the report of our work was highly behavioristic (McLeish & Martin, 1975). However, in our own 'minds' (we never used such mentalistic terms without connoting their dubious scientific status with inverted commas), we believed that we somehow had "missed the boat." We frequently fantasized about having privileged access to people's innermost thoughts and experiences while they interacted normally in the settings we studied. We came to believe (albeit somewhat privately—i.e., "just among ourselves") that we never would understand how social talk between teachers and students or between therapists and clients resulted in student/client change without some such privileged access. For us, understanding the mysterious transformation of social talk into personal change was the ultimate goal of our empirical enterprise.

Unfortunately, while privately flirting with Vygotsky, we remained publicly faithful to Skinner. After all, the only data we possessed were behavioral, and we did not wish to court the ridicule of our colleagues by running afoul of then widely accepted doctrines concerning the possible unscientific uses of hypothetical constructs. This desire was especially acute for me, given that Kenneth MacCorquodale from the University of Minnesota (a leading proponent of such views) was the external examiner at the oral defense of my doctoral research. As it turned out, Kenneth's personal charm and obvious intellectual prowess made such an impression on me that I continued to espouse (at least publicly) a highly behavioristic "line," long after I privately had abandoned any hope of understanding therapeutic transformations (i.e., therapeutic talk to client change) in Skinnerian terms. As a consequence of this intellectual "schizophrenia" (although other factors also were involved), I did very little research related to therapeutic transformations for several years following the attainment of my doctorate.

It was during my first professorial appointment at Simon Fraser University that I came to know and understand what eventually became known as the cognitive-mediational paradigm for research in applied psychology. Two colleagues and close friends at SFU, Phil Winne and Ron Marx, then were engaged in contributing to the development of this paradigm for research on teaching (cf. Winne & Marx, 1977). By taking the active cognitive agency of teachers and students as a conceptual given, and by adopting then novel methods such as stimulated recall, think aloud, and process tracing, Phil and Ron seemed to be getting close to my fantasy of gaining privileged access to the minds of therapists and clients (in their case, teachers and students) as they interacted in real-life settings. Their work helped fuel my vision of a program of cognitive-mediational research on counseling and psychotherapy that eventually would explain how therapy worked (i.e., how therapeutic talk resulted in client change).

Unfortunately, my personal and professional life in those early years at Simon Fraser was not conducive to launching a major research program. "House poor," with the arrival of three children in 5 years, I turned to university administration to acquire a needed salary supplement. However, I now knew the precise type of research on therapeutic practice that I wished to conduct, and did manage to draft a series of research proposals and plans that I filed away for future reference. Consequently, when in 1983 I accepted a non-administrative position at the University of Western Ontario, I was ready to spring into action. Using the research proposals I had drafted at Simon Fraser, I secured the first of several grants from the Social Sciences and Humanities Research Council of Canada, permitting me (at long last) to get on with the task of attempting to understand how psychotherapy works.

In this chapter, I give a retrospective, personal account of my method choices and inquiry processes as I have pursued my program of research on therapeutic practice over the past 10 years. I describe my research program in two distinctive phases. Within each phase, I attempt to convey something of my cyclic enthusiasms for and disenchantments with the conceptualizations and methods that have typified the various studies conducted. While I summarize major research results, I do so briefly, choosing instead to emphasize and explicate epistemological and methodological choices, and the personal and social contexts in which such choices were made. Of course, readily available, published reports of the studies I mention are referenced fully.

PHASE I: COGNITIVE MEDIATION AND NEOPOSITIVISM

The first academic work I did after arriving at the University of Western Ontario in 1983, and securing funding for a series of cognitive-mediational studies of counseling processes and outcomes, was to write a paper outlining a rationale, conceptual framework, and possible methodologies for the conduct of such research (Martin, 1984). (Throughout this chapter, I use the terms counseling and psychotherapy interchangeably.) In this piece, I argued for the necessity, when conducting research on counseling outcomes, of obtaining relatively direct data on therapists' and clients' cognitive processes during counseling. I presented a tentative theory that linked therapists' and clients' cognitive processing in therapy to the interactive behaviors of counselors and clients and to client learning outcomes. The formal points emphasized in this document were: (1) the cognitive activity of counselors and clients during therapy mediates the effects of their interactive behaviors on therapy outcomes; (2) clients' interactive behaviors are processed by (and therefore affect) therapists, just as therapists' interactive behaviors are processed by (and therefore affect) clients; and (3) knowledge of therapeutic effects will not advance until researchers examine the cognitive activity of therapists and clients as directly as possible in ecologically valid contexts. For me, this piece amounted to a sort of personal "cognitive/subjective/naturalistic" manifesto, through which I abandoned any remnants of the radical behaviorism I had imbibed as a graduate student.

From now on, my work would focus on the internal experiences of therapists and clients in "real-life" settings and would treat "subjects" as participants, expert with respect to their own thoughts and perceptions (at least with respect to the content of these, if not with respect to explanations of them). The 1984 article also functioned as a personal challenge and call to produce research that met the conceptual and methodological criteria I set out. Thus motivated, I embarked upon a hectic period of research activity so as to "put my money where my mouth was."

Before describing briefly the three major studies that constitute this first phase of my research program, I should make it clear that the foregoing conceptual and methodological commitments had no real basis in formal philosophical considerations. I subsequently have become very much interested in the philosophy of social science and am now an avid reader of the various debates that populate this area. However, at the time of the 1984 article, my proposals were based almost entirely on my dissatisfaction with my own graduate school work, my reading of applied psychological research in therapeutic and educational psychology, and my conversations with influential colleagues and friends.

The first major empirical study that instantiated the cognitive-mediational strategies I had proposed, employed methods of stimulated recall and structured content analysis to examine relations among counselor and client cognitions, behaviors, and ratings of outcome in 29 counseling sessions, involving 10 different counselor–client pairs (Martin, Martin, Meyer, & Slemon, 1986). In particular, it was hypothesized that consistency (matching) across different elements in the cognitive behavioral chain proposed by Martin (1984), that is, "counselor intention—counselor behavior—client perceptions of counselor intention and behavior—client cognitive processing—client behavior," would predict participant ratings of session effectiveness. Consistency across the elements in this chain was determined with the aid of a set of theoretically probable relations based on conceptual work concerning human information processing in therapy, such as that of Wexler (1974). For example, the therapist behavior of "stating goals" was associated theoretically with the likely client cognitive operation of "expecting." A comprehensive list of such theoretically probable relationships among various elements of the cognitive-behavioral chain described above appears in Martin and co-authors (1986).

A stimulated recall procedure, in which participants described their "in-therapy" thoughts while viewing selected segments of videotapes of "just completed" therapy sessions, was used to obtain data on the cognitive components of the cognitive-behavioral chain being tested. Behavioral components of the chain were coded directly from the videotapes. Structured interviews were associated with the stimulated recall procedure, and tightly defined coding systems were employed to place the data into distinct categories.

Two results were especially noteworthy. First, consistency across the various elements in the cognitive-behavioral chain did account for a significant proportion of the variance in counselors' ratings of session effectiveness. However, consistency between counselors' intentions and clients' accurate perceptions of their counselors' intentions was negatively correlated (rather than positively correlated, as predicted) with counselor ratings of session effectiveness. Second, consistency across elements in the cognitive-behavioral chain was lower for interpersonal cognitive than for interpersonal behavioral or intrapersonal cognitive-behavioral links. In other words, interpersonal cognitive links, such as the aforementioned link between counselor intentions and client perceptions of counselor intentions, displayed less consistency than links such as that between counselor behaviors and client behaviors, or that between counselor intentions and counselor behaviors.

On the basis of the results from Martin and co-authors (1986), I concluded that greater understanding and prediction of participants' therapeutic experiences (and the impact of these experiences on therapeutic change) might follow from a consideration of cognitive variables such as intentions, perceptions, and cognitive operations, in addition to behavioral variables alone. Since this conclusion essentially coincided with the cognitive-mediational thesis I had set forth in the 1984 piece, I was encouraged. However, the surprising result that counselor transparency (i.e., client accurate perception of counselor intentions) was not positively related to perceived session effectiveness was disturbing. It hinted that things may not be quite as straightforward and linear as the cognitive-mediational model (Martin, 1984) assumed them to be.

The next study in what I am now calling Phase I, the cognitive-mediational studies, partially replicated Martin and co-authors (1986), but employed theoretical models and coding systems specific to person-centered and rational-emotive therapies (Martin, Martin, & Slemon, 1987). In this second study, we predicted that consistency across the basic cognitive-mediational chain (counselor intentions, to counselor behaviors, to client perceptions and cognitive operations, to client behaviors, and ultimately to participant perceptions of session effectiveness and client change) would once again predict participants' session ratings. However, we also predicted that the previously noted negative correlation between counselor transparency and ratings of session effectiveness (Martin et al., 1986) would hold for the two person-centered dyads, but give way to a positive correlation between these same variables in the two rational-emotive dyads. The reasoning behind this latter, differential prediction was that in more directive therapies like rational-emotive therapy, therapists attempt actively to make their intentions for client therapeutic work more explicit than do therapists using less directive therapies such as person-centered counseling.

The results of the Martin and co-authors (1987) study were almost exactly the same as those from the previous Martin and co-authors (1986) study. Once again, prediction of participant ratings was greater when cognitive and cognitive-behavioral variables were added to behavioral variables alone. Second, the strong negative correlation between counselor transparency and session ratings held for both person-centered and rational-emotive dyads.

By this time, I and my colleagues were beginning to suspect that we had taken our original lock-step, linear model of cognitive mediation in therapy (Martin, 1984) about as far as we could take it. Cognitive self-report data on participants' experiences in therapy obviously seemed important to an understanding of how therapy works, in that such experiences (perceptions and cognitive operations) seemed to mediate significantly between participants' verbal behaviors and perceptions of therapy outcomes. However, beyond this general support for a cognitive-mediational perspective, we seemed to be learning relatively little about the precise mechanisms by which therapeutic talk transformed into client change.

We also began to understand that consistently troublesome results such as the negative correlation between counselor transparency and outcome ratings might be a result of how our methods of studying therapy interacted with participants' experiences of therapy. Our analytical gauge in the Martin and co-authors (1986, 1987) studies was very reductionistic (e.g., asking clients to comprehend the intentions that might lie behind separate counselor talking turns). It seemed entirely possible that clients could perceive and understand the "gist" of therapists' intentions without perceiving accurately the micro- or subintentions that lay behind every single therapist comment. In fact, it seemed likely that if clients attempted to do the latter, they might be distracted from more primary therapeutic work such as tracking, elaborating, and analyzing their own problematic experiences. If this were so, it made sense that the kind of microscopic counselor transparency we were coding would be negatively related to more global evaluations of session outcome.

However, a much more general concern began to emerge from considerations of this sort. Our method of attempting to study distinct, linear sequences of participants' cognitive and behavioral responses to therapy was grounded in neopositivist models of information processing similar to those employed in experimental cognitive laboratories where considerable experimental control over subjects' moment-to-moment experiencing and responding could be exercised. Tasks undertaken by therapists and clients in actual therapy settings seemed much more holistic, ill-structured, and laden with affect and personal belief than did the structured tasks studied in laboratory settings. We began to search for units and means of analysis and procedures of inquiry that would be better matched to the natural experiential units and themes employed by clients and therapists in identifying and negotiating therapeutic tasks.

At this point in our deliberations, I became very impressed by the "events paradigm" research on psychotherapy conducted and advocated by Rice and Greenberg (1984), and related work on "good moments" in therapy (Mahrer & Nadler, 1986) and "comprehensive task analyses" of therapeutic events (Elliott, 1984). For several months, I seriously considered adopting this paradigm as an alternative to the cognitive-mediational assumptions and methods I had employed to date. However, a third and final study in the first phase of our research program alerted me to several possible problems with "events paradigm" conceptualizations that still seemed to presuppose a highly deterministic theory of therapeutic change mechanisms.

Martin, Martin, and Slemon (1989) considered probabilities of frequently occurring sequences of counselor intentions, counselor behaviors, client cognitive operations, and client responses from 18 different therapy dyads. The aim of this study was to determine if sufficient stability and predictability in patterns of therapeutic actions (relationships between therapists' intentions and behaviors) and acts (relationships between therapists' behaviors and clients' cognitive responses to these behaviors) existed to warrant a deterministic social science of therapeutic psychology. Methods employed were similar to those cognitive-mediational methods employed by Martin and co-authors (1986, 1987).

While some interesting and understandable patterns of action–act sequences in therapeutic interactions were noted, our results were highly probabilistic. For example, when therapists in this study intentionally reflected the meanings and feelings they perceived in clients' interactions, clients responded in extremely variable ways—by "registering information" contained in the therapist reflection (29% of the cases studied), by "thinking about feelings" (19%), by "thinking about their own thinking" (13%), by "analyzing their experiences" (11%), and by "recalling something" from their past experiences (10%), together with a variety of much less frequently noted cognitive responses. These results led us to caution against assuming "a tighter brand of action–act determinism in therapeutic interactions than can be supported by a careful scrutiny of extant empirical results in this area" (Martin et al., 1989, p. 16).

At the start of the first phase of my research on psychotherapy, I believed that the answer to how therapy worked would reveal itself in the form of stable, highly predictable, linear patterns of relationships linking therapeutic interactions to therapy outcomes (Martin, 1984). I had embraced the importance of ecological validity and the subjective experiences of therapists and clients for an understanding of therapy. Unfortunately, I had put neopositivistic "straightjackets" on these conceptions by choosing to retain presuppositions and employing methods and procedures of inquiry better suited to an exploration of small-gauge, tightly controlled laboratory tasks, than to the naturalistic, experiential tasks of participants in psychotherapy.

Phase I of my research program, together with its methods and inquiry processes, had succeeded in demonstrating that the world of psychotherapy was too probabilistic and holistic to yield to neopositivist, information-processing conceptualizations and methodologies, at least with respect to my foundational question, "How does psychotherapy work?" Paradoxically, while incapable of moving very far toward a satisfying answer to this question, the cognitive-mediational studies had succeeded in making me much more aware of essential characteristics of the phenomena I wished to understand—their inherent complexities, subtleties, and uncertainties.

Of course, by this time I also was becoming more and more interested in, and spending more time reading and discussing, contemporary work in the philosophy and history of psychological and social science (e.g., Manicas, 1987). In fact, many of my lunch hours at the University of Western Ontario were spent in a faculty common room discussing recent work of this sort. It therefore is very likely that my dissatisfaction with the first phase of my research program was attributable not solely to the work itself, but to the work when viewed through "new lenses" created by such reading and conversation.

PHASE II: MEMORY MEDIATION AND CONSTRUCTIONISM

In 1987, while teaching a graduate course in theories of counseling and psychotherapy, I described to my students a vexing problem for research on psychotherapy. I stated that the problem was to find a unit of analysis that could be employed in naturalistic psychotherapy research that would be amenable to empirical research and yet properly represent clients' and therapists' phenomenological experience of therapy. The context in which I made this comment was a seminar discussion of constructivist theorizing about psychotherapy, as detailed in Mahoney and Freeman (1985). One of my students, Karl Stelmaczonek, who seemed to know something about recent cognitive research and theorizing in the area of episodic memory, wondered if it might be interesting to examine what participants recalled as important following therapy sessions. I immediately thought of Mahrer and Nadler's (1986) piece in the then recent special issue of the *Journal of Consulting and Clinical Psychology* devoted to psychotherapy research. Aloud, I expressed the opinion that the idea of examining participants' memories of therapy might dovetail nicely with recent work by Mahrer and Nadler on "good moments" in psychotherapy.

Shortly after this seminar, Karl and I met to discuss the research he would conduct as part of his master's degree requirements. We decided that participants' experiential or episodic memories (i.e., autobiographical memories of specific events experienced during therapy sessions) might be just the unit of analysis that I was searching for in my own research program. No previous research on therapeutic events had defined such events explicitly in terms of participants' memories. Consequently, adoption of episodic memories as experimental units would preserve and further my ongoing commitment to phenomenologically and ecologically valid research on therapy. Further, such memories were (on the basis of considerable research in the area of cognition and memory—cf. Ashcraft, 1989) notoriously driven by individuals' existing knowledge networks, personal theories, and world views. Memories of therapeutic events thus seemed to lend themselves to processes of selective perception, personal agency, and reconstruction over time, all of which were potentially important features in the more constructionistic speculations concerning therapeutic change in which I then was immersed.

During my discussion with Karl, I began to see how personal episodic memories of therapy might very well mediate between actual therapeutic transactions/discourse and participants' own personal theories about therapy, their problems, themselves, others, and life in general. For some time I had been interested in constructivistic accounts of human change that employed terms such as "personal constructs" (Kelly, 1955; Neimeyer, 1986) and "schemas" (e.g., Mandler, 1984). On the whole, I preferred the term "personal theories," because it seemed to provide a link between change processes in science/social science and in individual development. This link appealed to me (cf. Martin, 1988), although I previously had considered the more cognitivistic, less holistic term, "cognitive structure" (cf. Martin, 1985). I also wanted to use a term (i.e., personal theories) that would lend itself to a neo-Vygotskian perspective that viewed cognitive constructions as embedded in social-historical contexts and constructions (cf. Kozulin, 1986). I had a long-standing interest in Vygotsky's work that I inherited from John McLeish, my Ph.D. thesis advisor, and my "natural" inclination was to prefer social-cultural to biological origins of psychological phenomena. While I was committed to the reality of human capacities for cognitive construction, I realized that the "raw materials" for such cognitive work must come from somewhere. It made sense to me that these sources might be found in the social interactions, conversations, and practical activities in which all humans are embedded. At any rate, I now became taken with the idea that perhaps psychotherapy works by constructing conversations and activities, some of which become embedded in clients' memories and affect clients' personal theories and eventually their real-world (extratherapy) behaviors and experiences.

Eureka! The second phase of my research program had begun. The heirs of Skinner had finally given way to those of Vygotsky (1934/1986). As Harré (1984) had theorized earlier, the real question for psychology is to explain how the public and social can become private and personal, and eventually how the latter can "turn around" and influence the former. This question, as applied to the world of psychotherapy, became my new, updated version of "How does psychotherapy work?"

The first paper reporting our research on memory-mediated therapeutic processes and change was by Martin and Stelmaczonek (1988). In this report we described two studies that not only marked a shift to memory mediation and constructionist theorizing, but also began a more genuinely pluralistic choice of research methods. Exploratory research methods were joined with hypothesis-testing methods. The first study in Martin and Stelmaczonek (1988) explored three questions, none of which could be cast as formal hypotheses: (1) What kinds of events during psychotherapy do therapists and clients identify as important? (2) Does the nature of such events change over time in therapy? and (3) Do therapists and clients identify the same events as important? Therapists and clients in eight short-term therapeutic dyads (eight sessions each) were interviewed by a research assistant immediately following the completion of each therapy session and asked to identify "the most important things that happened during this session." Participants' recall and identification of important events were coded into categories derived from Mahrer and Nadler's (1986) system of "good moments" in psychotherapy.

The decision to employ Mahrer and Nadler's system for the foregoing purposes was taken after Karl and I had made independent and collaborative attempts to describe, without the aid of preselected categories, the events recalled by participants. We eventually adopted Mahrer and Nadler's "good moments" categories because our own descriptions of these events could be captured extremely well by those categories, and because the Mahrer and Nadler system already was documented in relevant, extant literature in psychotherapy research. We did, however, find it necessary to add one category of our own, "internalizing (learning about) therapeutic processes and constructions," to the Mahrer and Nadler categories.

Both therapists and clients most frequently recalled as important six categories of therapeutic events, which I subsequently organized under two major therapeutic task areas (Martin, 1992). Four types of events related to the therapeutic task of *enhancing clients' personal awareness:* (1) experiencing a good therapeutic relationship, (2) experiencing and exploration of feelings, (3) elaborating personal meanings, and (4) attaining personal insight. The remaining two types of events related to the therapeutic task of *revising personal theories:* (1) internalizing therapeutic processes and constructions, and (2) experimenting with, or experiencing, new ways of behaving and being. Thus, I interpreted results from the first study in Martin and Stelmaczonek (1988) to demonstrate a constructive therapeutic process involving the promotion of clients' awareness of current (and presumably, dysfunctional) personal theories and their subsequent revision (reconstruction or restructuring) of these personal theories (presumably with more functional consequences) (Martin, 1992).

Other findings from the first study in Martin and Stelmaczonek (1988) were that "no obvious patterns emerged in these descriptive data that led us to feel confident in ascribing differences in participant identification of important events in counseling to either time in counseling or individual differences in the dyads studied" (p. 386) and "counselors and clients . . . identified exactly the same events as important in roughly one third of the cases in which they reported important events" (p. 387). In other words, while therapists and clients identified the same six kinds of events as important, they did not tend to identify exactly the same events in the majority of cases. Further, the logical pattern of "enhanced personal awareness" followed by "revision of personal theories" did not appear to operate in any correspondingly simple, linear empirical pattern.

The second study reported by Martin and Stelmaczonek (1988) employed a very similar methodology, but combined exploratory and hypothesis-testing strategies. The hypothesis tested was that discourse during events recalled as important by clients would differ from temporally proximate, "control" events in ways consistent with experimental laboratory research on "determinants of memorability." (The method used to select control events ensured that both the specific topic and therapeutic work evident in these events differed from those in evidence during events recalled by clients.) To test this hypothesis, discourse during "recalled important" and "control" events from three dyads (seven or eight sessions each) was transcribed and coded for "depth of meaning," "elaboration of meaning through use of figurative language," "personalizing," "clarity," and "conclusion orientation." Results of inferential statistical comparisons revealed that client-recalled important therapeutic events were reliably characterized by significantly more "depth of meaning," "elaboration of meaning through use of figurative language," and "conclusion orientation." Thus, the events that clients recalled as important were ones in which therapists and clients attended to the meanings implicit (or explicit) in clients' experiences, elaborated these meanings through the use of figurative language (illustrations, images, metaphors, and so forth), and attempted to draw conclusions (i.e., entertained hypotheses and explanations, and formed insights and understandings) concerning clients' experiences.

These results, especially those related to the elaboration of meanings through the use of figurative language, encouraged me to pay much closer attention to psychotherapy research that focused specifically on such matters by employing intensive, interpretive analyses of psychotherapeutic dialogue (e.g., Angus & Rennie, 1988, 1989; McMullen, 1989). However, as will become clear later in this chapter, I only very recently am reaping the methodological/epistemological "yield" from my exposure to work of this kind.

The exploratory component of the second study by Martin and Stelmaczonek (1988) provided information concerning clients' ability to recall, at a 6-month follow-up, events they had identified as important immediately following the therapy sessions studied. To our knowledge, no one previously had attempted to provide data relevant to this question. The procedure employed was to cue clients' recall (after a 6-month period) by having them view a one-minute segment from the start of each of the therapy sessions in which they previously had participated. Results were that clients recalled accurately the exact same events they previously had identified as important in 73% of the cases tested (40% from the exact therapy sessions cued, 33% from a therapy session other than that cued).

I was greatly encouraged by the results from the Martin and Stelmaczonek (1988) studies. I interpreted these results to lend support to my emerging theory that psychotherapy worked by somehow embedding in the minds of clients relatively lasting episodic memories from therapeutic interactions that could be used as a basis for the reconstruction of clients' personal knowledge and theories, and eventually for altered "real-life" experiencing and actions. Further, if results from the second study could be confirmed, it might even be possible to identify general characteristics of therapeutic language and discourse that therapists might be able to manipulate in order to enhance clients' long-term episodic memories of therapy. My abandonment of the linear, microscopic "straightjackets" that had characterized the cognitive-mediational phase of my work (for more dynamic, larger-gauge alternatives) was beginning to pay dividends.

The next study, Martin, Paivio, and Labadie (1990), was devoted to a verification test of the results obtained from the hypothesis-testing portion of the second Martin and Stelmaczonek (1988) study. In this research, we studied six short-term therapy dyads (8 to 14 sessions each) in which experienced psychotherapists employed either cognitive or experiential forms of psychotherapy. As in Martin and Stelmaczonek (1988), clients recalled important therapeutic events immediately after therapy sessions were completed. Discourse from these events was compared with discourse from same session control events on the potentially memory-enhancing variables examined in the previous study. The control events were temporally proximate to the client-recalled important events, but were thematically and strategically distinctive from the client-recalled important events. Control events were matched to the recalled important events in terms of elapsed time and number of participants' talking turns. The psychometric properties of the instruments and procedures used for these purposes were examined formally and found to be adequate for our purposes. More substantively, results indicated that the scales developed to score the "depth of meaning," "elaboration of meaning through the use of figurative language," and "conclusion orientation" of the therapeutic discourse discriminated reliably and as predicted between client-recalled important and control events.

In addition, some limited support was obtained for a second hypothesis that "elaboration of meaning through the use of figurative language" would discriminate more reliably between client-recalled and control events during the experiential therapy sessions than during the cognitive therapy sessions. Finally, and of potentially significant clinical and theoretical relevance, it was therapists' language (interactions) that contributed most to these discriminations. Once more, the strong implication was that therapists could influence clients' encoding and recall of therapeutic content (discourse) through the nature of the language they employed during psychotherapy. Such a finding provided a strong basis for my growing conviction that psychotherapeutic conversations are appropriated by clients as a basis for personal theoretical and behavioral change, and that clients' experiential memories mediate this process of internalization. (Obviously, my interest in Vygotsky was now fully reawakened.)

In a more recent study, we (Martin, Cummings, & Hallberg, 1992) conducted a direct test of therapists' influence on clients' encoding and recall of therapeutic events through the intentional use of figurative, metaphorical language to enhance clients' episodic memories of therapy. Once again, we employed a combination of hypothesis-testing and exploratory strategies. However, in this study, the categories in the exploratory component of the study emerged entirely from our own discovery-oriented examination of natural language data from the therapeutic sessions and participants' self-reports of memorable events in those sessions. Therapists in four dyads of experiential psychotherapy (7 to

13 sessions each) attempted to use therapeutic metaphors whenever they judged that such metaphoric interventions might promote legitimate client therapeutic work and were appropriate to the current therapeutic context. Immediately after therapy sessions were completed, therapists and clients were asked to recall therapeutic events they found to be most memorable and to give reasons for the memorability of these events. Participants also rated each session in terms of its helpfulness and effectiveness.

Specific hypotheses were: (1) that clients would tend to recall events associated with therapists' intentional use of therapeutic metaphors, and (2) that clients would rate sessions in which they recalled therapists' intentional metaphoric interventions higher than sessions in which they did not recall therapists' intentional metaphoric interventions. The rationale for the second hypothesis was the assumption that clients tend to recall therapeutic events when they have encoded them "deeply" in terms of the "personal meanings" associated with them (cf. Craik & Tulving, 1975; Martin & Stelmaczonek, 1988). Thus, sessions during which therapists' intentional metaphoric interventions were recalled might contain more of such "deep, meaningful" processing than sessions during which therapists' intentional metaphoric interventions were not recalled (and, therefore, presumably not encoded deeply and meaningfully). Such deep, meaningful encoding and recall would seem to contribute significantly to client perceptions of session effectiveness and helpfulness.

In addition to the foregoing hypotheses, possible epistemic and motivational functions of metaphor use in therapy were examined by means of interpretive, natural language analyses, following a more open-ended, discovery-oriented research strategy. Epistemic functions referred to elaborations or alterations in clients' personal knowledge. Motivational functions referred to changes in clients' commitment to the process of personal, therapeutic change. Two research assistants and I independently examined clients' postsession, written accounts of their reasons for remembering the therapeutic events they recalled. We each attempted to describe these reasons in our own words. We then met to discuss our descriptions. These discussions led to a joint formulation of a small number of distinctive, epistemic and motivational functions upon which we could reach comprehensive, consensual understanding.

Results were that clients recalled therapists' intentional use of metaphor in approximately two-thirds of the sessions in which metaphors were employed intentionally by therapists. Not surprisingly, metaphors that were recalled tended, almost without exception, to be developed collaboratively through the active participation of both therapists and clients, and to be developed over considerable time, both within and across therapy sessions. With respect to clinical impact, clients rated sessions during which they recalled therapists' intentional metaphors as significantly more helpful than sessions during which they did not recall therapists' intentional metaphors.

Results from the discovery-oriented, interpretive analyses suggested that therapists' intentional metaphors served two distinctive epistemic and two distinctive motivational functions. Epistemic effects noted were: (1) enhanced emotional awareness, and (2) conceptual "bridging." Motivational effects noted were: (1) enhanced relationship with therapist, and (2) goal clarification.

I think that the study by Martin, Cummings, and Hallberg (1992) constitutes a rigorous verification test of the ability of therapists intentionally to manipulate characteristics of therapeutic discourse in ways that affect clients' encoding and recall of therapeutic content in predictable ways. As such, it confirms a central proposition with respect to my constructivist theorizing about how therapy works: *that therapeutic discourse can be constructed in the social, public domain with somewhat predictable effects on the cognitive, private constructions (memories) of clients.*

The memory-mediation, constructionist phase of the research program I have described is currently being continued by Anne Cummings and others at the University of Western Ontario. Cummings, Hallberg, Martin, and Slemon (1992) examined data from 11 dyads of short-term psychotherapy with respect to the relationship between accuracy of participants' memories of therapy and therapeutic outcome. Results obtained confirm our belief, based on our reflections on previous data obtained in our research program, that therapists are consistently more accurate than clients in their recall of therapeutic events. We also confirmed that clients' accuracy of recall correlates reliably and quite powerfully with therapeutic outcomes as measured by the Session Evaluation Questionnaire (cf. Stiles, 1980). Therapists were so accurate in their recall of events that there was insufficient variation in therapists' accuracy scores to permit a meaningful calculation of correlation with the SEQ measure.

CONVERSATIONS, MEMORIES, AND THEORIES: A MODEL OF HOW THERAPY WORKS

At this point in the evolution of my program of research on psychotherapy, I am prepared to outline a model in response to my long-standing curiosity about how psychotherapy works—that is, how the in-therapy talk between therapists and clients somehow promotes client change in extratherapy settings. My model is one that emphasizes

How Does Psychotherapy Work? 119

processes of social, public and of cognitive, private construction (see Figure 5.1).

To date, not all aspects of my model of the memory-mediated construction of therapeutic change have been researched. The social, interactive components of the model (represented in the small ovals and arrows at the sides of Figure 5.1 and by the cognitive/affective operations in the bottom thirds of the large ovals) were focal variables in the first, cognitive-mediational phase of my research program. The centrally located discourse characteristics and the memory variables (represented in the large ovals) have been focal variables in the second, memory-mediational phase of my research program. Other salient variables in the model (such as the personal knowledge and theory structures, and the individual epistemic and learning styles included in the large ovals) currently are being examined in a series of intensive case study researches I have begun to conduct since returning to Simon Fraser University in 1991.

In these studies, I am employing a form of interpretive discourse analysis that is targeted at explicating central meanings and "voices" across actual psychotherapeutic dialogues and participants' (especially clients') verbally reported recollection of these dialogues. At this writing, I am devising my own methods of qualitative discourse analysis, based on my reading and interpretation of methodological writings by Gee, Michaels, and O'Connor (1992) and Jacob (1992). The former emphasizes the interpretation of "socially situated texts." The latter focuses on neo-Vygotskian interpretations of "cognition in context." In adapting these methodologies for my own purposes, I am attempting to employ them in a theory-testing manner that will examine the extent to which clients' recollections of psychotherapy, and any changes to clients' personal theories, reflect a Vygotskian-like internalization of therapeutic conversations, expecially the "voice" of the therapist. This "new direction" in my research program really marks the first major shift in the epistemological commitments underlying my work. While previously discussed work by Martin and co-authors (1992) and Martin and Stelmaczonek (1988) was to some extent methodologically and strategically pluralistic, it still was dressed primarily in the trappings of quite traditional social psychological rhetoric. In my latest work, the rhetoric attempted is much more narrative and interpretive. I am interested to see how I fare in this more genuinely hermeneutic medium. Reports of this work will accompany an extended discussion of my theory of psychotherapeutic change (as the conversationally induced, memory-mediated revision of clients' personal theories) in my book, *The Construction and Understanding of Psychotherapeutic Change: Conversations, Memories, and Theories* (Martin, 1994).

Of course, the basic conceptualizations of therapeutic change that

120   Research as Praxis

FIGURE 5.1 A Model of How Psychotherapy Works

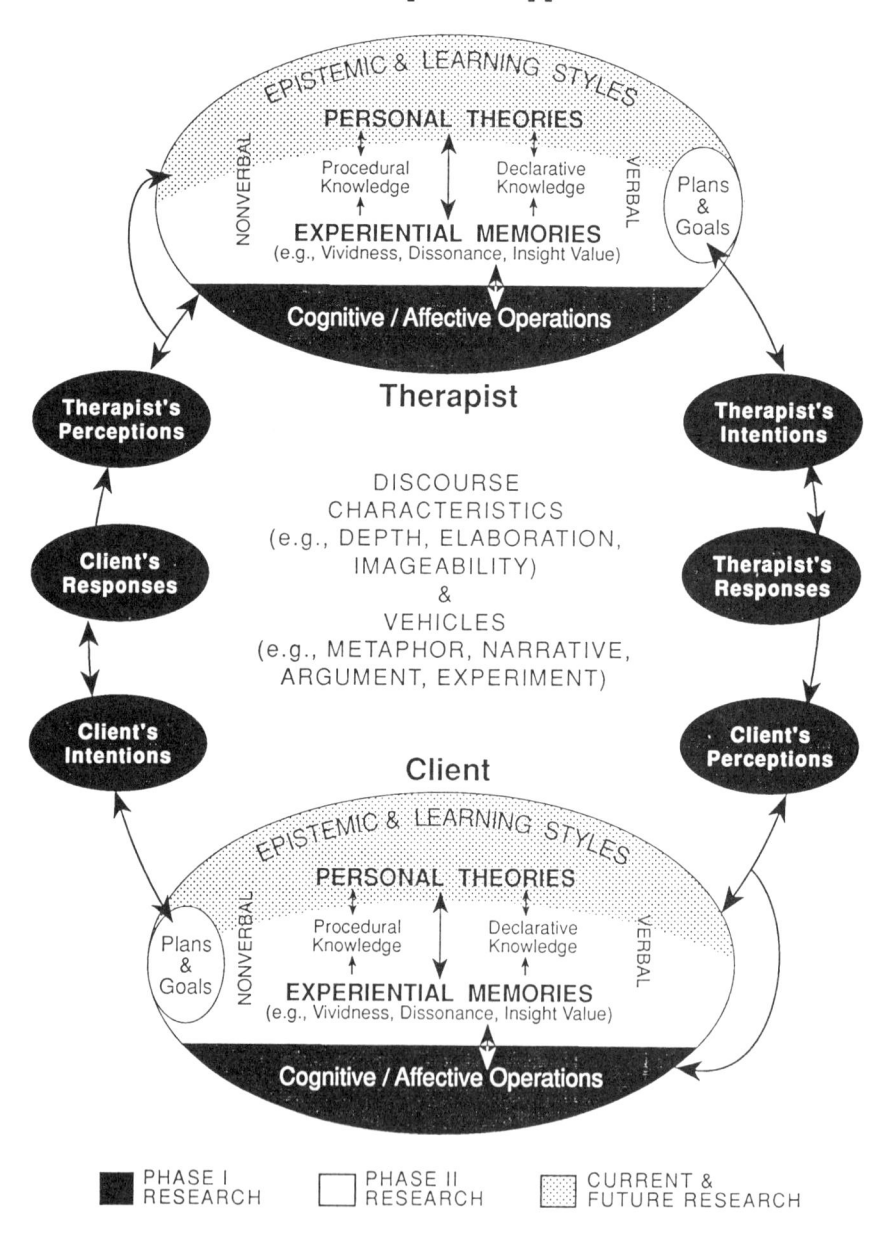

Therapist

EPISTEMIC & LEARNING STYLES
PERSONAL THEORIES
Procedural Knowledge ↔ Declarative Knowledge
NONVERBAL / VERBAL
EXPERIENTIAL MEMORIES
(e.g., Vividness, Dissonance, Insight Value)
Plans & Goals
Cognitive / Affective Operations

Therapist's Perceptions
Client's Responses
Client's Intentions

DISCOURSE CHARACTERISTICS
(e.g., DEPTH, ELABORATION, IMAGEABILITY)
&
VEHICLES
(e.g., METAPHOR, NARRATIVE, ARGUMENT, EXPERIMENT)

Therapist's Intentions
Therapist's Responses
Client's Perceptions

Client

EPISTEMIC & LEARNING STYLES
PERSONAL THEORIES
Procedural Knowledge ↔ Declarative Knowledge
NONVERBAL / VERBAL
EXPERIENTIAL MEMORIES
(e.g., Vividness, Dissonance, Insight Value)
Plans & Goals
Cognitive / Affective Operations

■ PHASE I RESEARCH   □ PHASE II RESEARCH   ▨ CURRENT & FUTURE RESEARCH

the model in Figure 5.1 attempts to convey are those already discussed during the foregoing presentations of the research program. As therapists and clients interact during psychotherapy, the responses of each partner reflect his or her underlying intentions, goals, and plans, which (in turn) are grounded in personal knowledge, theoretical, and memorial structures. A variety of affective and cognitive operations mediate between these private, personal structures and the public, interactive discourse, affecting both the communication and reception (understanding) of that discourse.

Of central significance are characteristics of the social, public discourse that enhance the memorability of that discourse. Participants' experiential or episodic memories of the therapeutic interactions and discourse are facilitated by cognitive operations such as encoding and recall. These same memories also affect the underlying personal knowledge and theories of therapists and clients by assimilating new information, insights, and understandings into these personal structures, and simultaneously forcing accommodations to the organization and content of the personal structures themselves. Such structural changes provide a basis for altered client perceptions, understandings, and actions outside of the therapy setting itself. It is through the action of these constructive processes that the social, public therapeutic talk of therapists and clients is transformed into client internal change that subsequently can be manifest in relevant extratherapy settings. This model (see Figure 5.1) constitutes my current best answer to the question of "how psychotherapy works," which has guided my entire research enterprise. Its more dynamic features clearly reflect the more constructionistic orientation of the second phase of my program of research.

REFLECTIONS

My research on psychotherapy has been driven consistently by my own curiosity concerning the "hows" of therapeutic change. This curiosity has remained relatively undiminished, albeit with the usual peaks and troughs that attend any human enterprise of long-term duration, over the entire course of the work I have attempted to describe. Without the motivation that stems from this curiosity, I could not have sustained a programmatic research effort.

The programmatic character of my research is, I think, the most important element in any progress I have attained toward my goal of understanding therapeutic change. Any of the single studies I have reported, by themselves, would be relatively unconvincing with respect to sustaining an overall theory of therapeutic change. Single studies beg multiple interpretations. However, when embedded in a research program, each study and its relevant presuppositions and theoretical/value contexts is informed by the overall logic of the program of research. Inevitable methodological and conceptual weaknesses and limitations of any single study are balanced by the strengths of other studies in the research program. In the program of research I have reported, quantitative testing of specific hypotheses accompanied both quantitative exploratory and qualitative discovery-oriented study of the phenomena of interest. Through the use of multiple research strategies and methodologies, a "triangulated," enriched perception and understanding of focal phenomena emerges. As focal phenomena are better understood, the models and theoretical frameworks of the researcher are inevitably altered. Thus, my initial cognitive-mediated framework eventually gave way to a more social constructionistic, memory-mediated framework.

At the same time, certain fundamental commitments have remained relatively constant across all phases of my work, although their mode of manifestation obviously has changed. These include my commitments to (1) ecological validity (the study of actual in-therapy interactions), and (2) subjective validity (knowledge of the perceptions, understandings, and judgments of therapists and clients). I do not believe that any program of research on psychotherapy that fails to attend to these two requirements ultimately can say much about the way in which psychotherapy operates. Therapeutic phenomena are highly contextualized and highly subjective/experiential. These fundamental characteristics of the phenomena under investigation must inform both the questions asked and the strategies employed to answer them.

In the final analysis, knowledge of fundamental qualities of focal phenomena and approaches to studying these phenomena must somehow evolve in tandem. I can identify no clear notion of what must precede what, although I have spent many hours considering this matter. I suspect that this is why research on therapeutic practice is inevitably intertwined with one's own personal, experiential knowledge of therapy, whatever its source (i.e., as a client, therapist, student, theorist, and/or researcher). However, our understanding of therapeutic phenomena will not evolve from immersion in therapy or the literature of therapy alone. The pursuit of knowledge arises from questioning. Questioning one's own understandings is (or should be) a common concern of participants, students, practitioners, and scholars in psychotherapy. Formal or informal empirical data always are collected and interpreted through our current understandings.

Two footnotes to this chapter are in order. First, I think it important to emphasize the unpredictable influence of chance factors and encounters on any researcher and research program. I and my research undoubtedly have been affected by numerous formal and informal comments and contributions of numerous colleagues and by seemingly "chance" occurrences. An example of the former was my unplanned meeting (for the first time) with George Howard at the 1986 APA Convention in Los Angeles, during which he (probably unwittingly) reinforced my firm commitment to understanding the perspectives of therapists and clients in therapeutic contexts and encouraged me to take a more constructionist view of these contexts.

The second footnote concerns the importance of environment to programmatic research. From 1983 to 1994, my research has been supported generously by the Social Sciences and Humanities Research Council of Canada, which seems willing to fund "less traditional" research in the social sciences. At the University of Western Ontario I benefited greatly from interactions with close colleagues and friends in the Counseling Psychology Research Group. The kindness and generosity of co-workers like Ted Hallberg, Anne Cummings, and Alan Slemon gave me consistent time, support, and encouragement with which to pursue my work in the face of the multiple, daily demands that beset any university-based researcher. In particular, the strong interests of both Ted and Anne in the practice of psychotherapy, and in the study of this practice, further encouraged me to keep my research embedded in the context of psychotherapeutic practice.

The overall environment within which I have worked also includes a wider network of colleagues who have pursued related research on psychotherapy with which I am familiar. There can be little question that the work of Clara Hill (cf. Fuller & Hill, 1985; Hill & O'Grady, 1985) and Robert Elliott (cf. Elliott, 1984, 1985) influenced and interacted with the earlier phase of the research program I have attempted to describe. The work of Al Mahrer (Mahrer & Nadler, 1986), Les Greenberg (Greenberg & Pinsof, 1986; Rice & Greenberg, 1984), and Lynne Angus and David Rennie (1988, 1989) has been especially helpful during the second phase of my work. I am pleased to count all these scholars and many others as personal acquaintances, and to note at least some similar findings across our research programs (cf. reviews of psychotherapy and counseling research by Hill, 1990; Wampold & Poulin, 1992). In the years to come, I look forward to working with new colleagues at Simon Fraser University as I attempt to extend my program of research on memory-mediated construction and change in psychotherapeutic, educational, and other applied settings.

REFERENCES

Angus, L. E., & Rennie, D. L. (1988). Therapist participation in metaphor generation: Collaborative and noncollaborative styles. *Psychotherapy, 25,* 552–560.

Angus, L. E., & Rennie, D. L. (1989). Envisioning the representational world: The client's experience of metaphoric expressiveness in psychotherapy. *Psychotherapy, 26,* 373–379.

Ashcraft, M. H. (1989). *Human memory and cognition.* Glenview, IL: Scott, Foresman.

Craik, F. I. M., & Tulving, E. (1975). Depth of processing and the retention of words in episodic memory. *Journal of Experimental Psychology, 104,* 268–294.

Cummings, A. L., Hallberg, E. T., Martin, J., & Slemon, A. G. (1992). Participants' memories for therapeutic events and ratings of session effectiveness. *Journal of Cognitive Psychotherapy, 6,* 113–124.

Elliott, R. (1984). A discovery-oriented approach to significant change events in psychotherapy: Interpersonal process recall and comprehensive process analysis. In L. N. Rice & L. S. Greenberg (Eds.), *Patterns of change: Intensive analysis of psychotherapy process* (pp. 249–286). New York: Guilford.

Elliott, R. (1985). Helpful and nonhelpful events in brief counseling interviews: An empirical taxonomy. *Journal of Counseling Psychology, 32,* 307–322.

Fuller, F., & Hill, C. E. (1985). Counselor and helpee perceptions of counselor intentions in relation to outcome in a single counseling session. *Journal of Counseling Psychology, 32,* 329–338.

Gee, J. P., Michaels, S., & O'Connor, M. C. (1992). Discourse analysis. In M. D. LeCompte, W. L. Millroy, & J. Preissle (Eds.), *The handbook of qualitative research in education* (pp. 227–292). San Diego, CA: Academic Press.

Greenberg, L. S., & Pinsof, W. M. (Eds.). (1986). *The psychotherapeutic process: A research handbook.* New York: Guilford.

Harré, R. (1984). *Personal being: A theory for individual psychology.* Cambridge, MA: Harvard University Press.

Hill, C. E. (1990). A review of exploratory in-session process research. *Journal of Consulting and Clinical Psychology, 58,* 288–294.

Hill, C. E., & O'Grady, K. E. (1985). List of therapist intentions illustrated in a case study and with therapists of varying theoretical orientations. *Journal of Counseling Psychology, 32,* 3–22.

Jacob, E. (1992). Culture, context, and cognition. In M. D. LeCompte, W. L. Millroy, & J. Preissle (Eds.), *The handbook of qualitative research in education* (pp. 293–336). San Diego, CA: Academic Press.

Kelly, G. (1955). *A theory of personality: The psychology of personal constructs.* New York: Norton.

Kozulin, A. (1986). Vygotsky in context. In L. Vygotsky, *Thought and language* (pp. xi–lvi). Cambridge, MA: MIT Press.

Mahoney, M. J., & Freeman, A. (Eds.). (1985). *Cognition and psychotherapy.* New York: Plenum.

Mahrer, A. R., & Nadler, W. P. (1986). Good moments in psychotherapy: A preliminary review, a list, and some promising research avenues. *Journal of Consulting and Clinical Psychology, 54,* 10–15.

Mandler, J. M. (1984). *Stories, scripts, and scenes: Aspects of schema theory.* Hillsdale, NJ: Lawrence Erlbaum.

Manicas, P. T. (1987). *A history and philosophy of the social sciences.* Oxford: Basil Blackwell.

Martin, J. (1984). The cognitive mediational paradigm for research on counseling. *Journal of Counseling Psychology, 31,* 559–572.

Martin, J. (1985). Measuring clients' cognitive competence in research on counseling. *Journal of Counseling and Development, 63,* 556–560.

Martin, J. (1988). A proposal for researching possible relationships between scientific theories and the personal theories of counselors and clients. *Journal of Counseling and Development, 66,* 261–265.

Martin, J. (1992). Cognitive-mediational research on counseling and psychotherapy. In S. G. Toukmanian & D. L. Rennie (Eds.), *Psychotherapy process research: Paradigmatic and narrative approaches* (pp. 108–133). Newbury Park, CA: Sage.

Martin, J. (1994). *The construction and understanding of psychotherapeutic change: Conversations, memories, and theories.* New York: Teachers College Press.

Martin, J., Cummings, A. L., & Hallberg, E. T. (1992). Therapists' intentional use of metaphor: Memorability, clinical impact, and epistemic/motivational functions. *Journal of Consulting and Clinical Psychology, 60,* 143–145.

Martin, J., Martin, W., Meyer, M., & Slemon, A. G. (1986). An empirical investigation of the cognitive mediational paradigm for research on counseling. *Journal of Counseling Psychology, 33,* 115–123.

Martin, J., Martin, W., & Slemon, A. G. (1987). Cognitive mediation in person-centered and rational-emotive therapy. *Journal of Counseling Psychology, 34,* 251–260.

Martin, J., Martin, W., & Slemon, A. G. (1989). Cognitive-mediational models of action–act sequences in counseling. *Journal of Counseling Psychology, 36,* 8–16.

Martin, J., Paivio, S., & Labadie, D. (1990). Memory-enhancing characteristics of client-recalled important events in cognitive and experiential therapy: Integrating cognitive experimental and therapeutic psychology. *Counselling Psychology Quarterly, 3,* 67–83.

Martin, J., & Stelmaczonek, K. (1988). Participants' identification and recall of important events in counseling. *Journal of Counseling Psychology, 35,* 385–390.

McLeish, J., & Martin, J. (1975). Verbal behavior: A review and experimental analysis. *Journal of General Psychology, 93,* 3–66.

McMullen, L. M. (1989). Use of figurative language in successful and unsuccessful cases of psychotherapy: Three comparisons. *Metaphor and Symbolic Activity, 4,* 203–225.

Neimeyer, R. A. (1986). Personal construct therapy. In W. Dryden & W. L. Golden (Eds.), *Cognitive-behavioral approaches to psychotherapy* (pp. 225–260). London: Harper & Row.

Rice, L. N., & Greenberg, L. S. (Eds.). (1984). *Patterns of change: Intensive analysis of psychotherapy process.* New York: Guilford.

Stiles, W. B. (1980). Measurement of the impact of psychotherapy sessions. *Journal of Consulting and Clincial Psychology, 48,* 176–185.
Vygotsky, L. (1986). *Thought and language.* Cambridge, MA: MIT Press. (Original work published 1934)
Wampold, B. E., & Poulin, K. (1992). Counseling research methods: Art and artifact. In S. D. Brown & R. W. Lent (Eds.), *Handbook of Counseling Psychology* (2nd ed., pp. 71–110). New York: Wiley–Interscience.
Wexler, D. A. (1974). A cognitive theory of experiencing, self-actualization and therapeutic process. In D. A. Wexler & L. N. Rice (Eds.), *Innovations in client-centered therapy* (pp. 49–116). New York: Wiley.
Winne, P. H., & Marx, R. W. (1977). Reconceptualizing research on teaching. *Journal of Educational Psychology, 69,* 668–678.

CHAPTER 6

The Poetics of Science: Creativity in the Construction of Causality

GEORGE S. HOWARD

While marveling at God's creative act, Alexander Pope exclaimed,

> And binding Nature fast in fate, Left free the human will (Pope, 1738/1967, Stanza, 3)

Had I been blessed with the gift, I surely would have chosen to become a poet. But I'm afraid I have neither the eye, the ear, nor the imagination for the tasks of gently crafting visions through the medium of words—which is, of course, the gift of the poet. My gift is of a baser nature. I sculpt demonstrations! For I've been called to the vocation of science.

When at their best, members of the scientific clergy breathe life into "facts" so skillfully that the person-on-the-street (or the apprentice scientist) might actually imagine that these new creations had "spoken for themselves." A well-turned demonstration shrieks its (created) reality to the reader so compellingly that, for an instant, one wonders, "How could I have earlier missed that reality?" Recall the dazzling colors of Stanley Milgram's (1974) portrait of obedience to authority—or hum the melody of Soloman Asch's (1951) ode to conformity to group pressure. Did you just now experience the wonder of those experimental creations? Did those scientifico-poetic demonstrations flash before your mind's eye? Or perhaps you have not yet been exposed to those masterpieces of empirical persuasion. Were I a giant of the hypothetico-poetic method (like Milgram or Asch) my remaining task would be quite easy. I would simply exclaim, "Behold my creation!" And all would be dazzled by the elegance of my experimental demonstration.

But, alas, as every minor poet knows so well, life isn't easy for us second-stringers. Helping you to understand how my studies of self-determination have proven that the human will was indeed "left free" will not be a simple task. I lack the artistic genius of Pope to simply claim (in 11 words!) that while the entities that populate the natural sciences (e.g., evolving species, orbiting planets, combining chemicals) are slaves to nonagential causal influences, human beings possess the unique capacity to self-determine their actions somewhat. That is, at certain points in time we might choose to act over and against the tendency to go with the flow of non-agential causal influences in our lives. You can see that it took me a long string of inelegant phrases to convey my understanding of (and conviction about) the freedom of the human will. However, since I lack the poet's fine hand, I beg each reader to bear with my plodding prose, as I am incapable of the penetrating poetics that you so richly deserve. I pray you will be patient with me.

ME AND BOURBON: FREE AT LAST! FREE AT LAST!

Have you ever driven during rush hour in Houston, Texas? Believe me, it's no picnic! Several years ago I was on the faculty at the University of Houston. My home was on the opposite side of the city from the University. By the time I arrived home from work each evening I was coiled as tight as a spring. Having a drink as I read the newspaper served to help me unwind from the pressures of the day—and the drive home. I had the good fortune to take a job at the University of Notre Dame a dozen years ago, and now there are few traffic jams in my life—but my habit of having a drink after work each day remained.

My wife, Nancy, is a therapist in private practice whose workday typically starts and ends a few hours later than mine. Like all good spouses she often comments about what she feels I am doing well, and what I might do differently. One day she mentioned that she would like it if I did not drink when I was alone—having a drink at home or out with others was fine. Since I enjoyed my end-of-the-workday drink, I demurred. Being persistent, she challenged me by asking why, when I urged others to gain volitional control over their behavior in my research, was I reluctant to test my own volition in this domain? I assured her that my after-work drink was perfectly under my control, and so there was no need to undertake the exercise. Knowing me as she does, and being the skilled clinician that she is, she settled the issue by hurling the one challenge that every true scientist is incapable of ignoring: "It's an empirical question, Sweetie! Prove it!!!"

Being hopelessly outwitted, I began designing my personal experiment on the volitional control of my after-work drink. I first suggested a 1-year baseline period during which we could assess the stability of the behavior in question. Nancy objected, asserting that we had very stable behavior indeed, and that I had my drink on about 90% of my work days. She was right, of course, so I determined that my "not drink" condition would begin the next day. I maintained this condition for a month and I was able to reduce my after-work drinks to about 30%. Of course, I was happy (with the reduction from 90% to 30%) but rather surprised that I had been unable to stop it totally. One day I had an interesting insight (Are research subjects allowed to have insights??) that suggested a way in which the study might be modified.

Bourbon is my favorite drink. It occurred to me that if there was no bourbon in the house, I might be less likely to have my after-work drink. This new phase of the study began when my last bottle of bourbon ran dry. Well, my hunch was correct; not having bourbon at home decreased the frequency of after-work drinks. What shocked me was the magnitude of difference it made—the frequency of after-work drinks went from 30% to 0%! The next interesting insight came several months later when I became convinced that the 0% in the "keep bourbon out of the house" condition would be maintained. The methodologist in me kept insisting that I reverse the condition by buying bourbon but still trying not to have my drink after work—or even a reversal to a "try to drink after work condition." But somehow I couldn't bring myself to perform either of these reversals. Consequently, I am sorry to inform you that this personal experiment had an incomplete design.

A little over a year after I began my personal experiment I read an intriguing little article entitled "The beneficial side of moderate alcohol use" in *The Johns Hopkins Medical Journal* (Turner, Bennett, & Hernandez, 1982). I immediately "became able" to reverse to a "bring bourbon back into the house" condition, and my best estimate is that I now have an after-work drink on about half my work days. Whenever I "catch myself" getting close to the 100% level of having a drink after work over a period of time (such as during tenure review, interviewing job candidates, and so forth), I "become concerned" and "force myself" to have a drink after work less often.

I used "scare quotes" liberally in the preceding paragraph to highlight the fact that a final cause (Rychlak, 1988), or phenomenological (Giorgi, 1970), or active agent (Harré & Secord, 1972), or volitional (Howard, 1984) explanation seems a more plausible (at least to my ear) interpretation of my action than any mechanistic, or psychodynamic, or biopsychological, or sociobiological account of my actions. The reality that you might find a different explanation more compelling highlights a fact known to every philosopher of science (e.g., Hanson, 1958; Kuhn, 1977; McMullin, 1983) and most psychologists (e.g., Cronbach, 1982; Gergen, 1982; Howard, 1984; Rychlak, 1988; Weimer, 1979): that the theoretical meaning of our data is *never* self-evident. Explaining the meaning of one's findings is an interpretive act that always involves a leap of faith that is underjustified by the data. As suggested earlier, while every experimenter struggles mightily to produce demonstrations where "facts" appear to "speak for themselves," they never really do. Each reader must agree to see the world through the conceptual lenses offered by the researcher.

This brief tale from my past highlights the paradox of freedom and constraint as it presents itself to each of us in our lives. That is, it depicts the paradox as your clients might experience it—namely, being free to act in some ways, while also being the pawn to various nonagential causal influences. Having heard the story of my struggle to control my bourbon drinking, you might now render a summary decision. Have I no control over bourbon? Do I have complete control over my consumption of bourbon? Imagine for a moment that I am in complete control of alcohol. What empirical demonstration would prove compelling to you? What would an imaginary research subject have to be able to do to convince you that she or he was simply choosing to drink (or not drink) rather than being compelled to do so? Would it be sufficient if a subject drank moderately for a week (or a month, or a year)? Would you be convinced if a person went without an alcoholic drink for a week (or a month, or a year)? Exactly what would it take for you to be convinced that a person is self-determining her or his actions?

Alcohol consumption represents a good example of the problems encountered in attempting to empirically support arguments for freedom of the will because many addictionologists are so convinced that alcoholism represents a non-volitional disease, that there is no piece of evidence that would shake their belief in this regard. For example, alcoholics can go entire decades without touching a drink and they are still seen as not cured of their disease. Such people are called "dry alcoholics." It is an act of faith of Alcoholics Anonymous (AA) that one is *never* cured of the disease of alcoholism. But my point is *not* to quibble with the AA view of alcoholism. Rather, I want to highlight how difficult (often impossible) it is to convincingly demonstrate the causal efficacy of freedom of the will. Many scientists assert that science can only demonstrate the influence of non-agential causal influences acting upon objects of scientific scrutiny. Berger (1963) highlighted this belief nicely.

> Freedom is not empirically available. More precisely, while freedom may be experienced by us as a certainty along with other empirical certainties, it is not open to demonstration by any scientific methods.... Every object of scientific scrutiny is presumed to have an ante-

rior cause. An object, or an event, that *is* its own cause lies outside the scientific universe of discourse. Yet freedom has precisely this character.... The individual who is conscious of his own freedom does not stand outside the world of causality, but rather perceives his own volition as a very special category of cause, different from the other causes that he must reckon with. This difference, however, is not subject to scientific demonstration.... There is no way of perceiving freedom, either in oneself or in another being, except through a subjective inner certainty that dissolves as soon as it is attacked with the tools of scientific analysis. (pp. 122–124)

While Berger's claims (that science could not study freedom) were originally correct, recent methodological refinements now make possible demonstrations of precisely what Berger claimed to be impossible. That is, we are now able to provide scientific evidence of self-determination (or volition, or behavioral freedom) in human actions.

RESEARCH METHODOLOGY TO THE RESCUE

Milgram's (1974) demonstration of obedience to authority was so memorable because he showed levels of obedience (to the command that subjects deliver electric shocks to inefficient learners) at levels far greater (and by greater percentages of subjects) than almost anyone would have believed possible. One way of creating an experimental masterpiece is to create a demonstration of human action that people would find shocking (pun intended). To a certain extent, every psychologist harbors some degree of belief that she or he understands human nature. Any surprising experimental demonstration of human action challenges each psychologist with the question, "If I *really* understood human nature, how could I have been so wrong in predicting how this group of human subjects would act in this experiment?" Such compelling demonstrations of heretofore unrealized or underappreciated sources of causal influence immediately challenge the psychologist to revise somewhat his or her view of human nature. Thus, one category of compelling experimental demonstrations involves those studies that capitalize on a causal influence (like the high level of obedience that authority figures can sometimes command) to an extent that psychologists had previously thought unachievable.

Experiments also can be compelling for reasons other than the revelation of unexpected patterns of human behavior. *Demonstrations can be compelling because they force surprising conclusions upon us with compelling rigor.* If my work on self-determination deserves any notice at all, it lies in the ability of the program of research to force the fair-minded skeptic to a rather startling conclusion: namely, that humans have substantial powers to self-determine their actions when all other possible nonagential causes of these actions have been methodologically controlled and thus eliminated as possible explanations of the behavior in question. Notice that I identified you, the reader, as a member of the fair-minded, skeptical group. You should take a "prove-it-to-me" attitude toward my claims and be willing to have your beliefs altered by compelling arguments that are backed up by supportive data. If one makes it an act of faith that science can*not* provide evidence of human freedom, then no proof is possible to this sort of true-unbeliever. But I trust my readers possess the basic scientific value of being open-minded (although with great skepticism) to new ideas and arguments.

My argument's compellingness rests on basic concepts in research methodology (e.g., the logic of random assignment, the elimination of rival hypotheses to experimental hypotheses). What the research to follow does, is to demonstrate in a series of experiments the proportion of variance in human behavior that is attributable to freedom of the will. What these studies will show is that there is no possible non-agential factor that you can name that might possibly have caused the observed behavior. Quite a remarkable claim to make, you must be thinking. Thus, I hope you are willing to skeptically follow my line of reasoning and the demonstrations that support my claims. Then you will be able to judge for yourself whether I have justified my radical claim.

The most fruitful construal of the notion of free will turns upon the following question: When a person chooses and then performs an action, might that person have done otherwise, *ceteris paribus* (that is, if all other things had been equal). This description speaks to the issue most of us believe to be at the heart of free will. Namely, could the action have been self-determined to occur differently, even if all characteristics of the situation had been identical except the agent's choice to behave differently. But the *ceteris paribus* assumption can never be met because time marches on and as the pre-Socratic philosopher Heraclitus said, "One can never step in the exact same river twice." There is no way of knowing for sure, once a person makes a choice and acts upon it, that he or she might have chosen to do otherwise. But we believe that these problems in satisfying the conditions of the *ceteris paribus* assumption occur only because thinkers restrict their consideration to single choices and acts. In fact, this is precisely where free-will advocates foundered in the free will–determinism debate. Thus, while freedom of choice has long been perceived by acting agents as an inner certainty, for many years this human power could not be demonstrated experimentally with compelling rigor.

Conversely, advocates of determinism (who see themselves as free-will opponents) are continually heartened by the evidence of science suggesting that numerous non-agential mechanisms (biological, environmental, cultural, etc.) are implicated in human action. Thus, until lately, the free will–determinism debate has gone quite badly for free-will advocates.

AN EXPERIMENTAL OPERATIONALIZATION OF THE *CETERIS PARIBUS* ASSUMPTION

It is generally conceded that among the most important strategies developed by modern sciences are those that deal with experimental control—control over extraneous variables that might obfuscate the relationship of interest; control of plausible rival interpretations to the experimental hypothesis. Among the many successful control procedures developed, two forms of control that emerge are: (1) control through elimination, and (2) control through equalization. The development of vacuums represents an example of control via elimination. By reducing the density of the medium through which objects fall to near zero, one can study the effects of gravity in a "purer," less contaminated manner. But some variables cannot be eliminated from a study. If one is interested in the relationship between a particular chemical fertilizer and crop yield, then the amount of water and light that plants receive are critical factors to be controlled. But one cannot eliminate water and light without killing the plants; therefore, a control through equalization strategy is indicated.

Between-Subject and Within-Subject Methods of Equalization

Random assignment of experimental subjects to research conditions represents the optimal equalization control strategy. The rationale behind the random assignment procedure is that two groups will be created that are *equal on the average on all conditions* save the independent variable and any other variable inadvertently correlated with the independent variable (usually due to bad experimental procedure). Assuming all such correlated variable problems are handled properly, it follows that differences on the dependent variable between the two groups logically can be attributed to the independent variable, since the effect of all other possible causes is controlled by the formation of two equivalent groups through the random assignment procedure. Behavioral scientists are virtually univocal in acknowledging the power of equalization via random assignment in isolating discrete causal relationships. But many variables of interest to social scientists (referred to as subject-variables—e.g., intelligence, motivation, personality traits, etc.) cannot be randomly assigned in a non-trivial manner. Take intelligence as an example. One cannot randomly assign subjects to be highly intelligent or low in intelligence. Thus, intelligence cannot be studied as an independent variable by employing random assignment—although random assignment can be used to control for intelligence when the effects of other variables (e.g., teaching styles) are being investigated.

Yet another strategy for controlling extraneous variables experimentally involves employing within-subject designs. In such studies each subject is exposed to more than one condition of the independent variable. The famous "Pepsi challenge" capitalizes upon within-subject strategies, since each subject tastes and rates the flavor of both Pepsi and Coke. In such studies, each subject serves as his or her own control and thus all subject-variables are equivalent for the two groups when the ratings of Pepsi and Coke are made. Of course, proper design procedures (e.g., counterbalancing the order of presentation of stimuli) must also be employed to eliminate specific threats (e.g., novelty effects, carryover effects, etc.) to valid inference. The new operational definition of volition (or will, or behavioral freedom, or self-determination, or personal causation) described below represents a hybrid approach that employs the logic of random assignment in a within-subject design.

A Method for Studying Self-Determined Behavior

The crucial aspect of the new methodology for investigating volitional behavior is that it requires the active cooperation of the research subject. If, for whatever reason, the subject chooses not to cooperate fully with the experimenter, a serious underestimate of that subject's degree of volitional control will be obtained. (We performed several process checks in a few studies and found levels of subject cooperation to be quite high. Most subjects believe they have some power to self-determine their actions—and they welcome the opportunity to prove it.) One of the first procedures developed involves the experimenter dividing the total time for the experiment into a large number of equal-length time blocks. The experimenter then randomly assigns each of the time blocks to either "try to _____" or "try not to _____" conditions. For example, if one considered subjects' ability to control between-meals snacks, as a part of their ability to lose weight, the instructions for each subject on half the studies' days would be to "eat as many snacks as you wish," whereas on the other half of the days, subjects would be instructed to "try not to eat any snacks." Differences in mean number of snacks consumed on "eat" versus "not eat" days are a reflection of the subjects' ability to volitionally control snacking behavior.

The studies to be reviewed below probed subjects' capacity to volitionally control their actions. Is this teleological account the only interpretation that can be given for the data reported herein? Definitely not. One might choose to argue for a Humean-type, efficient cause explanation. For example, if subjects eat more peanuts on "try to eat" days than they do on "try not to eat" days, a critic might claim that such evidence does not imply volitional control of that action. Rather, the critic might assert that subjects have been socialized to play "good subject" roles in scientific studies. Thus, the difference in amount of peanuts eaten on "eat" versus "not eat" days is best attributed to conformity by the subjects to the demands of the experiment, rather than being evidence of volitional control. While at first blush this might appear to be a serious criticism of this group of studies, closer inspection reveals that such interpretive difficulties are endemic to all research (although this fact is rarely acknowledged by psychological researchers). The problem is referred to by philosophers of science as the underdetermination of theory by evidence (Hanson, 1958; Kuhn, 1962, 1977). In its weakest form, the underdetermination thesis suggests that the meaning of a research finding is never transparent. Does this mean that there are no criteria whereby scientists can make objective (if fallible) judgments as to the probable meanings of research findings? Not at all. Cronbach (1982) points toward a partial solution to this dilemma by expanding the traditional notion of the concept of the "validity" of an experiment.

> Validity depends not only on the data collection and analysis *but also on the way a conclusion is stated and communicated.* Validity is subjective rather than objective: The plausibility of the conclusion is what counts. And plausibility, to twist a cliché, lies in the ear of the beholder. (p. 108, emphasis added)

The position espoused herein is that humans possess capacities that enable them to behave volitionally. If that position is correct, then individuals might be expected to be able to control their behavior in meaningful ways. But note that another investigator might see that same behavior as being under the control of stimuli, both internal and external. Such an individual might actually design the exact same studies as will be reviewed here (and, hopefully, would have obtained a similar set of results). But the account of the *meaning* of the findings would have been quite different—and perhaps equally plausible. No amount of evidence ever "proves" a theory, and, relatedly, there can be multiple theoretical interpretations of any body of evidence. Hence, one is forced to a position like Cronbach's where the scientific community evaluates the plausibility of various competing accounts of empirical findings. This chapter argues for the plausibility of a volitional account of a growing body of research evidence. However, other interpretations of these findings are also plausible.

While my research has implications for therapeutic psychology, it should now be clear that I had an audience of theoretical psychologists, research methodologists, and philosophers of science in mind as I developed the research strategy to demonstrate the capacity of humans to self-determine their actions. In fact, I even wrote a philosophical fantasy (Howard, 1989, Chapter 8) wherein I imagined that the moon really was a person who freely chose to orbit the earth. However, just to prove his/her power of agency, astronomers and philosophers could ask for one action on the moon's part that would convince them of his/her power to self-determine. Throughout that fantasy it is clear that I was struggling to find a research strategy that mechanists (among theoretical psychologists, research methodologists, or philosophers of science) would be unable to refute. My interest in the implications of self-determination for therapists came much later—after the smoke from the methodological and conceptual battles had cleared.

Eventually, I came to see psychotherapy as often containing instances where people lost their normal ability to self-determine their actions in some domains (e.g., alcohol consumption, food consumption, level of depressive affect, anxiety-provoking thoughts, etc.). Successful therapy helps the client to re-establish a more normal level of control over troublesome behavior. I tried to identify a model of optimal therapist strategies in aiding clients to reassert proper levels of self-determination in their lives (the ACT model, Howard, Nance, & Myers, 1987), which will be described subsequently.

THE EVIDENCE FOR SELF-DETERMINATION

What data suggest the importance of volitional control in human action? Using subjects' self-control as a warrant for volitional behavior, my colleagues and I (Howard & Conway, 1986; Howard, Curtin, & Johnson, 1991; Howard, DiGangi, & Johnson, 1988; Howard, Youngs, & Siatczynski, 1989; Lazarick, Fishbein, Loiello, & Howard, 1988; Steibe & Howard, 1986) conducted a series of studies that considered what proportion of a particular eating behavior was due to particular external, efficient-cause influences, and what part was due to volitional control. Several studies dealt with subjects' ability to control eating peanuts. Peanut eating was chosen because it provided a non-controversial dependent measure, and because eating peanuts was an activity subjects tend to enjoy, but which they should be able to control. Here (Howard & Conway, 1986, Study 1) the effect size (partial Eta squared) for volitional control was .56, while the effect size for whether the food was kept in sight or out of sight was .13. Comparable figures for the second study of Howard and Conway (1986) were .57 for volition and .16 for whether the subject received a written reminder or not. Finally, in a third study (Howard, Youngs, & Siatczynski, 1989, Study 1) the effect size for volition was .53, while the effect size for a written reminder was .03. Therefore, in studies on the control of eating behavior, volition appears to be about five times more influential than certain (sight and reminder) external, efficient-cause influences (i.e., the average effect size for volition was .56, while the average effect size for the efficient causes was .11).

Great care should be taken in interpreting the above findings. The major point is that we now are able to assess the influence of volition in eating in a rigorous, empirical manner. Beyond that, interpretation becomes difficult. For example, the ratio of the effect size of volition to the effect size of external factors should be viewed with extreme caution. Had we considered other and/or more non-volitional factors in our studies, that ratio likely would have been reduced. Therefore, if one really was interested in volitional versus non-volitional factors in eating behavior, these studies would represent but a first step toward developing a more complete understanding of the phenomenon, which might be obtained by investigating additional external and/or organismic variables. Conversely, one might consider whether various self-control enhancing techniques might actually increase the volitional-to-non-volitional ratio in our account of the phenomenon.

Criticisms of a "Volitional" Interpretation

A second set of investigations probed the plausibility of the volitional account of the findings of the peanut-eating studies, as opposed to a nonagential explanation of the data. Specifically, it was suggested by some that the differences in the amount of peanuts consumed on days when subjects were instructed to "eat" versus when they were told to "not eat" did *not* represent evidence for volitional control. Rather, critics saw these differences as confirming that peanut-eating behavior was under the control of the experimenter, since the subjects obeyed the experimenter's instructions. Or as one commentator put it, "the psychologist reader, steeped in behavioristic lingo, 'sees' in the experimental instruction to eat or not eat a *nonvolitional* control or manipulation directing behavior."

Two objections, which are really two ways of wording the same problem, were raised. These explanations suggest that the subject is either trying to be a good subject (Orne, 1962; Weber & Cook, 1972) or is trying to avoid being "socially sanctioned" for being an inconsistent and, therefore, a poor subject (Hayes, 1987).

First, let me address the contention that subjects are responding to demand characteristics, that is, that subjects determined the experimenter's hypotheses and are behaving in such a manner as to confirm the hypotheses (and thus be good subjects). Note that the force of this position evaporates if one sees subjects volitionally choosing whether to adopt "good subject" or "bad subject" roles (see Howard, Youngs, & Siatczynski, 1989, Study 2). But, it also is worth mentioning that Howard & Conway (1986) note enormous differences among subjects, such that several subjects did not show any evidence of trying to play the role of "good subject."

Next, Hayes's (1987) reply focuses on research on "social standard setting" that speaks to our findings. Hayes believes subjects are able to behave in particular ways in experimental settings because they are "public" settings. But in "private" (read, non-experimental) contexts, these subjects would be unlikely (perhaps even unable) to behave in the same manner. Although Hayes's research highlights an interesting factor in this domain, what remains unclear is exactly how important the public versus private nature of the data is in our studies.

Consider the following thought experiment. You set a jar of peanuts on your desk and flip a coin each day to determine whether it will be an "eat" or "try not to eat" day. Then you choose a colleague to tell which set of instructions you are entertaining, and you show him or her your daily results (public phase). Our data suggest that you might consume about six times the weight in peanuts on "eat" days as on "try not to eat" days. Next, you inform your colleague that your personal experiment has been completed, but you continue the same set of procedures without letting anyone else know (private phase). I would not be at all surprised if you found that the effect of volitional control remained unchanged in the private phase. Nor would I be concerned if, for example, your average weight consumed on "eat" days was only (for example) four times the amount consumed on "try not to eat" days. The decline (from a sixfold to a fourfold advantage for "eat" days) represents an estimate of the impact of the "private" versus "public" nature of the experimental context.

When I conducted this experiment on myself, the advantage of "eat" days in the private phase was actually greater than the advantage of the "eat" days in the public phase. But I am completely confident that if Hayes conducted the same experiment on himself, he would be perfectly able to show no effect of volition in the private phase—if he wanted to demonstrate such an effect. What would surprise me is if you (the typical reader) were unable to eat more peanuts on "eat" days than on "try not to eat" days in the private condition.

Of course, there is a simpler way of thinking of Hayes's public versus private challenge to our studies of volition. If one considers the issue to be one of external validity, the findings might be summarized as follows: In public settings (such as therapy) subjects are able to achieve their agential goals more satisfactorily than in private contexts (such as self-improvement efforts) (see Howard, DiGangi, & Johnson, 1988). Thus, if one is interested in public, psychological activities (such as psychotherapy), the public studies we presented likely possess greater external validity than the private research alternative.

Empirical Investigations of the Obedience Hypothesis

Because of the possible plausibility of the conformity objection to the original volition studies, the following series of investigations explicitly attempted to test the volitional interpretation versus the "control via the experimenter's instructions" interpretation. In one study (Howard & Conway, 1986, Study 2) subjects sometimes received their daily "eat" or "not eat" instructions via a coin toss, and the experimenter was unaware as to what condition the subject was in for that day. Subjects still demonstrated a strong effect of volition. At other times, subjects simply chose and recorded whether that particular day would be an "eat" or a "not eat" day (and also did not let the experimenter know the condition they chose). In this condition, subjects also showed strong volitional control. Therefore, subjects showed volitional control in two different types of situations where the experimenter not only did not give the "eat" and "not eat" instructions, but also was not even aware of whether subjects were in an "eat" or "not eat" condition on any day.

In yet another study, Howard, Youngs, and Siatczynski (1989, Study 2) had subjects choose and record each day whether they would "follow instructions" or "do the opposite" of the instructions given (the meta-volitional factor). Subjects were then told by the experimenter either to "eat" or "not eat" peanuts that day. As expected, the volition by meta-volition interaction was significant and accounted for 65% of the within-subject variance. That is, subjects ate many more peanuts on "eat" days than on "not eat" days (135 g. vs. 10 g.) when they had chosen to follow the instructions. However, when they decided to "do the opposite," they consumed far more peanuts in the "not eat" condition than in the "eat" condition (120 g. vs. 3 g.). These studies serve to lessen the plausibility of the efficient-cause objection (that, "they were compelled to obey the experimenter's instructions") to the volitional interpretation of the above studies.

The intriguing aspect of the studies of volition reviewed above is that through the random assignment of conditions of volitional control (e.g., "eat–not eat," "binge–not binge," "initiate conversations–do not initiate conversations," "exercise–do not exercise," etc.) to time blocks, all but two possible explanations for mean differences between the two conditions are rendered implausible. The two possible explanations are: (1) that these mean differences reflect the agents' power of self-determination (or behavioral freedom, or volition) in this particular instance; and (2) that subjects were compelled to obey the experimenter's instructions and could not do otherwise (or, similarly, they had been so thoroughly socialized into a "good subject" role and therefore could not choose to disobey). Thus, the crux of the difference between these two explanations involves whether subjects obey their own directives or the directives of the experimenter. Howard, Myers, and Curtin (1991, Study 1) addressed the above question of who causes the subject's behavior (the subject him/herself or the experimenter through the experimental instructions to the subject) by *collapsing the distinction between the subject and the experimenter*. Thus, I served as both experimenter and subject for the study. Enormous volitional control of alcohol consumption was evident in this study. But if as both experimenter and subject I was merely conforming to the experimental instructions, then I was conforming to my own commands—but this is precisely the character of volition.

One last study addressed the rival, conformity explanation to our volition interpretation of our data. Most readers by now must wonder why yet another demonstration of this point is necessary. The reason is that conformity is the only viable alternative explanation offered for these data. If conformity can be shown to have no force, a fair-minded theorist must (either willingly or grudgingly) see the differences on the dependent measure between "try to _____" and "try not to _____" days as evidence for self-determination—no other explanation appears possible, thanks to the effects of random assignment. So one more spear to the heart of the "Conformity Monster" will be thrown.

Howard, Myers, and Curtin (1991, Study 2) gave subjects commands to "try to _____ " or "try not to _____" in three separate domains on each day of this study. If conformity to the experimenter's authority was primarily responsible for differences between conditions on the dependent measure (and self-determination an illusion, as the extreme non-agential mechanist would argue), then similar amounts of self-determination would appear on all three dependent measures. But I believe humans can self-determine in most domains and choose to go along with the experimenter's request that they prove (experimentally) their ability to self-determine. But in some value-laden domains, subjects will choose not to prove their ability to self-determine because behaving in that manner would violate their sense of ethics, taste, and the like. Thus, despite equal power of conformity, subjects will show great differences in their ability to self-determine in domains that are: (1) not value-laden, (2) moderately value-laden, and (3) highly value-laden. Since ethics and taste are often idiosyncratic, each subject identified one target behavior in each value-ladenness domain. Thus, a daily instruction for one subject might be: "try to eat a lot of celery (not value-laden); try not to read psychology (moderately value-laden); and try to strike your child as often as possible (highly value-laden)." To no one's surprise, subjects showed an enormous ability to self-determine in the not value-laden domain; a moderate ability to self-determine in the moderately value-laden condition; and a negative effect for self-determination (i.e., "try not to _____" days slightly higher than "try to _____" days) in the highly value-laden domain. While the conformity hypothesis is completely unable to explain these results, the pattern is exactly what would have been predicted by the free-will advocate.

Volition as a Factor in Therapeutic Interventions

We will now turn to applied and/or therapeutic investigations and applications of the above designs. Many psychologists have observed that self-determination is a critical factor in counseling and psychotherapy. Schultz (1977) concludes, after drawing from the collected theories of Gordon Allport, Carl Rogers, Erich Fromm, Abraham Maslow, Carl Jung, Viktor Frankl, and Fritz Perls, the following:

> Perhaps the only point on which they agree fully is that psychologically healthy persons are in conscious control of their lives. Healthy persons are capable of consciously, if not always rationally, *directing their behavior and being in charge of their own destinies.* (p. 143, emphasis added)

Thus, it has long been held by therapists that many clients' troubles stem from their inability to control either their environment or their response to the environment (Mahoney & Thoresen, 1974). The process of therapy often involves the process of re-establishing such control.

After accepting the validity of our methodology for empirically assessing volitional effects in a series of studies on peanut eating, one reviewer wondered whether the concept of volition generalizes beyond the shell of a peanut. Indeed, my colleagues and I have considered the role of volition in domains that are of more interest to practicing psychologists. Many practitioners (e.g., clinical, counseling, industrial/organizational, and school psychologists) often are involved in consulting on behavior that their clients have difficulty controlling. At first blush it might appear that volition would not be a useful construct to aid these applied psychologists in their ministrations. For example, simply telling a schizophrenic to "stop hearing those voices," or instructing a depressed client to "feel less depressed," would seem to be singularly unhelpful. However, a slight modification of the procedures employed in the "peanut studies" of volition has yielded some interesting findings in several clinically important domains. Rather than attempting to volitionally control the problem behavior directly, these studies adopted a strategy similar to that practiced by most experienced clinicians. Namely, subjects were encouraged to exercise volitional control *over the conditions that serve to maintain the problem behavior.*

I would like to suggest that the following studies be viewed as the beginning of a bridge-building process that will establish a direct link between research and the practice of therapy from a volitional perspective. The following are examples of the range of issues addressed by volition research to date.

Frequency of Heterosexual Interaction. In one study (Howard & Conway, 1986, Study 3) college students, who wished to increase the frequency of their heterosexual social (heterosocial) interactions, were recruited for a study in which they were encouraged to exert volitional control over three factors related to heterosocial interactions: (1) the number of conversations initiated with members of the opposite sex; (2) the amount of time spent in places where social interactions frequently occur (e.g., dining hall, student center, parties, etc.); and (3) the frequency of positive self-statements made about themselves and their social skills. Control of all three factors was structured in the same "try to _____/try not to _____" paradigm used in the peanut studies. It should be noted that, while few subjects in the previous "peanut studies" doubted their ability to control peanut consumption, the subjects in this study identified heterosexual social skills as an area of concern.

The data revealed that on the group analysis level, subjects were able to control all three of these conditions related to the number of heterosocial interactions, and that in so doing they were extremely effective in achieving their goal of having more (and more satisfying) heterosocial interactions.

Control of Snacking and Exercise. Lazarick and co-authors (1988, Study 1) considered the degree to which eating and exercise habits are under an individual's volitional control (for control of exercise, see also, Howard et al., 1988). Subjects were divided into two groups, those who wanted to lose weight and those who did not particularly care to lose weight. After an initial baseline observation period, subjects were given a container of vegetables and one of four sets of instructions: (1) To snack on as many vegetables as he or she liked but try not to exercise; (2) try not to snack on the vegetables and also try not to exercise; (3) snack on vegetables and exercise as much as he or she wished; and (d) try not to snack on the vegetables but exercise as much as he or she wished. The results indicated that subjects could control both snacking on vegetables and exercising.

Control of Time Spent Researching Vocational Information. In another study reported by Lazarick and co-authors (1988, Study 2), the researchers considered how pursuing two types of information, vocational and personal, affected career indecisiveness. Subjects were assigned to one of three conditions: (1) search for personal information, (2) search for vocational information, and (3) try not to search (purposely avoid attempting to discover information about oneself or the world of work). The dependent measure was time spent engaged in the searching activity. Results indicate that not only do subjects have a considerable amount of control over their behavior, but they were able to follow the "try not to search" instruction even though they reported dissatisfaction with this condition.

Control of Binging Behavior by Bulimics. Two studies (Lazarick et al., 1988, Study 3; Steibe & Howard, 1986) in this series obtained strong evidence for the efficacy of a volitional treatment of binge eating and bulimia by using a "try not to/act normally" paradigm. The findings demonstrate that frequency of binge eating episodes can be reduced and subjects can replace high caloric foods with vegetables. Thus, binge eating is modifiable in the short run by efforts of will, but other issues remain unresolved, making long-term control unlikely.

Control of Social Consumption of Alcohol. Finally, Howard (1986), Howard, Myers, and Curtin (1991) and Howard, Curtin, and Johnson (1991) showed, with a slight variation in methodology, that social drinking is, indeed, under volitional control. In Howard, Curtin, and Johnson (1991, Study 1), subjects exerted control over their consumption of alcohol. The study had two phases. First, the subjects were to undergo a baseline, monitoring period. The second phase was the target hitting period in which they were to drink only as many glasses of alcohol as were indicated by the predetermined targets. Inaccuracy scores for the target hitting period could then be compared with inaccuracy scores for the monitoring period. The latter were determined by comparing "normal" drinking patterns with a set of randomly selected targets.

To operationalize volition, then, subjects converted a significant message (FREE WILL), via Morse Code, into target numbers. That is, a two drink target represented a "dash," a one drink target depicted a "dot," a zero drink target represented a space between letters, and two consecutive zero drink targets signaled a break between words. The subjects' volition was measured by how close they came to spelling "FREE WILL" and by how much they improved their accuracy from the baseline period to the target hitting period. (It should also be noted that half of the subjects knew that they were spelling the words "FREE WILL" (high meaning condition), while the other half only knew the target numbers (low meaning condition). The role of meaning will be discussed below.)

The results were striking. For example, those in the high meaning condition achieved 100% accuracy, and those in the low meaning condition, while unable to spell the words precisely, improved their accuracy from baseline to intervention by up to 86%. Thus, these results invite another round in the controversy over whether the increased use of alcohol over time by non-addicted individuals is best understood as a form of progressive physical addiction, a breakdown of volitional control, or both. Future research in this area with special populations and with the control of diverse environmental variables should prove both interesting and fruitful.

Self-Determination and Psychotherapy

One might think of psychotherapy as instances in which people find that they are unable to achieve the level of self-determined control in a domain (e.g., alcohol consumption, excessive negative affect, thought disorders) that most other people at their stage and state in life achieve, and that their efforts at self-change have proven unsuccessful (Howard, Curtin, & Johnson, 1991; Schachter, 1982). This perspective seeks to "normalize" psychopathology. That is, all of us from time to time can find ourselves drinking a little too much, becoming a bit depressed, putting on a few too many pounds, getting a little paranoid, and the like. When we notice these shifts in the direction of inappropriate thoughts, behaviors, and lifestyles, we initiate a host of self-change efforts designed to bring our lives back to a more appropriate course of action (e.g., initiating diets, taking vacations, discussing our problems with members of our support systems). In most cases these self-initiated change strategies yield results that render the problem less troubling. But what about those instances when a succession of efforts to reverse the negative pattern in one's life all prove unsuccessful? This becomes the occasion for one to seek professional help in dealing with a recalcitrant problem. From this perspective, psychopathology is seen as especially difficult cases of the loss of a reasonable degree of volitional control in some domain. The challenge of therapy, then, is "How can this client be helped back to the normal degree of self-control in this domain?"

Therapeutic interventions are ways that professionals have found to be effective in aiding clients to re-establish reasonable levels of self-determined control in particular domains (e.g., lithium has proven to be an effective adjunct in controlling bipolar depression; desensitization and flooding techniques are helpful in treating phobias; support groups such as AA have been successful with alcohol abuse). The research on self-determination that was reviewed above suggests two general strategies that can enhance a client's ability to self-determine in a troublesome domain: (1) an attempt to change the meaningfulness of a particular course of action (cf. Frankl, 1965); or (2) an attempt to restructure the circumstances of a person's life to enhance the likelihood that he or she will achieve desired goals and patterns of action (e.g., building a support system makes debilitating depression less likely; regular exercise and proper diet fight depression; minimizing time spent with unfriendly people combats depressive affect). Thus, one might choose to see therapy from the perspective of efforts to re-establish proper levels of self-determination in a domain.

But are all therapeutic techniques equally effective at all times and for all problems in aiding clients to regain lost control or in learning appropriate amounts of self-control that have never before been learned? Of course they are not! Much of what therapists learn in their training and through their practice is the pragmatic, practical, "how to" knowledge of what interventions are best suited to achieve what results, for which types of clients, at what point in their recovery process, from which types of problems. That such grounded knowledge is fundamentally different from the theoretical knowledge we learn in graduate courses has been argued by Hoshmand and Polkinghorne (1992). If you want to know how to do therapy, that practical knowledge must come in large part from the practice of therapy. But in saying this, one does not imply that one's practice cannot profit from conceptual analyses of (or reflections upon the experience of) the practice of psychotherapy as aided by research such as described here.

Adaptive Counseling and Therapy (ACT)

Pennie Myers and Don Nance are two of the most skilled therapists that I have ever had the pleasure of knowing. Because they supervised my therapy efforts when I was an intern, the three of us had long been engaged in conversation about when (and where, and by whom, and why) therapy is effective, ineffective, and sometimes harmful. Don and Pennie then suggested a model of therapy that saw all therapeutic methods as potentially helpful, but more for certain clients than others (or, more precisely, for clients at certain levels of task readiness, i. e., the client's level of competence, confidence, and motivation to change). I saw that the model had great promise for bringing some degree of conceptual order to the therapeutic tower of babel caused by the hundreds and hundreds of different therapeutic approaches that clamored for our attention. Additionally, I was attracted to ACT because it downplayed the stigmatizing aspects of psychopathology and posited as the ultimate goal of therapy that the client would achieve the normal ability to self-determine her or his thoughts, actions, or affect in the target domain (e.g., social skills, depression, alcohol consumption, thought disorders). Here is a thumbnail sketch of the ACT model.

Howard, Nance, and Myers (1986, 1987) see counseling and psychotherapy as a developmental process wherein the client is helped to grow from a lower level of developmental maturity (vis-a-vis the particular tasks designated as the target issues of counseling, such as assertiveness, social skills, depression, antisocial behavior) to a higher level of maturity. The counselor is advised to choose a style of therapeutic intervention believed to be optimally effective in moving the client from his or her current maturity level to the next higher level. Rather than maintaining a constant style of counselor behavior throughout counseling, ACT theory recommends that once initial progress in counseling has been achieved, and the client has progressed to the next higher maturity level, the counselor should switch his or her style of interaction to the style predicted to be optimally effective (by ACT theory) for achieving the next round of therapeutic growth in task-relevant developmental maturity. Thus, ACT theory recommends the use of a slowly evolving progression of therapeutic styles that are theoretically hypothesized to be optimally effective in facilitating client development from lower to higher levels of task-relevant developmental maturity. Like all such scientific theories, value judgments as to optimal therapist styles are offered by ACT theory. To the degree that such claims are supported by research, and are productively used by practitioners, these prescriptions will be justified.

The heart of ACT theory involves the concept of *match and move*.

Properly matching the client's current needs (as determined by their current level of task-relevant readiness) is believed to optimally enhance therapeutic progress (maximize client movement toward higher maturity levels). Slight mismatches are thought to lead to retarded rates of therapeutic change. Finally, when the chosen counselor style badly mismatches the client's level of readiness, either no progress, or even client deterioration, occurs.

The counselor styles alluded to earlier consist of differing combinations of levels of counselor attention to (1) task/directive behaviors, and (2) relationship/supportive behaviors. The optimal matching of counselor behavior to client task-relevant developmental maturity shown in Figure 6.1 is a slightly different depiction of relationships found in Howard and co-authors (1987).

In Figure 6.1 there are four categories of counselor styles (Q1, *telling;* Q2, *teaching;* Q3, *supporting;* Q4, *delegating*). Immaturity (or low task-relevant readiness) is found at the left-hand side of the figure, and high levels of client maturity are found at the right side. The bell-shaped curve transversing the four counselor styles represents the optimally effective counselor style for clients at that particular maturity level, as predicted by ACT theory. This curve is actually the smoothing of a stepwise process of moving back on (decreasing) structure or direction and up on (increasing) support through Q1 and Q2. For Q3 and Q4 the curve is a smoothed stepwise process of decreasing both direction and support as the client assumes more and more responsibility for the maintenance of the targeted task behaviors. ACT theory not only predicts the optimal therapeutic style for each maturity level, but also suggests the probability of success of the other three counselor styles when applied to that situation.

Roughly speaking, the probable success of each style is a function of its distance from the predicted "best style" along the bell-shaped curve. Styles at a greater distance stand less of a chance of success than do styles nearer to the recommended counselor style for that maturity level. See Howard and co-authors (1987) for a thorough analysis.

Thus, one can see that the heart of the ACT model lies in recommending to therapists a progression of therapeutic styles (e.g., telling to teaching to supporting to delegating) if the client enters therapy with a very low maturity level. This progression is believed to optimize the client's progress through the successive maturity levels that lead her or him back to appropriate levels of self-determination in the target domain. Obviously, the ACT model was the perfect vehicle to tie my basic research on self-determination to the domain of therapy. I don't believe I will ever be able to properly thank Pennie and Don for all they've done for me. Their impact on my personal and professional development far exceeds

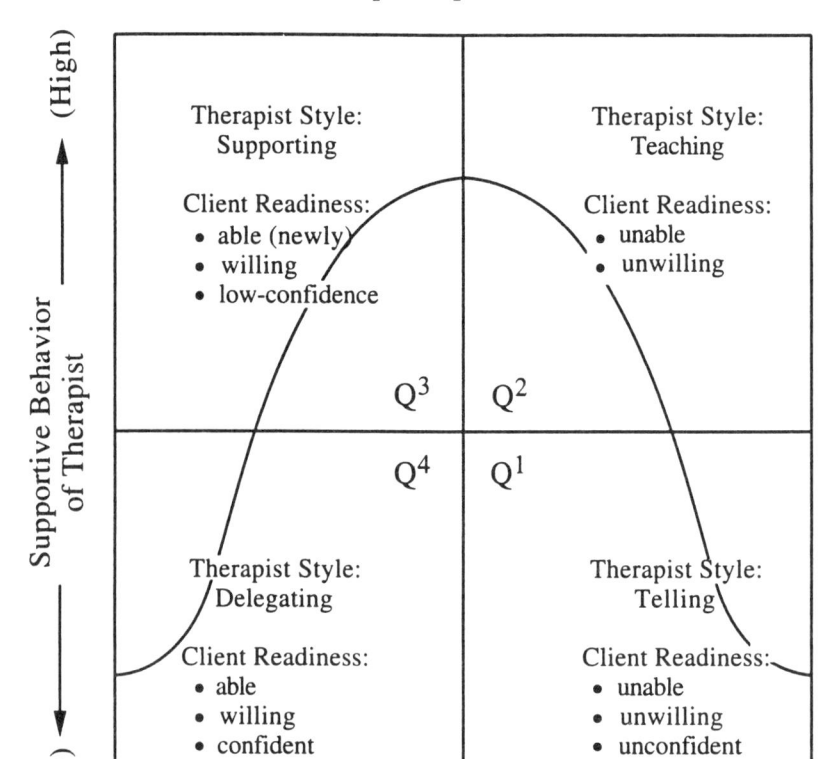

FIGURE 6.1 **Effective Therapist Styles**

Supportive Behavior of Therapist (Low) ↔ (High)

Directive Behavior of Therapist (Low) ← → (High)

Q³ — Therapist Style: Supporting
Client Readiness:
- able (newly)
- willing
- low-confidence

Q² — Therapist Style: Teaching
Client Readiness:
- unable
- unwilling

Q⁴ — Therapist Style: Delegating
Client Readiness:
- able
- willing
- confident

Q¹ — Therapist Style: Telling
Client Readiness:
- unable
- unwilling
- unconfident

their understanding of how they have changed me over the years—and greatly exceeds my ability to express my gratitude to them in words.

But what of the empirical adequacy of the ACT model? Did the research evidence suggest its efficacy? Yes! The data were extraordinarily supportive. Gabbard, Howard, and Dunfee (1986) presented the results of a study that considered the psychometric adequacy of the measure (the Counselor Behavior Analysis, CBA) that we designed to assess the central construct of ACT theory—namely, therapist adaptability. The CBA evidenced fantastic reliability and construct validity. But, of course, the crucial question for ACT theory is to what extent does therapist adaptability predict positive change in therapy? The data were stunning—therapist adaptability correlated with therapeutic improvement .98! This validity coefficient dwarfs the coefficients typically found for traditional predictors of therapy outcome (e.g., therapist empathy). Usually the results of our studies yield findings that are somewhat (at times even extremely) disappointing—this is especially true for incorrigible optimists like myself. Of the more than 300 studies I've conducted over the last 20 years, this is the only instance where the data came out better than I'd imagined. Clint Gabbard and I went over every data point and every analysis many times, as we could not believe that the data Gods would ever be that generous with us. We also decided not to try to replicate our finding, as there seemed no place to go from .98 but down.

WHAT DOES IT ALL MEAN?

It is difficult to say what my program of research means, as I feel I am far from the program's end. After all, it will be another 4 years before I'm half way along the journey between receiving my doctoral degree and retirement. I may be mistaken, but I am convinced that my best work still lies ahead. But I've made sufficient progress to be able to see the outlines of my scientific contribution. I think I finally can see clearly the direction in which I'm traveling. Let me try to nest my contribution within a broader view of the thrust of twentieth-century psychology.

Like William James, my intellectual demon is the specter of complete non-agential determination in human actions. James and I shudder at the prospect that human beings might be nothing more than rudderless pawns tossed about by the tides of non-agential causes that pull and push at our lives. Perhaps our actions are completely out of our control, and humans' sense of freedom of the will is a pathetic illusion. James's psychological and philosophical systems (and much of my research program) are offered in the hope that the human will contributes original causal force in the genesis of human actions and in the conduct of our lives. My data certainly buttress James's claim that the human will is an important element that must be included in any explanation of human actions and lives. Support of the Jamesian construct of "will" has been sparse in the past hundred years of experimental research in psychology, as most researchers have been greatly influenced by the mechanistic, behavioristic, and positivistic excesses that have plagued psychological theorizing. Unfortunately, the sorts of psychologists most sympathetic with the Jamesian vision of human nature (e.g., humanistic, gestalt, and phenomenological psychologists) shared James's aversion for strict experimental and laboratory research. However, I believe (Howard, 1992, 1993) that James would have been quite thrilled with the experimental support that his ideas receive in my research on self-determination (and the evidence for the freedom of the will reviewed above).

Lastly, recall my earlier apology for being unable to produce a dramatic experimental demonstration (a la Milgram or Asch) of the role of self-determination in the genesis of human action that virtually would compel belief by all. Lacking the creative genius to produce a single experimental masterpiece, I offer instead a workman-like program of research that I hope suggests belief in the existence of some degree of freedom of the will in the genesis of human actions in many important domains of our lives. In this world where so much feels out of our control, all humans need a *dramatic* reminder that our efforts do make important differences in our lives. The actions of the pilot of the ship of our lives (the self) does matter in the course our lives take. We are not the helpless pawns of various non-agential winds and tides—we are not completely out of control. The time is long overdue for psychology to highlight and appreciate the role of the will in the creation of happy and healthy human lives. Are there a few experimental poets out there who care to join me in this endeavor?

REFERENCES

Asch, S. E. (1951). Effects of group pressure upon the modification and distortion of judgments. In H. Guetzknow (Ed.), *Groups, leadership, and man*. Pittsburgh, PA: Carnegie University Press.

Berger, P. L. (1963). *Invitation to sociology: A humanistic perspective*. New York: Doubleday.

Bernstein, R. J. (1976). *The restructuring of social and political theory*. Philadelphia: University of Pennsylvania Press.

Cronbach, L. J. (1982). *Designing evaluations of educational and social programs*. San Francisco: Jossey-Bass.

Frankl, V. (1965). *Man's search for meaning*. New York: Harper and Row.

Gabbard, C. E., Howard, G. S., & Dunfee, E. J. (1986). Reliability, sensitivity to measuring change, and construct validity of a measure of counselor adaptability. *Journal of Counseling Psychology, 33*, 377–386.

Gergen, K. J. (1982). *Toward transformation in social knowledge*. New York: Springer-Verlag.

Giorgi, A. (1970). *Psychology as a human science: A phenomenologically based approach*. New York: Harper & Row.

Hanson, N. R. (1958). *Patterns of discovery: An inquiry into the conceptual foundations of science*. Cambridge: Cambridge University Press.

Harré, R., & Secord, P. F. (1972). *The explanation of social behavior.* Oxford: Basil Blackwell.

Hayes, S. C. (1987). Contextual determinants of "volitional action": A reply to Howard and Conway. *American Psychologist, 42,* 1029–1030.

Hoshmand, L. T., & Polkinghorne, D. E. (1992). Redefining the science–practice relationship and professional training. *American Psychologist, 47,* 55–66.

Howard, G. S. (1984). A modest proposal for a revision of strategies in counseling research. *Journal of Counseling Psychology, 31,* 430–442.

Howard, G. S. (1986). *Dare we develop a human science?* Notre Dame, IN: Academic Publications.

Howard, G. S. (1989). *A tale of two stories: Excursions into a narrative approach to psychology.* Notre Dame, IN: Academic Publications.

Howard, G. S. (1992). William James: Closet clinician. In M. E. Donnelly (Ed.), *Reinterpreting the legacy of William James* (pp. 293–312). Washington, DC: American Psychological Association.

Howard, G. S. (1993). Why William James might be considered the founder of the scientist-practitioner model. *The Counseling Psychologist, 21,* 118–135.

Howard, G. S., & Conway, C. G. (1986). Can there be an empirical science of volitional action? *American Psychologist, 41,* 1241–1251.

Howard, G. S., Curtin, T. D., & Johnson, A. J. (1991). Point estimation techniques in psychological research: The role of meaning in self-determined action. *Journal of Counseling Psychology, 38,* 219–226.

Howard, G. S., DiGangi, M. L., & Johnson, A. J. (1988). Life, science, and the role of therapy in the pursuit of happiness. *Professional Psychology: Research and Practice, 19,* 191–198.

Howard, G. S., Myers, P. R., & Curtin, T. D. (1991). Can science furnish evidence of human freedom? Self-determination versus conformity in human action. *International Journal of Personal Construct Psychology, 4,* 371–395.

Howard, G. S., Nance, D. W., & Myers, P. (1986). Adaptive counseling and therapy: An integrative, eclectic model. *The Counseling Psychologist, 14,* 363–442.

Howard, G. S., Nance, D. W., & Myers, P. (1987). *Adaptive counseling and therapy: A systematic approach for selecting effective treatments.* San Francisco: Jossey-Bass.

Howard, G. S., Youngs, W. H., & Siatczynski, A. M. (1989). Reforming methodology in psychological research. *Journal of Mind and Behavior, 10,* 393–412.

Kuhn, T. S. (1962). *The structure of scientific revolutions.* Chicago: University of Chicago Press.

Kuhn, T. S. (1977). *The essential tension.* Chicago: University of Chicago Press.

Lazarick, D. L., Fishbein, S. S., Loiello, M. J., & Howard, G. S. (1988). Practical investigations of volition. *Journal of Counseling Psychology, 35,* 15–26.

Mahoney, M. J., & Thoresen, C. E. (1974). *Self-control: Power to the person.* Monterey, CA: Brooks/Cole.

McMullin, E. D. (1983). Values in science. In P. D. Asquith & T. Nickles (Eds.), *Proceedings of the 1982 Philosophy of Science Association* (Vol. 2). East Lansing, MI: Philosophy of Science Association.

Milgram, S. (1974). *Obedience to authority.* New York: Harper & Row.

Orne, M. T. (1962). On the social psychology of the psychological experiment:

With particular reference to demand characteristics and their implications. *American Psychologist, 17,* 776–783.

Pope, A. (1967). The universal prayer (Stanza 3). In *The works of Alexander Pope.* New York: Gordian Press. (Original work published 1738)

Rychlak, J. F. (1988). *The psychology of rigorous humanism* (2nd ed.). New York: New York University Press.

Schachter, S. (1982). Recidivism and self-cure in smoking and obesity. *American Psychologist, 37,* 436–444.

Schultz, D. (1977). *Growth psychology: Models of the healthy personality.* New York: Van Nostrand.

Steibe, S. C., & Howard, G. S. (1986). The volitional treatment of bulimia. *The Counseling Psychologist, 14,* 85–94.

Turner, T. B., Bennett, V. L., & Hernandez, H. V. (1982). The beneficial side of moderate alcohol use. *The Johns Hopkins Medical Journal, 148,* 53–63.

Weber, S. J., & Cook, T. D. (1972). Subject effects in laboratory research: An examination of subject roles, demand characteristics, and valid inference. *Psychological Bulletin, 77,* 273–295.

Weimer, W. B. (1979). *Notes on the methodology of scientific research.* Hillsdale, N.J.: Lawrence Erlbaum.

CHAPTER 7

Methods and Metaphors: The Study of Figurative Language in Psychotherapy

LINDA M. McMULLEN

Reflecting on Barbara McClintock's unconventional habit of becoming intimately familiar with the genetic make-up of each kernel of maize she was studying, Evelyn Fox Keller (1985) states that

> the kinds of questions one asks and the explanations that one finds satisfying depend on one's a priori relation to the objects of study.... Questions asked about objects with which one feels kinship are likely to differ from questions asked about objects one sees as unalterably alien. (p. 167)

To this statement we might add that the kinds of questions one asks also depend on one's epistemological beliefs (see Conway, 1992) and research training, and that these questions, in turn, dictate one's choice of methods.

In my own case, research training was exclusively in the hypothetico-deductive paradigm and in quantitative methods. As a consequence of this training, I came to believe that objectively measurable phenomena should be the targets of study. However, as someone with a keen interest in the humanities, particularly in English literature, I also believe that investigating human experiences and questions about the meaning of human actions through qualitative methods is valuable, although I have never received any formal instruction in these methods. As I hope to demonstrate, the interconnection of research training (and lack of exposure to certain methods), epistemological beliefs (and the tension between, at times, competing values), familiarity with the objects of study, and question formulation, has been particularly salient for me as I have moved back and forth in the use of quantitative and qualitative methods in my work on figurative language in psychotherapy.

BACKGROUND OF MY RESEARCH PROGRAM

When I became interested in this topic in 1979 the literature was, by today's standards, comparatively sparse. It consisted primarily of three groupings of articles and books. One group comprised conceptual and/or theoretical papers and books in which the author(s) attempted to specify the functions that figurative language serves in psychotherapy (e.g., Aleksandrowicz, 1962; Arlow, 1979; Gore, 1977; Lenrow, 1966; Rice, 1974). Among the many functions proposed, the ones most consistently identified were that it (1) allows clients and therapists to talk about problems in an indirect, non-intrusive manner, (2) facilitates problem setting and problem solving, (3) helps "unblock" clients and aids them in communicating what they actually may be experiencing, (4) reveals a great deal about the client and can function as a diagnostic tool, and (5) serves as a vehicle for therapeutic communication and the development of a working alliance.

The second group consisted of practice-oriented articles and books in which suggestions for the use and interpretation of metaphor as a therapeutic tactic was provided (e.g., Bauer & Modarressi, 1977; Gordon, 1978; Mosher, 1979; Rossel, 1977). Typically, the primary focus was on the use of metaphor by the therapist, and the intervention was illustrated by a brief excerpt from a therapy session. The third group comprised a few small-scale empirical studies that were based on single sessions or a few sessions from a single case (e.g., Barlow, Pollio, & Fine, 1977; Pollio & Barlow, 1975; see Pollio, Barlow, Fine, & Pollio, 1977). As it was from these latter studies that I took my lead, I will briefly describe the kinds of questions they were designed to answer and the method chosen to do so.

The primary goal of the researchers was to examine "the frequency of occurrence and significance of figurative language" (Pollio & Barlow, 1975, p. 236) and the relationship between figurative language and therapeutic insight (Barlow et al., 1977; Pollio et al., 1977). In selecting and analyzing the instances, the researchers relied heavily on the distinction between frozen and novel figures (Barlow, Kerlin, & Pollio, 1970). The former are clichéd expressions or those words and phrases that are commonly used, accepted parts of speech, such as "the legs of a chair." The latter are figures that are considered by the receiver to be original contributions within the context of the speaker's communication, such as describing one's life as "a thread ready to break." In examining the frequency of occurrence of figurative language in a single session of gestalt therapy, Pollio and Barlow (1975) found that while frozen figures were produced by the client at a fairly regular rate, novel figures tended to occur in extended bursts. These bursts were typified by the continued use of the same piece of figurative language and were found to relate to (1) problem setting or development of major themes and (2) problem solving. A further examination of the session in terms of the relationships between the occurrence of figurative language and judged instances of insight, revealed that novel figurative activity tended to co-occur significantly with regions of therapeutic insight, while no such pattern occurred for frozen figurative activity (Barlow et al., 1977). Similar results were found in a study that investigated the occurrence of figurative language and insight in five interviews selected from a lengthy case of successful psychoanalytic therapy (Pollio et al., 1977). These researchers concluded, then, that it was novel figurative language that was of most significance in problem description and resolution.

Considering that these studies were the first systematic empirical analyses of the occurrence of figurative language in psychotherapy, it is not too surprising that they were based on a fairly simple methodology and conceptual model. The authors chose for analysis "a single highly successful hour of gestalt therapy" featuring "a highly intelligent and highly articulate" female client (Pollio & Barlow, 1975, p. 237) as well as five interviews from a lengthy case of successful psychoanalytic therapy. They did so in order to maximize their chances of finding several instances of figurative language to document and analyze. In addition, they used only simple quantitative measures such as overall frequency counts and rates of production as the basis for comparing the use of novel and frozen figures and their relationships to insight. These choices are understandable given that, at the time, so little was known about the use of figurative language in psychotherapy. However, the sampling of only successful cases precluded any statements about the relationship between figurative language usage and therapy outcome (although the implication that novel figurative language was an important therapeutic tool was clear). In addition, the use of simple quantitative measures moved the focus of the analysis away from the *content* of novel instances in the study by Barlow and co-authors (1977) and rendered all frozen instances equally unimportant.

Having the benefit of these early studies, I became interested in alternative ways in which the use of novel figurative language in psychotherapy might be studied. I reasoned that more might be learned about the functions of such language if cases differing in outcome were compared and if we analyzed systematically more complex elements of usage, such as (1) patterns of use over the course of therapy, (2) development of figures over time (i.e., as single instances, repetitions, or elaborations), (3) degree of "sharing" or mutual use of figures by a client and a therapist, and (4) how figures cluster according to content themes. For my first study, I chose for comparison two cases of short-term psychotherapy (fewer than 15 sessions)—one in which the therapist had judged the client to have made only "slight improvement," and the other, "significant improvement." I then compared the two cases on the four elements of usage that I had proposed, using quantitative analyses (McMullen, 1985). Before presenting the main features and summarizing the findings of this study, let me try to articulate the factors that influenced my choice of method at this early stage.

FACTORS INFLUENCING THE INITIAL PHASE OF MY WORK

Perhaps most fundamentally, my initial choice of method was influenced by my research training (and accompanying epistemology) and by my almost complete unfamiliarity with how clients and therapists actually used figurative language. As is the case for nearly all graduate students enrolled in clinical psychology programs in which the Ph.D. is awarded, I was trained exclusively in a specialized version of the hypothetico-deductive method and taught to analyze quantitative data with statistical procedures. Specifically, I was trained to proceed (1) by proposing causal theories from which (2) particular hypotheses are derived, which (3) can be tested by reference to publicly observable events (Harré & Lamb, 1986, p. 93). Further, I was taught to believe in and to value objectivism—the contention that (1) an objectively separate "real world" lies beyond the organism and exists independently of being perceived, (2) true or valid knowledge about that world is ultimately rendered through sensory experience, and (3) such knowledge can be totally separated from the individual knower (Mahoney, 1989, p. 1374).

Partly as a result of my training, I did not know how to make use of the conceptual or practice-oriented papers that constituted most of the literature at the time. These papers contained interesting ideas about the functions that figurative language served in psychotherapy and potentially useful suggestions for clinical practice, but there were no easily derivable hypotheses that could be tested with the tools with which I was most familiar. Consider two examples. Wexler (1975) stated that

> whereas a therapist response with a flat vocal style and dull lifeless words may have little impact, the same meaning poignantly conveyed in an active voice with vivid figurative language, rich in terms of evoked connotations and associations is likely to be far more effective to evoke an enriched range of inner experience in the client. (p. 487)

And Fine, Pollio, and Simpkinson (1973) proposed that

> if the therapist fails to understand [words] in [a] metaphorical sense, he is not hearing all that is being said, and thus blocks the patient's attempt at resolving the discrepancy [between what the patient is able to communicate about how he feels and what he may actually be experiencing]. (p. 87)

These are two examples of only a very few stated or implied hypotheses that existed in the literature of the 1970s, and both require access to the client's or therapist's subjective experiences. Being trained to value objectivism and to believe that data available to third-person external observers are most appropriate to the enterprise of the behavioral scientist, and having no familiarity with alternative methods, I felt unable to take my lead from the few hypotheses that could be found in the conceptual literature.

Another way in which my training influenced my choice of method at this early stage of my research was through my well-developed belief in the power of quantitative analyses. Given that only a few basic questions about the occurrence of figurative language in psychotherapy had been investigated in the empirical literature, I began my work with the contention that more could be learned about clients' and therapists' use of figurative language by applying sophisticated quantitative procedures to more complex questions. Underlying this belief were two convictions: (1) that regularities in the objects of study would be revealed if the complexity of the research questions and procedures for analyzing the data more closely approximated the assumed complexity of the subject matter, and (2) that these regularities were primarily quantitative in nature.

Perhaps a more indirect way in which my background influenced my choice of methods was through my unfamiliarity with the objects of study. I had had no direct experience in studying how clients and therapists used figurative language. Because of the absence of a formalized model or theoretical framework from which to derive specific predictions or even relevant questions, I relied partly on my clinical knowledge of psychotherapy and partly on the scant empirical literature in determining the nature and form of the questions I wished to ask. Ultimately, my unfamiliarity with the subject matter led me to formulate questions about quantitative differences in the four content domains I had specified (i.e., patterns of usage over time, development of figures over time, degree of "sharing" of figures by clients and therapists, and clustering of figures according to content themes). My research training led me to use the judgments of external third persons as my data. In the absence of personal knowledge of the subject matter, I had only my research training and general clinical experience to guide me.

DETAILS OF MY FIRST STUDY

The specific questions that I posed in the first study were: (1) Does the successful case differ from the unsuccessful according to the patterns of usage over time or the location of figures over time? Do the client and the therapist in the successful case increase their use of novel figures during times when the development of understanding and the expression and communication of experiences are occurring, for example, during the middle phase of therapy, or do they maintain a continuously high rate of usage from the beginning to the end of therapy? Do the client and the therapist in the unsuccessful case decrease their use of novel figures over time or simply maintain a low rate of usage? (2) Are there differences in how the figures are developed in the two cases? Do the client and the therapist in the successful case use more repetitions and elaborations of their own and the other member's figures than their unsuccessful counterparts? (3) Is there greater contiguity in the use of each other's figures by the client and the therapist in the successful case compared with their unsuccessful counterparts? and (4) Do the client and the therapist in the successful case use figures to develop major therapeutic themes to a greater extent than their unsuccessful counterparts?

To investigate these questions, three judges independently documented the occurrence of novel and frozen figures in transcribed 15-minute segments of the first two, middle two, and last two available sessions from both cases. In both cases, the clients were middle- to upper-middle-class women and the therapists were male, doctoral-level clinical psychologists. Following Barlow and co-authors (1970), only those instances agreed upon by the three judges, either independently or through discussion, were used as data. The data were analyzed using techniques and statistics such as regression analysis, chi square, z scores, and cluster analysis.

Findings from My First Study and the Next Choice of Method

As I mentioned previously, the major purpose of this first study was to suggest alternative ways in which the use of novel figurative language in psychotherapy might be studied and to illustrate them in a comparison of a successful and an unsuccessful case. In the single comparison, differences were found in the four aspects of usage that I had proposed. For the most part, these differences were between the two clients, rather than between the therapists or between a client and a therapist. Specifically, the client in the unsuccessful case used most of her own novel figures in the beginning phase of therapy predominantly as descriptors of external circumstances; the client in the successful case used both her own and the therapist's novel figures at a fairly constant rate across all phases of therapy, predominantly as vehicles for describing her own inner experiences. The only difference between the therapists was in the extent to which their use of figurative language followed that of their clients, with this pattern occurring significantly more often in the successful case.

On the one hand, I was encouraged by these findings. It seemed that the questions I had posed had served to highlight differences in the use of novel figurative language in the two cases. On the other hand, I was troubled by the novel/frozen distinction and by the assumption that novel figures play a more significant role in psychotherapy than do frozen figures or common, clichéd expressions. In looking over the transcripts that were used in this first study, it seemed to me that some instances of novel figurative language were not therapeutically "useful." That is, they did not appear to facilitate the expression and communication of critical experiences or to promote new awareness and understanding on the part of the client. Others did not seem to be "therapy-relevant," in the sense of relating to the major themes of therapy. Furthermore, some frozen figures seemed to reveal a great deal about clients' major concerns; their perceptions of self, others, and interpersonal relationships; and their affective experiences.

I decided, then, to abandon the use of the novel/frozen distinction. However, doing so had significant consequences for my future work in the area. There was no longer any easy way of selecting instances of figurative language for analysis, and I was forced to think more about what I considered to be a therapeutically useful or therapy-relevant instance. What was to be the *unit of analysis* and how was it to be defined? I realized that I still did not know much about what kinds of instances clients and therapists used (particularly because I was now including common, everyday figures of speech as potential units of analysis) and, perhaps more important, what questions were appropriate to ask. In other words, because I was unfamiliar with what the objects of study were to be, I found it difficult to formulate any specific hypotheses. The standard approach of proceeding from theory and/or previous empirical findings to the formulation of hypotheses (based on quantitative differences between groups) and the testing of these hypotheses (with statistical procedures) was not appropriate at this point.

Although I did not specify precise research questions for my second study, I also did not begin my investigation in an "unmotivated way." In other words, I did not see where observations of the data would go without considering the question of what I was going to end up with, as would be the case for some ethnomethodologists and conversation analysts (see Sacks, 1984). Rather, I was guided by three major goals: (1) to specify more meaningful and *context-sensitive* criteria for selecting therapeutically useful or *therapy-relevant* instances for analysis, (2) to document these instances, and (3) to determine if there were any characteristics or patterns (such as changes in the content of figures over time or the use of self- versus other-generated figures) that differentiated successful from unsuccessful cases. Given these goals, there were at least three ways in which I could proceed. The unit of analysis could be determined from the *perspectives* of (1) both participants (client and therapist) and external judges, (2) the participants only, or (3) third parties only (external judges and/or me).

Several pragmatic and personal factors influenced my choice of the third alternative. At this point, I was in the early stage of my career, had only a modest amount of external grant money, and, as a result of having collected audiotaped sessions of psychotherapy for my dissertation, knew how time-consuming, expensive, and difficult it was to amass the sort of data to which I needed access. For these reasons, I chose to use archival data, which meant that I could not involve the clients and therapists as participants in my research.

In addition, as mentioned previously, I had only a passing familiarity with the range of figurative expressions produced by clients and therapists. Although instances of frozen figurative language had been documented in my first study, I had paid very little attention to them because they were not the focus of analysis. In the second study, I wanted a complete documentation of the range of figurative expressions so as not to exclude any frozen figures that might be deemed therapy-relevant. I also reasoned that if the participants were asked to identify what they considered to be the therapeutically useful or therapy-relevant instances through, for example, a method such as tape-assisted recall (Elliott, 1984; Kagan, 1975), my goal of knowing the domain of instances might not be realized because the participants likely would identify only a limited number of figures. Similarly, I thought that considering the perspectives of the participants and third-party observers might direct the focus of the study to an analysis of the similarities and differences between perspectives. In essence, then, an important factor that influenced my choice of method for the second study was my desire to know, *for myself,* what *I* considered to be "therapeutically useful" or "therapy-relevant" instances of figurative language, that is, to gain firsthand knowledge of the phenomenon. I felt that I first had to discover what *I* would consider to be the objects of study before I focused on the perspectives of others. One way to do so was through an intensive, descriptive-interpretive study of several cases of psychotherapy.

Before describing briefly the details of this study, I want to say a little more about one additional factor that I think influenced my decision to use a descriptive-interpretive approach at this point in my research program. Like many scientist-practitioners, I hold both scientific and humanistic values. In Kimble's (1984) terms, I sometimes place more value on increasing knowledge than on improving the human condition, on analyzing human behavior at a molecular rather than a molar level, and on developing nomothetic rather than idiographic laws; that is, I sometimes lean more toward the scientist half of the scientist-humanist dimension. At other times, however, I am drawn more toward intuitionism than objectivism as a source of basic knowledge and more toward individual uniqueness than universalism. That is, sometimes I am more interested in understanding the meaning of human actions in their social context. My choice of method can be seen as being influenced, then, not only by factors that are external to me (e.g., the state of existing literature in the area) but also by my epistemic beliefs.

DETAILS OF MY SECOND STUDY

The material for the second study (McMullen, 1989) consisted of all available and audible sessions ($N = 95$ of a total of 112 sessions held) of six cases of psychotherapy—one successful and one unsuccessful case from each of three therapists—gleaned from the Vanderbilt I Psychotherapy Project (see Strupp, 1980a, 1980b, 1980c, for detailed clinical descriptions and analyses of these cases). Briefly, the Vanderbilt I project was a large controlled study of process and outcome that was largely intended to address the question of the influence of specific versus non-specific factors in psychotherapy (see Strupp & Hadley, 1979). The clients were single, male students from a southern university in the United States who suffered from anxiety, depression, and difficulties in relating comfortably to peers, predominantly members of the opposite sex. The trained therapists were five male, highly experienced professional psychotherapists, each of whom treated a minimum of three clients in individual, time-limited psychotherapy (usually up to a maximum of 25 hours in twice-a-week sessions). Prior to beginning therapy, the clients were assessed by independent clinicians; these assessments were repeated at termination and at follow-up (approximately 1 year after intake). Evaluations were also provided by the client and the therapist. The assessment battery included the Minnesota Multiphasic Personality Inventory (MMPI), videotaped assessment interviews (following the format of the Psychiatric Status Schedule), global change ratings, ratings of target complaints, an adapted form of the Barrett-Lennard Relationship Inventory, clients' retrospective accounts of their therapeutic experience, and ratings of the third videotaped therapy sessions using the Vanderbilt Psychotherapy Process Scale.

Because I wanted to begin with a complete record of all instances of figurative language used by the clients and therapists, I had judges listen to the audiotapes of entire sessions and document all instances. Consistent with some aspects of discourse analysis, I was interested, at this stage, in producing a body of instances and not in trying to set limits to that body (see Potter & Wetherell, 1987). Consequently, judges were instructed to be as inclusive as possible, that is, to document borderline instances as well as those that would likely be excluded because they were not relevant to the task of therapy. This procedure resulted in the production of a very large corpus of data (approximately 12,000 instances) that included many common, everyday figures of speech that did not have any particular importance within the context of therapy. I then faced the question of how to reduce this corpus to only those instances that did seem to be of importance.

I decided that determining which instances to retain required that I become intimately familiar with all of what the judges had documented. I immersed myself in the data by listening to every audiotape and examining each documented instance in the context in which it occurred. In making my decisions, I also relied on my knowledge of and ever-increasing experience in doing psychotherapy. This procedure resulted in the exclusion of three broad categories of figures: (1) common, everyday figures of speech that had no special significance in the context of psychotherapy, such as container metaphors (e.g., *"I want to go into the past a little bit," "I put that out of my mind"*) and common idioms (e.g., *"Keep your chin up," "Make yourself stick with it"*); (2) figures that were unrelated to the major themes in each case (e.g., descriptions of other people's experiences that did not bear directly on the client); and (3) figures that were frequently used by clients and therapists in general and that seemed to have lost any particularity (e.g., *"fight," "lose/win,"* and *"put on an act" / "a role"*). Instances retained for further study were vehicles for the major tasks of therapy, for example, for the description of events, actions, behaviors, or cognitive-affective states; for the expression and exploration of inner experiences and emotional reactions; for the communication of one's views or perceptions of self, others, interpersonal relationships, and the therapy process; and for the description of change.

After selecting this subset of instances for intensive study, I engaged in a descriptive-interpretive approach to analyzing and understanding the instances. Specifically, I attempted to engage myself in the subject matter, to participate actively in it, in an effort to note underlying patterns and themes. I spent many hours reading and rereading the phrases and passages that I had culled for analysis, and frequently found myself going back and forth from the short transcribed segments of tape that contained figures of speech to the "live" segments on the audiotape, and constantly moving between the original data and the emerging description of the patterns. Some of the descriptive work, such as documenting the most frequently used, therapy-relevant figures and detailing the repetition and elaboration of instances in bursts of figurative language, was relatively straightforward. However, attempting to describe changes over time (or lack thereof) and to construct some meaning out of the instances, required many long hours of struggling with the data and many false starts before a systematic patterning emerged. Although I allowed myself to be guided by my goals for the study, I tried to challenge my own presuppositions about what I "should" look for and to remain open to unexpected discoveries. At all times, I tried to be sensitive to uniqueness as well as to similarities in the data. That is, in much the same way that discourse analysts search for patterns (see Potter & Wetherell, 1987), I tried to be sensitive both to variability (differences in the content or form of the instances across cases) and to consistency (the identification of features shared by the cases).

In communicating my findings, I tried to let the instances of figurative language "have their own say" by reporting as accurately as I could what had been selected and detected, and by describing as accurately as possible the patterns I had noted. In addition, I tried to present the reader with as much of the original data as was feasible, to allow for a judgment on the faithfulness and coherence of my description and interpretation. In contrast to quantitative research where the reliability and validity of the findings are often determined through measurement data, the criteria for assessing the reliability (i.e., dependability) and validity (i.e., the strength or groundedness) of a descriptive-interpretive analysis include *coherence, believability,* and *fruitfulness* (Bruner, 1984; Polkinghorne, 1988; Potter & Wetherell, 1987). The report of the analysis also constitutes part of the confirmation and validation procedures. In the tradition of discourse analysis, then, I considered it important to include a representative set of examples along with a reasonably detailed description and interpretation of the data in order to allow the reader to assess my claims (Potter & Wetherell, 1987).

Findings from My Second Study and Lessons Learned

Let me highlight a few of the major findings that emerged from this study. First, regardless of outcome status, clients always used more of their own than therapist-introduced figures. Each therapist was remarkably consistent *within himself* and used either his own and the client's figures to roughly the same extent in both the successful and the unsuccessful case, or many more of his own figures in the two cases. In general, however, there was not a great deal of "sharing" of figures between a client and a therapist.

Second, figures produced by the clients often revealed a great deal about their major concerns, their interpersonal relationships, their perceptions of self and others, and their affective experiences. On the other hand, therapist-introduced figures did not seem to reveal much about the therapists' views of the client or about their own perceptions of the client's world. The generally limited and unremarkable use of figurative language by the therapists in this sample is likely related, in part, to their theoretical orientation, which was predominantly psychoanalytic or psychodynamic.

Third, there were three features of figurative language that seemed to differentiate the successful and the unsuccessful cases. In the successful cases, there was evidence of (1) the elaboration of major therapy themes via bursts of figurative language or the development of a metaphor over time, (2) the existence of a well-developed central metaphor or metaphors as evidenced by the use of several conceptually related figures that fit the metaphor, and (3) the expression of some positive personal change in figurative language. These features were not evident in the unsuccessful cases.

Alternating between engagement and critical distance in an effort to detect and describe patterns in the data, allowed me to have a clearer sense of how the clients and therapists in my sample had used figurative language. By "used" I do not mean what functions it served or what meaning it had for the participants. Rather, by observing *and* engaging in the data, I was able to discover features of clients' and therapists' use of figurative language that may not have been discovered through either a positivistic approach or a participant-centered approach (such as tape-assisted recall by clients and therapists). One such feature was the presence of a well-formed central metaphor(s) in the talk of successful as compared with unsuccessful clients. In addition, many of the instances that were documented were conventional everyday expressions that, despite revealing a great deal about clients' experiences, perceptions, and thoughts, were unlikely to be heard or commented on by the therapist. If I had focused exclusively on novel figurative language (as had been done in previous empirical literature) and/or chosen to focus on a few metaphors that were deemed by the participants to be particularly meaningful, I would not have discovered *for myself* the value of studying the pervasive use of conventional figurative expressions.

Using an approach in which I tried to be critical of my own assumptions and to enter the data without firmly set categories in mind also helped me to establish criteria for selecting therapeutically "useful" or "therapy-relevant" instances. I now feel that I am more familiar with what I think are the objects of study.

CURRENT RESEARCH: MULTIPLE PARADIGMS

I turn now to a brief description of our current research in this area, the methods we are using, and our decisions regarding choice of methods. After completing the second study and presenting my findings, it became apparent through discussions with colleagues, including my husband, who are familiar with interpersonal theory that many of the figurative expressions used by the clients in my study could be placed on the interpersonal circumplex (e.g., Wiggins, 1982). My husband and I then set out to determine if the interpersonal circumplex would be of heuristic value in the study of clients' metaphors of self and others' actions (McMullen & Conway, 1994).

We set out a broad criterion by which the heuristic value or utility of employing an interpersonal coding scheme would be assessed. We reasoned that a useful application should produce a pattern of results that is theoretically consistent with other assessments of clients' interpersonal functioning and therapy outcomes. For example, consistent with Strupp's (1980a, 1980b, 1980c) conclusions that deeply rooted personality problems, particularly negativism, hostility, and resistance, are associated with negative therapeutic outcomes, we expected that more of the figurative language of clients with poorer outcomes would be coded on the hostile half of the circumplex compared with that of their more successful counterparts. Similarly, in keeping with interpersonal conceptions of poor psychological adjustment as consisting (in part) of inflexible, rigid patterns of social behavior and conceptions of self and/or others (Leary, 1957), we expected that the metaphors for self and/or others produced by clients with poorer outcomes would be less evenly distributed around the circumplex (i.e., clustered in a few segments).

We selected 21 cases (15 female and 6 male clients with predominant diagnoses of major depression, dysthymic disorder, generalized or atypical anxiety disorder, and other or mixed personality disorder, ranging in age from 24 to 62 years) from phase 1 (therapy-as-usual) of the Vanderbilt II Psychotherapy Research Project. Therapy was short-term (to a maximum of 25 sessions) and was conducted by experienced psychologists and psychiatrists (self-described as psychodynamically oriented). Outcome was assessed by a variety of measures and ranged from very positive to very negative.

As in my previous work, we had external judges listen to all usable audiotaped sessions ($n = 471$) and document every therapy-related instance of figurative language generated by the clients ($n = 9,904$). Following this documentation, three other judges independently read all instances selected by the first judges and selected only those that pertained to the self's and others' actions toward the self or others. All instances judged as acts of self or others ($n = 3,854$) were then coded independently by two coders using Kiesler's (1985) Acts Version of the Interpersonal Circle. We then calculated dominance and nurturance scores for both self and other metaphors for each client and determined into which part of the circumplex each client's metaphors of self actions and metaphors of others' actions fell (see McMullen & Conway, 1994, for specific details). Use of this quantitative procedure revealed theoretically consistent findings for metaphors of self but not others' actions.

I think that there are two interrelated reasons for my use of (1) a preexisting theoretical framework, (2) a coding scheme that employs a third-party perspective, and (3) quantitative methods. First, as was noted previously, there continues to be a lack of conceptually based or theoretically grounded empirical investigations in this area. Part of the reason for the dearth of such investigations has been the lack of a theory or conceptual framework that is specific to the context of psychotherapy. Interpersonal theory has been found to be useful and informative in this context (e.g., see Henry, Schacht, & Strupp, 1986). In addition, the presence of a large number of references to self and others in clients' figurative expressions made the selection of this framework and Kiesler's (1985) coding scheme seem appropriate. The aim of this third study was to use interpersonal theory and the interpersonal circumplex as heuristic devices for organizing some of the voluminous data I had collected, with the eventual goal of helping me to learn more about the data than I was currently able to see, and to formulate new questions for future investigation.

The second and related reason for using this approach is that after immersing myself in the data for so long without any clearly defined guiding structures, I felt a strong need for some organizing principles.

That is, although I felt more familiar with the objects of study after using qualitative methods, and had been able to describe some similarities and differences in the cases, my goal had not been to construct what is referred to as grounded theory. Consequently, I still lacked a conceptual or theoretical structure that would allow me to go beyond my own analysis. Whether it is premature to adopt a pre-existing framework at this time is a question with which I continue to wrestle. At the same time, I am interested in assessing the empirical and conceptual yield from the merger of figurative language and the interpersonal circumplex.

In addition to revealing clients' conceptions of self-and-other relationships, figurative expressions also tell us about clients' intrapersonal experiencing. They can inform us about felt experiences, emotional reactions, perceptions, thoughts, and attitudes. Currently, we are identifying these intrapersonal metaphors in the 21 cases from which we had previously selected instances of self and others' interpersonal actions. However, because we do not have a sophisticated, well-used system (similar to the interpersonal circle) for classifying non-interpersonal acts such as thoughts, expectations, and emotional experiences, we will be using a descriptive-interpretive approach (similar to that used by Lakoff and Johnson, 1980) for conceptualizing these domains. After selecting these non-interpersonal instances from clients' protocols, we will immerse ourselves in the data and try to abstract patterns in the meanings of these instances.

Our choice of a combination of different methods of analysis (quantitative and qualitative) and methods of inquiry (theory-driven and descriptive-interpretive) in this project is influenced by the different kinds of questions we are posing and by the various degrees of familiarity we have with the subject matter we are studying. Increased familiarity with clients' use of figurative language to describe self-and-other relationships and the availability of a pre-existing coding scheme for studying this realm of behavior led to a desire to test some specific notions with traditional empirical methods. At the same time, however, a desire to understand more about other aspects of the subject matter with which we are unfamiliar leads us to adopt an approach in which we actively immerse ourselves in the data.

FINAL COMMENTS

The research program described in this chapter illustrates what Evelyn Fox Keller (1985) maintains is "the diversity of values, methodological styles, and goals that, to varying degrees, always exist in science"

(p. 160). The decision to ask particular kinds of questions, to use a particular method (or methods), resides in the combination of the researcher's values, goals, training, and experience with the subject matter that is present at a given point in time.

In trying to recapture and articulate the factors that I think have influenced my choice of methods in this research program, I have become aware of the interplay between the development of my research program and the development of myself as a researcher. I am convinced that my "movement" from quantitative to qualitative methods and, subsequently, to an integration of these methods is not a linear path. Rather, I expect that over the next 10-year period I will revisit each of these approaches. The exact sequence in which I will do so is unknown to me and will depend, to a large extent, on what I am able to discover from my own work, how I am able to use the work of others, and the way in which my personal beliefs and values about knowledge develop.

REFERENCES

Aleksandrowicz, D. R. (1962). The meaning of metaphor. *Bulletin of the Menninger Clinic, 26,* 92–101.

Arlow, J. A. (1979). Metaphor and the psychoanalytic situation. *Psychoanalytic Quarterly, 48,* 363–385.

Barlow, J. M., Kerlin, J. R., & Pollio, H. R. (1970). *Training manual for identifying figurative language* (Tech. Rep. 1). Knoxville: University of Tennessee.

Barlow, J. M., Pollio, H. R., & Fine, H. J. (1977). Insight and figurative language in psychotherapy. *Psychotherapy: Theory, Research and Practice, 14,* 212–222.

Bauer, R., & Modarressi, T. (1977). Strategies of therapeutic contact working with children with severe object relationship disturbance. *American Journal of Psychotherapy, 31,* 605–617.

Bruner, J. (1984, August). *Narrative and paradigmatic modes of thought.* Invited address to the annual conference of the American Psychological Association, Toronto.

Conway, J. B. (1992). A world of differences among psychologists. *Canadian Psychology, 33,* 1–24.

Elliott, R. (1984). A discovery-oriented approach to significant change events in psychotherapy: Interpersonal process recall and comprehensive process analysis. In L. N. Rice & L. S. Greenberg (Eds.), *Patterns of change: Intensive analysis of psychotherapeutic process* (pp. 249–286). New York: Guilford.

Fine, H. J., Pollio, H. R., & Simpkinson, C. (1973). Figurative language, metaphor, and psychotherapy. *Psychotherapy: Theory, Research and Practice, 10,* 87–91.

Gordon, D. (1978). *Therapeutic metaphors.* Cupertino, CA: META Publications.

Gore, N. (1977). Psychological functions of metaphor. *Dissertation Abstracts International, 38,* No. 6B, 2861.

Harré, R., & Lamb, R. (Eds.) (1986). *The dictionary of personality and social psychology*. Cambridge, MA: MIT Press.

Henry, W. P., Schacht, T. E., & Strupp, H. H. (1986). Structural analysis of social behavior: Application to a study of interpersonal process in differential psychotherapeutic outcome. *Journal of Consulting and Clinical Psychology, 54*, 27–31.

Kagan, N. (1975). *Interpersonal process recall: A method of influencing human interaction*. East Lansing: Michigan State University.

Keller, E. F. (1985). *Reflections on gender and science*. New Haven, CT: Yale University Press.

Kiesler, D. J. (1985). *The 1982 Interpersonal Circle: Acts Version*. Unpublished manuscript, Virginia Commonwealth University, Richmond.

Kimble, G. A. (1984). Psychology's two cultures. *American Psychologist, 39*, 833–839.

Lakoff, G., & Johnson, M. (1980). *Metaphors we live by*. Chicago: University of Chicago Press.

Leary, T. (1957). *Interpersonal diagnosis of personality*. New York: Ronald Press.

Lenrow, P. B. (1966). The uses of metaphor in facilitating constructive behavior change. *Psychotherapy, 3*, 145–148.

Mahoney, M. J. (1989). Scientific psychology and radical behaviorism: Important distinctions based in scientism and objectivism. *American Psychologist, 44*, 1372–1377.

McMullen, L. M. (1985). Methods for studying the use of novel figurative language in psychotherapy. *Psychotherapy, 22*, 610–619.

McMullen, L. M. (1989). Use of figurative language in successful and unsuccessful cases of psychotherapy: Three comparisons. *Metaphor and Symbolic Activity, 4*, 203–225.

McMullen, L. M., & Conway, J. B. (1994). Dominance and nurturance in the figurative expressions of psychotherapy clients. *Psychotherapy Research, 4*, 41–55.

Mosher, D. L. (1979). The Gestalt experiment in sex therapy. *Journal of Sex and Marital Therapy, 5*, 117–133.

Polkinghorne, D. E. (1988). *Narrative knowing and the human sciences: Systems of inquiry*. Albany: State University of New York Press.

Pollio, H. R., & Barlow, J. M. (1975). A behavioural analysis of figurative language in psychotherapy: One session in a single case study. *Language and Speech, 18*, 236–254.

Pollio, H. R., Barlow, J. M., Fine, H. J., & Pollio, M. R. (1977). *Psychology and the poetics of growth: Figurative language in psychology, psychotherapy and education*. Hillsdale, NJ: Lawrence Erlbaum.

Potter, J., & Wetherell, M. (1987). *Discourse and social psychology: Beyond attitudes and behaviour*. London: Sage.

Rice, L. N. (1974). The evocative function of the therapist. In D. A. Wexler & L. N. Rice (Eds.), *Innovations in client-centered therapy* (pp. 289–311). New York: Wiley.

Rossel, R. D. (1977). The use of metaphors in the negotiation of group issues. *Group Analysis, 10*, 43–46.

Sacks, H. (1984). Notes on methodology. In J. M. Atkinson & J. Heritage (Eds.), *Structures of social action: Studies in conversation analysis* (pp. 21–27). Cambridge: Cambridge University Press.

Strupp, H. H. (1980a). Success and failure in time-limited psychotherapy: A systematic comparison of two cases: Comparison 1. *Archives of General Psychiatry, 37*, 595–603.

Strupp, H. H. (1980b). Success and failure in time-limited psychotherapy: A systematic comparison of two cases: Comparison 2. *Archives of General Psychiatry, 37*, 708–716.

Strupp, H. H. (1980c). Success and failure in time-limited psychotherapy: Further evidence (Comparison 4). *Archives of General Psychiatry, 37*, 947–954.

Strupp, H. H., & Hadley, S. W. (1979). Specific versus nonspecific factors in psychotherapy: A controlled study of outcome. *Archives of General Psychiatry, 36*, 1125–1136.

Wexler, D. A. (1975). A scale for the measurement of client and therapist expressiveness. *Journal of Clinical Psychology, 31*, 486–489.

Wiggins, J. S. (1982). Circumplex models of interpersonal behavior in clinical psychology. In P. C. Kendall & J. N. Butcher (Eds.), *Handbook of research methods in clinical psychology* (pp. 183–222). New York: Wiley.

CHAPTER 8

On the Process of Studying the Process of Change in Family Therapy

MYRNA L. FRIEDLANDER

Perhaps all theoretical interests are rooted in the personal. In my own personal relationships, I have found that when we can get under the words, when we understand the emblematic context as opposed to the merely literal, we can better respond to each other's motivations and agendas, conscious and unconscious. Doing so ultimately enhances our relationships.

Most of my scientific explorations are the result of a long-held conviction that while language in psychotherapy is often imprecise, with effects ranging from exhilaration to devastation, an understanding of the discourse between client and therapist has important implications for effective treatment. I hope to elucidate this belief in this chapter. The purpose of the account, as I understand it from the editors, is to describe the reasoning behind the various methodological decisions I have made in the course of developing my research program on change processes in family therapy. In general, my primary focus in the past 10 years has been, and continues to be, the interchange between and among family members and therapist. I am concerned with what language—this imperfect reflection of thought and feeling—can tell us about how to facilitate the family healing process. Language is, however, meaningless without a social context. So too is my research program. To understand it, you, the reader, will need to spend some time with the context—that is, with what came before.

PRECURSORS

In my earliest research on psychotherapeutic processes, for my dissertation, I tested the effects of an audiotaped role induction on the process and outcome of time-limited individual therapy (Friedlander &

Kaul, 1983). The questions I posed, the method of inquiry, and the selection of process measures were an outgrowth of three interrelated interests: the application of social influence theory to psychotherapy, the comparison of different theoretical approaches, and the study of language and communication processes. My research in family therapy continues to reflect these interests.

The theoretical model of greatest appeal at Ohio State during the period of my doctoral work there was Stanley Strong's (e.g., 1968) view of psychotherapy as a social system in which change is brought about by specific processes of interpersonal influence. Various faculty and doctoral students at Ohio State had tested the tenets of Strong's theory, most often using laboratory analogues in which therapist characteristics (e.g., expertness) were manipulated for their effects on "clients"—typically, undergraduates observing a role-played counseling vignette. In 1979 as I was beginning my dissertation, several Ohio State faculty and students, Corrigan, Dell, Lewis, and Schmidt (1980) had just completed a critical review of the social influence literature. They concluded that despite the heuristic value of Strong's theoretical model, few meaningful inferences about therapeutic influence could be drawn from the almost exclusive reliance on contrived analogue methods. For this reason, I was determined to construct a well-designed experiment using actual clients in treatment. (It should be noted that, in the field at that time, experimental research tended to be favored over *ex post facto* designs.)

I was particularly impressed by the literature on role induction in psychotherapy. Providing prospective clients with specific information about the client role had repeatedly been predictive of therapeutic outcome. Role induction can be viewed as a form of interpersonal persuasion that relies not on the personal characteristics of the therapist (a la social influence theory) but on the assumption that socialization is crucial for competent performance. This assumption seemed valid from my clinical experience. Veteran clients, those with previous experience in the client "role," seemed to be able to take advantage of the therapeutic situation more rapidly. Comparing a cognitively based to an affectively based role induction, I predicted that both would be superior to the control, a manipulation designed only to enhance clients' expectations of receiving help with their problems. I expected the clients exposed to the cognitive induction to use more "thinking" language, and those exposed to the affective induction, more "feeling" language.

It seemed essential to consider the effects of the role induction manipulation not merely on clients' perceptions of the therapist but on the actual process and outcome of treatment. Contemporary reviews of the psychotherapy literature had decried the paucity of research linking process to outcome. If role inductions do, indeed, persuade clients to take a more active role in expressing their thoughts and feelings, I reasoned, these effects should be evident in the language of psychotherapy. Specifically, clients should become more active in initiating topics, talking more, being more involved, and so forth.

My interest in language and culture has been lifelong. Having been a high school French teacher prior to studying psychology, I was excited to discover a keen interest in "language as social policy" on the part of Harold Pepinsky, a distinguished faculty member at Ohio State whose work on "tracking" and "convergence" in therapeutic discourse provided an interesting perspective on psychotherapy. "Pep" (as he prefers to be called) encouraged me to scan the literature on discourse analysis. There I discovered sociolinguistics—a perspective on how social rules are embedded in natural discourse. According to sociolinguists, language both reflects and creates social reality. Rules of discourse have to do with implicit assumptions regarding social relations among people. Rules override the content (or the substance) of the message, having more to do with who says what, when, how, and toward what end (Friedlander, 1984).

For my dissertation research I adapted a sociolinguistic coding system that had been developed to study the ways in which parents use language to socialize their children. The Discourse Activity Analysis System (DAAS; Friedlander, 1984), as I called it, estimates the "communicative involvement" of clients and therapists in initiating and sustaining topics. If role inductions enhance clients' socialization, I reasoned, those exposed to a role induction should become more involved in the psychotherapeutic process—responding more actively, introducing more new topics, and so forth. Significant changes in DAAS "activity levels" from pre- to post-role induction would support my hypothesis, I believed— and they did (Friedlander & Kaul, 1983).

Immersing myself in transcripts for the dissertation, I discovered several interesting phenomena about therapeutic discourse that did not concern the specific effects of role induction but that seemed, nonetheless, important. These discoveries confirmed some of my own clinical hunches, suggested the need for new theory (Friedlander & Schwartz, 1985), and provided guidance for my later investigations. What was most evident to me in the transcripts was the tremendous variability in discourse patterns across dyads, even with the same therapist. This, of course, corresponded to my own clinical experience. Each client drew out something different from me. The pace varied, the language varied, the tone varied. With some clients I was quiet and reflective, with others active and encouraging, with others wary and cautious. Thus, it seemed clear that the unidirectional view of therapist as actor and client as target was only half of the clinical picture. Indeed, my dissertation data suggested that clients who were positively affected by my role induction may have been more attractive to their therapists. I noted that the influence of clients on their therapists' attitude and behavior was strikingly absent from Strong's original model.

Believing that *mutual* influences needed to be investigated, I reanalyzed the discourse activity data (DAAS) from my dissertation study using a sequential analysis, Markov chain (Friedlander & Phillips, 1984), to test the reciprocity of influence, that is, *A* influencing *B*, *B* influencing *A*, and so forth. In the results I was struck by certain patterns of verbal behavior that, from a sociolinguistic perspective, were illuminating. In particular, the sequence of topic shift initiation followed by topic shift initiation in the DAAS coding suggested a "struggle for control" between client and therapist. I wondered if the struggle was due to the timing of the interviews (all being early sessions) or because the therapists lacked experience or skill.

Results of this sequential analysis and of a subsequent case study along the same lines (Friedlander & Phillips, 1985) supported the notion of reciprocity of social influence in psychotherapy and confirmed for me a growing suspicion that *ex post facto* designs may be more informative than experiments for practitioners. Without a thorough understanding of what occurs naturally in psychotherapy, experimental manipulations of the process (as I had attempted in my dissertation) seemed premature.

What led me to the next step was the realization that the results of sequential analyses could not be fully understood in the absence of information about how participants view the process of change. Do *they* see the negotiation of topics as a struggle for control? This question prompted a new investigation, one that involved selecting sessions for study based on clients' and therapists' perceptions of their value or impact. The study was based theoretically on Jay Haley's (1963) interactional view of psychotherapy. Reading the work of Haley and his contemporaries (e.g., Watzlawick, Beavin, & Jackson, 1967) for my graduate course on family therapy (I was now on the faculty at the University at Albany, State University of New York), I was impressed with the fact that these theorists view interpersonal influence as reciprocal and intimately tied to language. Haley (1963) postulated that the therapist must not struggle for control with the client, since the client would need to continue to be symptomatic in order to win the struggle. Rather, therapists must establish meta-complementary relations with clients, ones in which, on one level, the therapist appears to be more passive but is actually directing the therapeutic action at another, more covert level.

In our test of Haley's (1963) assertions about meta-complementarity in therapy (Friedlander, Thibodeau, & Ward, 1985), my interest was the "proximal" outcome, that is, clients' and therapists' perceptions of the value of each session. Rather than manipulate the treatment experimentally, we simply recorded each session and solicited participants' post-interview perceptions on the Session Evaluation Questionnaire (Stiles,1980). Stiles, among others, had argued, rather convincingly I thought, that "distal" outcomes such as reduced depression or enhanced self-esteem were too far removed from the ongoing process of treatment to be meaningful. Clinicians tend not to select specific strategies or interventions in their sessions based on a long-range view of outcome. Rather, they evaluate the process of change at the level of the intervention, the episode within a session, or the session itself. A succession of "good" sessions is one of the most valuable indicators of therapeutic progress for the practicing therapist.

Comparing "good" with "bad" sessions (as rated by client and therapist) from eight dyads, we observed differences in the DAAS activity levels, the distribution of talk, and the therapist response modes. Analyzing the data, I was struck anew by the great variability in the linguistic data across dyads. Knowing that a sample of eight did not provide adequate statistical power for hypothesis testing, we followed the group analysis with a close inspection of each case. Our observations suggested that important differences were obliterated when averages were compared statistically. With respect to the distribution of talk and DAAS activity levels, for example, some therapists were "too passive, too unstructuring" in their bad sessions, whereas others were "too active, too structuring" (Friedlander, Thibodeau, & Ward, 1985, p. 640). As another example, in the group analysis there were no significant differences in the frequency of confrontation. In one dyad, however, there were markedly more confrontations in the "good" session as compared with the bad, while in another dyad the reverse was true. We concluded that

> each dyad evaluates the culture it creates phenomenologically.... In other words, a "policy of treatment" is formulated in the early stage of therapy (Meara et al., 1981). Thereafter, client and therapist assess the value, or impact of each session in light of what has already transpired (cf. Stiles, 1981), so that interactions that typify a good session for one dyad may characterize the bad session for another. (p. 641)

My interest in sociolinguistics also led me to semantic cohesion analysis, a method developed by Halliday and Hasan (1976) to study coherence in literary texts. Whereas the DAAS had provided me with a relatively content-free means of assessing communicative activity levels—one measure of social influence—it did not take into account actual semantic content. I knew, as a therapist, that if my client adopted my words to describe her experience, I felt that my intervention had been influential. More coherent sessions seemed more productive. Using semantic cohesion analysis, one can observe the nature and frequency of "ties" (or coherent links) between sentences or, as I adapted the measure to psychotherapy, from one speaking turn to the next.

Encouraged again by Pep, who had recently employed cohesion analysis in a study of classroom dynamics, I recognized the possibilities of this coding scheme for studying reciprocal influence in psychotherapeutic discourse. I explored the utility of semantic cohesion analysis for understanding therapeutic processes by observing the frequency of ties in the transcripts of four time-limited psychotherapy groups (Friedlander, Thibodeau, Nichols, Tucker, & Snyder, 1985). The study involved an experimental comparison of self-disclosing and non-disclosing group therapists. We hypothesized that disclosing and non-disclosing "leaders would elicit and sustain [conversational] involvement in different ways and that the resultant cohesive discourse would be an important indicator of a group's ultimate success or failure" (p. 286). While the outcome data did support these hypotheses, the cohesion analysis proved to be of greatest interest to me, underscoring my growing disillusionment with group experimental designs and with the tenuous link between verbal process variables and distal client outcomes.

THE SHIFT TO FAMILY THERAPY

The results of the studies described above had some important effects on my subsequent endeavors, the most obvious being a shift in focus to family therapy. It became clear to me that interactional dynamics, particularly those that could be observed in natural discourse, were more integral to theories of family therapy than to those of individual or group therapy. In traditional theories (e.g., cognitive-behavioral, experiential, psychoanalytic, etc.), dysfunction is viewed largely as intrapsychic. Among social influence buffs, interpersonal constructs are invoked to provide a pantheoretical understanding of the change process. They do not reflect a coherent theoretical approach to treatment, they are not a way of conceptualizing dysfunction, and they do not suggest specific strategies or techniques that practicing therapists can apply to various client problems. Family systems theorists (e.g., Minuchin, 1974), by contrast, have developed theoretical models and techniques based directly on interactional concepts. Furthermore, these theorists pay specific attention to the dynamics of interpersonal power and control. Indeed, the notion of reciprocal social influence is an explicit, defining feature of family systems theories. Clients' symptoms are viewed as metaphorical expressions of dysfunctional systems of influence, ones in which, for example, children have more power than parents, or in which a covert coalition between one parent and a child alienates the other parent (cf. Minuchin, 1974).

Surprisingly little research had been conducted to test notions of interpersonal influence in family treatment. Indeed, my review of literature in 1982 suggested that, the plethora of theories notwithstanding, there were precious few studies on *any* aspect of family therapists' in-session behaviors with their clients. Despite many studies of family problems, of the communication patterns of distressed couples, and of treatment outcomes, I located only a handful of published studies on mechanisms of change in family therapy. Compared with the abundant research on processes of change in individual therapy, the research on therapeutic processes in family treatment was woefully inadequate, particularly when one considers the vast clinical literature on the topic.

So, where to begin? Two challenges were apparent to me. First, we had little knowledge of how experienced family therapists actually behave with their clients. Do their behaviors reflect theory? Are there common features that cut across various orientations? Are the distinctive features in the theories truly distinctive in practice? Second, there was an obvious need for a study of family therapy processes that would be faithful to the systemic perspective, using instruments that take into account multiple, interacting behaviors, that is, reciprocity among family members and between therapist and family system.

These two challenges led me to conduct a series of comparative investigations of "master" family theorists/therapists (Friedlander & Highlen, 1984; Friedlander, Highlen, & Lassiter, 1985; Friedlander, Ellis, Raymond, Siegel, & Milford, 1987). By addressing the first challenge, I hoped to avoid the limitations I had encountered in my earlier research with novice therapists. The therapists I had sampled in Friedlander, Thibodeau, and Ward (1985) and in Friedlander, Thibodeau, et al. (1985)—psychology interns and psychiatry residents—were more advanced than the novices I had sampled in my dissertation research (Friedlander & Kaul, 1983). In analyzing the linguistic data in these studies, I had wondered whether similar results would have been obtained by highly experienced clinicians, particularly since I found myself questioning the wisdom of some of the interventions I observed when I analyzed these transcripts.

Obtaining a sample of family therapy interviews with master therapists proved to be easier than I had expected. In my reading, I discovered that a training film series had been developed, the Hillcrest Family Series, in which four well-known, expert family therapists conducted consultation sessions with the same family. The idea of comparing and contrasting the work of these master therapists was prompted by the substantial and long-standing interest among process researchers of the "Gloria" films with Carl Rogers, Albert Ellis, and Fritz Perls. The assumption was, I thought, reasonable—comparing the behavior of different therapists with the same client(s) allows one to draw inferences about differences and similarities in the therapists' approaches. The validity of such comparative inferences is less threatened than when each therapist is observed working with a different client. (Actually, I had pursued a similar strategy in a research project to validate the Supervisory Styles Inventory [Friedlander & Ward, 1984]. Comparing the work of four master supervision theorists with a single trainee proved to be an excellent method for demonstrating theoretically relevant distinctions among supervisory styles.)

Although the Hillcrest films were created in the early 1960s, the therapists were among the earliest and best-known theorists in the field: Nathan Ackerman, Murray Bowen, Don Jackson, and Carl Whitaker. I reasoned that their work, even if different from contemporary family therapy (only Whitaker is alive today), was recognized as pioneering by their peers, thereby influencing successive generations of family therapists.

The second challenge, that of finding an instrument that would reflect reciprocal interpersonal influence, proved more difficult. Although several measures of dyadic behavior existed, I could locate no instrument that took into account the interpersonal behaviors of a group of individuals. Here serendipity played a part. I had attended a colloquium in organizational psychology in which multidimensional scaling (MDS; Kruskal & Wish, 1978) was described and illustrated. MDS is a statistical paradigm that takes into account the interrelations of multiple stimuli. Simply put, MDS allows the researcher to create a spatial "map" of distances among stimuli. The distances between points reflect the observed measure of proximity, and the map (the MDS "output") is the best geometric representation of the distances between all pairs of stimuli considered simultaneously.

To create a "map" of the interpersonal dynamics of a family therapy session, distances between participants needed to be measured. To do so, I selected frequency of interaction ("who-talks-to-whom") because structural theorists (e.g., Minuchin, 1974) propose that interpersonal proximity between family members is reflected in the amount of interaction—more frequent interaction signaling greater closeness, less frequent interaction signaling greater distance. I reasoned, therefore, that if I created a matrix of interactional frequencies among all speakers in an interview and subjected this matrix to MDS, a spatial map of the underlying interpersonal dynamics of the session would emerge. The results (Friedlander & Highlen, 1984) were surprisingly clean. Not only did the MDS statistics (the "stress" values) show that the two-dimensional spatial maps were an excellent fit to the interactional data, but the four Hillcrest maps themselves (one per session) were quite similar, and they were highly intercorrelated.

While fascinating to me, the results of this study had limited clinical value. Although the underlying structures had certain important features in common, nothing could be said from this research about similarities or dissimilarities in the actual content of the sessions. Therefore, we (Friedlander, Highlen, & Lassiter, 1985) undertook a re-examination of the Hillcrest data, a content analysis using several dimensions of Pinsof's (1980) Family Therapist Behavior Scale (FTBS). The FTBS was the best available coding system for classifying family therapists' verbal behaviors. Many of its dimensions reflect aspects of language that are meaningful to family therapists (e.g, "interpersonal structure," "system membership," "route," etc.). In addition to the FTBS, in order to compare these family therapists' interventions with those of individual therapists, we included a more generic measure of therapist response modes (e.g., confrontation, information, etc.).

Results showed some remarkable similarities across approaches as well as differences that seemed consistent with each therapist's theoretical writings. A number of the findings underscored my suspicions about the fundamental differences between family therapy and individual therapy. The Hillcrest therapists were, for example, notably more directive and authoritative and less feeling-oriented than traditional individual psychotherapists. In considering our results, I found that little attention had been paid, either in the theoretical or the clinical literature, to the therapeutic relationship in family therapy. But more on that later.

Other problems haunted me. Were the observed similarities due to actual similarities in theoretical approach or to the fact that the four Hillcrest therapists consulted with the same family? Were the differences due to real theoretical or technical differences or simply to artifacts of the experience, that is, a contrived series of consultation interviews? My observation of the films suggested that the family members were affected by each interview in succession. Order effects seemed to be a problem. Equally problematic was external validity, that is, generalizing beyond this one family and therapeutic context.

These issues prompted me to conduct another investigation of master family therapists (Friedlander et al., 1987), one that put the "convergence hypothesis," as I called it (p. 335), at greater risk. Rather than observing the same family with different therapists, I opted to maximize the heterogeneity of the families and the settings. If different expert therapists used similar interventions with markedly different families, there would be a stronger basis for concluding that some features of family therapists' work are common across theoretical approaches.

At the time we began the study in 1985, the two therapists I selected, Salvador Minuchin and Carl Whitaker, were among the most highly reputed in the field. Committed to training, both had made available to the professional public many videotaped demonstration interviews. Furthermore, their interpersonal styles and theoretical writings were quite different, Minuchin being notably more "left brain," Whitaker more "right brain." Using the same indices as in the Hillcrest investigations, we contrasted six consultation sessions by each therapist. Results of this analysis showed remarkable consistencies on all measures. Again, as in the two Hillcrest studies, the most notable differences seemed congruent with the therapists' theoretical differences.

While the results of the latter two studies were somewhat more relevant to the practicing family therapist than the MDS comparison (Friedlander & Highlen, 1984), something was still missing. The therapists' behaviors did reflect the technical aspects of their theories (e.g., Minuchin's use of direct guidance and advice, Whitaker's use of self-disclosure), but none of the measures we had used could elucidate precisely how therapeutic change evolves in family systems. Family members' immediate responses to the therapist needed to be taken into account, I thought, and an instrument reflecting interpersonal communication patterns needed to be applied to clients' verbal behavior as well as to the therapists'. With such a measure one would be able to determine (1) whether therapist/family member interactions are a reflection of within-family interactions and (2) if (and how) changes in the former facilitate changes in the latter. This ideal measure would reflect interactional processes that are theoretically meaningful, that is, congruent with a systemic perspective on family dysfunction and therapeutic change.

RELATIONAL CONTROL IN FAMILY THERAPY

These ideas for studying the therapeutic relationship as constituted in communication were evolving as I was analyzing the second Hillcrest study and planning the more extensive study of Whitaker and Minuchin. Throughout these early research endeavors, I was plagued by the feeling that the indices I had chosen were not sufficiently congruent with family systems theories and that the data, while interesting, did not address the nature of the relationship between therapist and family members, or how interpersonal change actually comes about in family therapy.

The answer to these bothersome problems came in the form of a productive collaboration with Laurie Heatherington, a clinical psychologist who joined the faculty at Williams College in 1984. Meeting at an APA poster session (we were presenting our work side by side), Laurie and I discovered some mutual interests—family therapy, the sequential analysis of verbal behavior, and process research—and, equally exciting, the fact that we lived only 50 miles apart. Laurie had the same experience as I—since no other faculty in our respective departments were conducting process research, we had no local colleagues with whom to collaborate or discuss our research agendas. This fortuitous meeting occasioned the beginning of a close friendship and a continuing collaboration on family therapy process research.

Laurie's dissertation research (Heatherington & Allen, 1984), the study she was presenting when we met, involved the application of Edna Rogers's Relational Communication Control Coding System (RCCCS; Rogers & Farace, 1975) to individual psychotherapy. The coding system had evolved from the study of communication processes at Palo Alto, California, specifically the systemic view of human interaction proposed by Gregory Bateson (1936/1958), Sluzki and Beavin (1965/1977), Watzlawick and co-authors (1967), and Jay Haley (1963). (Indeed, the seminal work on communication by these early theorists has continued to influence the field, having spawned many theories of family therapy over the past 3 decades.)

Rogers's RCCCS had several of the qualities I had been searching for in an instrument—it was derived from and thus was consistent with a systemic perspective on interpersonal behavior in families. The language codes could be applied to any speaker (therapist or family member) and would allow us to study the therapeutic relationship in family therapy. It had, however, been developed to study dyads and was not applicable to social contexts with three or more speakers.

When Laurie Heatherington used the RCCCS in her dissertation research, it had only once before been applied to the study of individual psychotherapy. The majority of the previous RCCCS research concerned marital communication. Over lunch one afternoon, Laurie and I considered the potential value of modifying the coding system so as to take into account relations among three or more individuals, that is, families. We anticipated that such a measure would help us elucidate the process of change in family therapy as well as the nature of the therapist/family member relationship.

In our first collaborative effort (Heatherington & Friedlander, 1987),

Laurie Heatherington and I extended the RCCCS to the family therapy context. As we argued in the article introducing our Family Relational Communication Control Coding System (FRCCCS; Friedlander & Heatherington, 1989), psychometrically sound measures are needed that "preserve the assumptions inherent in the systemic perspective" (p. 139) in order to test the tenets of interactional approaches to family therapy. Relational, or interpersonal, control refers to the use of language as social influence. It concerns *how* messages are delivered and responded to rather than their semantic meaning. Bateson (1936/1958), considering the reciprocal interaction between individuals as the essential unit of behavior, identified *complementary* and *symmetrical* relationships. In the former, *A*'s dominance moves ("one-up") are matched by *B*'s submissive moves ("one-down"), and vice versa. In the latter, both *A* and *B* maneuver toward either dominance or submission. These maneuvers are reflected in natural language, for example, *A* orders (↑), *B* obeys (↓) (complementarity) or *A* orders (↑), *B* refuses (↑) (symmetry). The notion of relational control is important in many approaches to understanding and treating dysfunctional family systems. Theoretically, symptoms or other family problems are maintained by the family's characteristic communication patterns. Changes in these patterns are necessary in order to alleviate symptoms and promote the well-being of the family as a whole.

Extending the original RCCCS to family (or any group) contexts proved to be more complex than we had anticipated. First, we realized the need to take into account a major distinction between dyadic and group interaction. In a group, sequences of verbal messages are not necessarily reciprocal. Whereas in a dyad the sequence of talk is *ABABABAB* ..., in a group, it may be *ABCABDBDABDC*. . . . Obviously interruptions are a major controlling maneuver in group talk. Second, we recognized that the individual who is interrupted, although not directly addressed by the speaker, is nonetheless involved in a control dynamic. Third, we noted several other "triadic" situations in which a family member may be indirectly controlled by another's behavior. When a question is ignored because the recipient (the target) of the question opts to speak to someone else in the group, the first speaker's definition of the social situation has indirectly been challenged.

Indeed, indirectness proved to be a major aspect of the FRCCCS. In creating the coding system (Heatherington & Friedlander, 1987), we recalled the results of my earlier research (Friedlander, Highlen, & Lassiter, 1985; Friedlander et al., 1987) in which expert family therapists frequently used indirectness to make a point. In coding their response modes, I had been unable to account for situations in which an interven-

Change in Family Therapy

tion to one party was actually a challenge to another (e.g., "How do you think you can get your husband to be more affectionate?").

Recognizing that these group aspects of relational control would need to be incorporated into the FRCCCS, we used an inductive strategy to create the coding rules. We selected a videotaped demonstration session by Carl Whitaker (one that had been used in Friedlander et al., 1987) in which the issue of interpersonal control was clinically meaningful. That is, the entire session was characterized by explicit struggle for control between Whitaker and one of the family members, the father. Indeed, other family members described the father as excessively controlling and domineering. We found that the constant interruptions, challenges, disqualifications, and indirect interventions that were observable clinically in this interview provided us with many suitable examples from which to create our coding rules.

As we began developing a coding manual for the FRCCCS based on our experiences with the Whitaker interview, we realized that a larger sample of interviews was needed to be certain that the coding rules covered all possible interactional dynamics among speakers in a group context. To do this, we wanted to sample actual, experienced therapists (i.e., non-experts) in their ongoing work with families. In planning this research, which was conducted at a hospital outpatient clinic, we sought to refine the coding system as well as to identify the kinds of communication patterns, in relational control terms, that typify systemic family therapy. Because of the interesting interactional patterns that we had observed between Whitaker and individual family members in our development of the coding rules, we speculated that different FRCCCS patterns might be reflected in clients' perceptions of the session and in their views of the therapeutic alliance.

We sampled 29 family sessions conducted between the third and fifth weeks of treatment. Family members (over age 10) completed Pinsof and Catherall's (1986) alliance scales immediately following each session, along with the Session Evaluation Questionnaire (Stiles, 1980). Results did not support the hypotheses, but a statistical trend suggested that complementarity in which the family member was dominant (↑) and the therapist submissive (↓) predicted a less favorable alliance. This finding was interesting in light of the descriptive analyses that showed that, in couples sessions as well as family sessions, the predominant control pattern was the reverse, that is, Therapist ↑/Family Member ↓ (Heatherington & Friedlander, 1990b).

While the verbal patterns were not strongly predictive of the alliance, the latter was related to family members' perceptions of the session's value (Heatherington & Friedlander, 1990c). We suspected that the leap from verbal patterns in one session to these "intermediate" (Greenberg, 1986, p. 4) outcome variables was too large. What was more likely to be observed—and possibly more meaningful—was a shift in the quality of the communication patterns themselves. We wondered if the father in Whitaker's interview would learn to behave differently with his wife and son over the course of treatment. If so, the competitive symmetry we observed in the session might occur less frequently or might alternate with other communication patterns. These questions drew us away from group research, toward a more microscopic view of change over time.

Changes over Time

One of my dissertation advisees, Lily Raymond, was interested in conducting a case study on the structural treatment of anorexia nervosa. Based on our common interest in anorexia, we began to discuss the kinds of changes in family members' interactional patterns one could expect to observe over the course of structural treatment with these kinds of families. We discovered that the clinical literature on the family treatment of anorexia lent itself well to testing specific hypotheses based on the FRCCCS indices.

Lily was able to secure permission to study a single family treated by a leading structural therapist, John Sargent, at the Philadelphia Child Guidance Clinic. This 15-session inpatient treatment had been recorded on videotape for training purposes. Although the family members declined to be interviewed about their perspective on the process of change (an important element, we thought), they did give Lily permission to transcribe and analyze their sessions. Here was an opportunity to study shifts in family relational control patterns over the course of treatment.

Consistent with our earlier findings on relational control in family sessions (Heatherington & Friedlander, 1990b), results of this case study (Raymond, Friedlander, Heatherington, Ellis, & Sargent, 1993) showed that Therapist "one-up"/Family Member "one-down" complementarity predominated. Furthermore, as in my previous study of structural therapy using multidimensional scaling (Friedlander et al., 1987), we found that the therapist maintained an active, central position in the therapeutic system.

The major aspect of the research concerned changes in family members' interactions with each other over time. Because there was an unexpectedly low frequency of communication within the family, several of the hypotheses could not be tested. A close inspection of the FRCCCS patterns did suggest, however, that some changes in the family's rigid interactional style may have occurred over the course of treatment. Specifically, over time the parents seemed to engage in more competitive symmetry with each other and greater complementarity with their anorexic daughter.

While this intensive study of a single case provided some clinically meaningful information, Lily and I suspected that there were key moments, particularly during the family lunch session, in which therapeutically important changes were occurring. The next logical step, it seemed to me, was to take a more microscopic look at exceptional moments in family therapy.

Validity of the FRCCCS

Before detailing the next stage in my evolving program of family therapy research, I would like to briefly describe three validation studies of the FRCCCS. Although the original RCCCS had been subjected to several validation tests, we believed that the coding rules we had created for the family context deserved similar attention. The FRCCCS interjudge reliabilities were satisfactory, suggesting that trained coders tended to view therapy interactions similarly. But did the codes indeed measure interpersonal control? To answer this question, three studies were undertaken, all of which supported the validity of the coding system.

Two studies were essentially criterion validity studies, that is, studies of observer accuracy. First, in Gaul, Simon, Friedlander, Heatherington, and Cutler (1991), we constructed two videotaped vignettes in which the "triadic" indices of the FRCCCS (the three-or-more person interactions that distinguish the FRCCCS from the original RCCCS) were embedded within the script. Therapists, experienced in working with families, viewed each vignette and then rated specific verbal messages as either "one-up" (a move to gain control), "one-down" (a move to relinquish control), or "one-across" (neutral). Similarly, after having created a nonverbal component to the FRCCCS, we constructed brief vignettes in which specific verbal and non-verbal messages were crossed. Experienced family therapists observed each videotaped vignette and rated the final, total message as a move toward either gaining or relinquishing control (Siegel, Friedlander, & Heatherington, 1992).

Analogue experiments were used in these studies to maximize internal validity. External validity, that is, generalizability to actual family treatment, was of minimal concern. Our sole interest was testing the validity of the coding system. (We did, however, pilot the vignettes to ensure their realism.) In the third study (Friedlander, Heatherington, & Wildman, 1991), the balance shifted somewhat; we paid greater attention to external validity—family therapy as it is actually practiced.

While results of the two criterion validity tests indicated that the FRCCCS control codes do reflect observers' perceptions of interpersonal dynamics, the third study was needed to ensure that the FRCCCS indices reflect clinically relevant behaviors. To do this, we contrasted two well-known but distinct approaches to families, structural therapy and Milan systemic therapy (Friedlander et al., 1991). We coded three published transcripts by different experts from each camp. Various FRCCCS indices differed significantly, as expected. The Milan therapists, for example, used significantly more complementarity and indirect, neutral messages, whereas the structural therapists used significantly more competitive symmetry and coalitionary moves. These results not only supported the validity of the coding system but encouraged us to continue pursuing our study of relational control.

THE APPEAL OF TASK ANALYSIS

While we now had a fairly good notion of the kinds of relational interactions that tend to characterize family therapy sessions, I knew that this descriptive information, while interesting conceptually, had little to offer the practicing family therapist. That is, the relational level of communication is important, but, as I was beginning to suspect, it may be overrated. I (as therapist) might be clear about the importance of a solid interpersonal relationship with my clients, but—simply put—what do I talk about with them? If a family is trying to come to terms with domestic violence, what kinds of interventions do I make at what points to help move them through the healing process?

Just as I was beginning to feel dissatisfied with our research program for its limited clinical appeal, I had the opportunity to spend a day with Leslie Greenberg, a prominent process researcher who, with Laura Rice, first applied "task analysis" (which originated in industrial psychology) to the study of therapeutic change processes (e.g., Greenberg, 1984). Les came to Albany for a colloquium in my department, and we spent some time consulting with Laurie Heatherington and with my student research group on various projects. At that time Laurie and I were working on our field study of relational control dynamics in family therapy. Les predicted—accurately, as it turned out—that the therapeutic alliance was too far removed from moment-to-moment therapy processes to correlate significantly with the FRCCCS control patterns. He suggested that we look at our data microscopically, and he encouraged our cautious musings about applying task analysis to family therapy. I say "cautious" because, while I admired Les's work on intrapsychic splits in gestalt therapy, the qualitative aspects of his research program were vastly different from the traditional designs I had employed to date. Yet the clinical relevance was clear-cut.

An aside is needed here to describe task analysis, one variant on change event research. According to Greenberg (1984), recurrent, important "episodes" in psychotherapy during which client and therapist engage in specific "tasks" are potentially the most meaningful aspects of the therapeutic process for clinicians. Like "incident[s] in a novel," episodes are experienced as "intrinsically complex and composed of interconnected activities in a changing pattern . . . occur[ring] within a continuous period of time and com[ing] to some closure in the session" (p. 138). An episode, which can range in length from a few speaking turns to an entire session, is readily identifiable. It has a clear beginning and ends either when the "task" is successfully "resolved," when another task begins, or when the session ends. Tasks—behavioral, affective, or cognitive—might involve setting guidelines for a child's misbehavior, discussing feelings about the family's relocation, considering a problem from a new perspective, and so on. Arguably, successful treatment is made up of a series of "resolved" tasks that occur over time.

Consider the couple dealing with domestic violence. It may be meaningful for me, as therapist, to know that I need to engage the family members in a warm, secure, trusting relationship, that a strong alliance is necessary for a positive outcome, that I should interact in a complementary manner with each spouse, and that indirect challenges can be effective. This information does not help me much, however, when—in an early session— the husband challenges his wife, yelling that her poor housekeeping is wholly responsible for his violent outbursts. How am I to proceed when I know that the immediate task at this point in the session (and in the treatment) is to challenge the husband's view that violence is a legitimate response to frustration? From a task analysis viewpoint, this man's challenge of his wife is a "marker," a signal to me that an important episode is beginning for this couple. The marker calls for some specific interventions on my part. But, what interventions? To whom? What steps need to occur at this moment for there to be a successful "resolution," that is, a change in this man's views on violence?

Unfortunately, as Greenberg and others have pointed out, our theories and our research efforts have been woefully inadequate in helping therapists answer these kinds of questions. Yet these are the kinds of questions that students ask when learning to conduct therapy. To answer them, even the most dedicated scientist-practitioner has difficulty citing the research literature; she has to rely instead on her own clinical expertise.

Encouraged by Les Greenberg, Laurie and I became enthusiastic over the prospect of trying our hand at change event research in family therapy. (Laurie, in fact, spent a semester at York University the following year so as to be able to consult more closely with Les and Laura Rice.) We had a vague sense that some reconceptualization of the task analysis methods needed to take place before we could embark on a research program. To do this, we used the same method that had been successful in creating the FRCCCS, that is, developing guidelines inductively from an intensive analysis of videotapes of master family therapists.

Among the tapes available to us from previous research efforts were two demonstration sessions conducted by Salvador Minuchin. In each interview Minuchin pursued a specific agenda, and in each case the results of his efforts were clear—a dramatic turnaround from the beginning of the interview. Thus both sessions could be viewed, in task analysis terms, as having successful "resolutions." There were other similarities. The tasks in both sessions involved encouraging an adolescent to take responsibility for his acting out behavior. Both episodes began with Minuchin requesting the parent(s) to talk over the problem with the boy while he observed their interactions. These angry parent–child communications went nowhere, yet both sessions ended with emotional outbursts by the boys and surprised reactions on the part of their parents.

Because, from a clinical standpoint, we could see that the family "dance" (Minuchin, 1974) had changed over the course of each session, we began by coding the interactions on the FRCCCS. Indeed, the potential relevance of the FRCCCS was clear because Minuchin (1974) theorized that shifts in family interactional patterns are the aim of treatment and that power relations between parents and children are critical factors to take into account in assessment. In addition to the coding, we used our clinical experience to identify the strategies Minuchin seemed to be pursuing to bring about closure in the sessions. We concluded that his interventions were congruent with those described in his theoretical writings.

In this intensive qualitative analysis of the two sessions, we recognized three distinctly different periods or "phases." During the first, the marker phase, Minuchin observed the family members' interactions without intervening himself. During the second period, the task environment phase, Minuchin was actively involved, using many of the techniques he has become known for, such as challenging, reframing, and so forth. During the resolution phase, beginning with a dramatic change on the part of the adolescent, Minuchin supported the boy's disclosure and challenged the parents to understand and respond differently to him.

Next, dividing Minuchin's two demonstration sessions into the three

Change in Family Therapy

phases that we had identified clinically, we closely scrutinized the FRCCCS data. The results were clear-cut and underscored what we had observed clinically—there were notable changes in the within-family control dynamics over the course of the session, and Minuchin's interpersonal relations differed somewhat with each family member. In one session the pattern shifted from complementarity, with Mother "one-up"/Son "one-down" in the marker phase, to Mother "one-down"/Son "one-up" in the resolution phase. In the other session, the nature of the interactions shifted between the two parents as well as between each parent and the adolescent.

We realized that although the two families were very different, as were their problems, in each session Minuchin's behavior seemed geared toward facilitating a productive discussion among family members about the boy's problems. Thus, the "task" was identical in each session. By the end of both events family members were clearly collaborating in the therapeutic process. The clinical "task"—to promote sustained engagement in problem solving—was successfully "resolved," even though no consensus was achieved about how to proceed with the boy's problems.

One interesting aspect of this research provided guidelines for our subsequent project. This was the realization that the similarity at a latent level was obscured by differences at a manifest level. In the marker phase of one session the mother angrily interrogated her son about his delinquent behavior, while he meekly responded, offering little. In the other session, by contrast, the parents almost begged the boy to open up about his problems. He angrily refused, directing them to his therapist for the answers. The two resolution phases also differed at a manifest level. In one session the boy's disclosure was met by curiosity and encouragement on the part of his mother, while in the other session the mother disqualified her son's feelings. Yet at a latent level, both families had moved off the pursue-distance cycle and were communicating more effectively.

The FRCCCS results underscored this interesting observation. The parent–child control patterns in the marker phase differed in the two episodes. The patterns in the resolution phases also differed. Yet in both events the FRCCCS patterns that characterized the marker phase no longer predominated in the resolution phase, suggesting that a shift in the family's rigid mode of relating had occurred. In other words, while the events were manifestly different from one another, they were similar in that both involved notable underlying changes in the family's interpersonal dynamics.

In a task analysis, there is an iterative process between empirical observation and clinical model building (Greenberg, 1984). Based on our analysis of Minuchin's two demonstration sessions, we believed that facilitating family engagement was an important task, not only in structural family therapy, but across treatment approaches. Thus our next step was to find a new sample of events and construct a conceptual model of the process of interpersonal change. To do this, we were interested in sampling experienced family therapists in the field, not experts or theorists. In short, we wanted to elucidate the sequence of behaviors that practicing therapists use to help family members begin to collaborate with one another in problem solving.

The resulting research (Friedlander, Heatherington, Johnson, & Skowron, 1994) involved creating a conceptual model of the process of change based on a qualitative analysis of a small sample of *sustaining engagement* (SE) change events. We constructed a preliminary conceptual model of the SE event based on the literature and our previous analysis of Minuchin's sessions. Then, from a pool of videotaped sessions, we identified SE events using inductively generated operational definitions. "Successful" SE events were defined as having a resolution phase beginning with a notable shift in the quality of family members' interpersonal behaviors from "disengagement" to "sustained engagement."

A comparative analysis was undertaken of four clearly successful and four clearly unsuccessful episodes. The resulting conceptual model of the successful SE event depicted five interrelated change processes. In short, in the successful event therapists help family members focus on their thoughts and feelings about their disengagement impasse, on the potential benefits of engagement, and on their cognitive constructions of one another's behavior. Doing so in a succession of steps seems to facilitate the family's movement from disengagement to sustained engagement in a specific problem-solving activity within the session.

COGNITIVE CONSTRUCTIONS

My next (and most current) program of change process research, which involves tracking shifts in clients' constructions of their problems, evolved from our initial work on the sustaining engagement event. In the SE model, one of the key factors is a shift in family members' constructions about their interpersonal impasse. Having observed many sessions for this project, we were struck by the fact that new constructions, or attributions, seemed to precede interpersonal behavior change. Indeed, one of the key elements in Minuchin's two sessions had been "reframing." In one interview Minuchin reframed the boy's delinquent behaviors as irresponsibility in response to his mother's over-responsibility. In the other, Minuchin reframed the boy's behavior as a response to his mother's depression. Noting Minuchin's strategy in our argument for applying task analysis to family therapy research, we identified another event that seems to be common across approaches—"systemic conceptualizing"— that is, when "[the] family therapist focus[es] on one person with the goal of changing his or her construction of the family problem from a linear to a circular view" (Heatherington & Friedlander, 1990a, p. 39).

In the late 1980s the constructivist perspective on behavior had been infused into many approaches to family therapy (e.g., Boscolo, Cecchin, Hoffman, & Penn, 1987; White & Epston, 1990) and was gaining popularity among family therapists as it was among psychoanalysts and, indeed, among scholars in many disciplines. There was a growing literature in social-clinical psychology applying attribution theory to an understanding of therapeutic discourse. We noticed, however, that despite the apparent clinical relevance to family therapy, there were no instruments tapping clients' constructions from a family systems perspective. To fill this gap and allow us to conduct change event research on shifts in family members' constructions, Laurie Heatherington and I initiated a program of method development research. Laurie took the lead in creating a self-report questionnaire, the Clients' Constructions of Family Problems Scale (CCFPS), while I—somewhat later—began developing an observational coding scheme, the Cognitive Constructions Coding System (CCCS; Friedlander & Heatherington, 1993).

One advantage of a self-report measure over a coding system is privacy. If family members have differing constructions of the problem, written self-report information may be more veridical than that obtained by coding their publicly expressed views during a family session. On the other hand, the structured format of the CCFPS does not allow clients to generate their own explanations for problematic behavior. Furthermore, when clients are asked to complete the questionnaire after therapy with respect to the same problem they had described prior to treatment, we are unable to observe changes in their construal of the problem itself. Valuable information is lost.

With these considerations in mind and with our long-standing interest in observing changes in the language of therapy, we proceeded to develop an observational coding system of clients' constructions. In my own clinical work, even in individual therapy, and even well beyond the initial session, a fair amount of time seems to be devoted to discussing the various possible causes of my clients' problems. I have become convinced that changes in constructions are a common, non-specific curative factor in *all* forms of psychotherapy. While the importance of changes in an individual client's constructions has been emphasized recently by theorists, family therapists are at the forefront of the constructivist trend, probably due to the obvious fact that different family members tend to construe events and relationships differently.

Taking into account the limitations and recommendations of social-cognitive psychologists who had attempted to study attributions in psychotherapy, we developed the CCCS to code clients' descriptions of and explanations for their problems on four dimensions. Problems and explanations are coded within the context of Problem Elaboration (PE) episodes, that is, segments of verbal interaction that are located in the verbatim transcripts of family therapy sessions. Within the PE episode, clients' problem statements are coded on the intrapersonal–interpersonal dimension, reflecting the emotional configuration in the client's views of the problem; causal explanations are coded on the internal–external, responsible–not responsible, and linear–circular dimensions. Clients' constructions are further identified with respect to the perspective of the speaker. Perspectives can be simple constructions (e.g., "I drink because I'm bored"), meta-constructions (e.g., "She thinks I drink because I'm bored"), or meta-meta-constructions (e.g., "She thinks that I think I drink because I'm bored") (Laing, Phillipson, & Lee, 1966).

To test the validity of the CCCS, we considered comparing clients' postsession perceptions of their constructions with the CCCS coding of their explanations by external judges. However, we realized that what is said publicly is not necessarily identical to one's actual constructions. Even when the client does not intend to deceive, his or her verbally expressed explanations may differ from unexpressed constructions. One way to get around this problem, we reasoned, was to manipulate what a client construes and then test the degree to which his or her explanations are "accurately" perceived and coded by external judges. This, of course, could not be done (either ethically or realistically) with actual clients. Instead, we created videotaped vignettes in which we coached the "family members" (actors) to construe a family problem in a particular manner. Validity was then assessed by comparing the coached "constructions" with the CCCS coding of the transcripts for these vignettes.

At present, there are two ongoing projects with the CCCS. The first is a dissertation study by one of my doctoral students, Robin Coulehan. This project is a qualitative analysis of the "systemic conceptualizing" (Heatherington & Friedlander, 1990a) change event, one in which parents' constructions of their children's problems shift from an intrapsychic to an interpersonal view. The second project is an intensive qualitative and quantitative analysis of a sample of family therapy interviews conducted by constructivist theorists. Undoubtedly, future efforts along these lines will be forthcoming.

FURTHER MUSINGS

Writing this memoir of the development of my research program in family therapy has been illuminating for me. Before discussing the salient general assumptions underlying my efforts, a few cautionary words seem in order. First, I have not been able to credit the hundreds of theorists, researchers, and clinicians whose ideas have influenced me, directly and indirectly, over the years. Nor have I described the long-term influence of the feedback, positive and negative, I have received from the many colleagues who read my work in its published or unpublished form. Furthermore, the present account of my work is incomplete, since I have focused only on my process research in family therapy and its relevant precursors. The methods and results of research projects on other topics that I undertook simultaneously with the studies described here undoubtedly also influenced my thinking.

These considerations notwithstanding, there are some aspects of my thinking (one may also call them biases) of which I became acutely aware while writing this account. First and foremost is my belief, being a psychotherapist as well as a researcher, that the only program of psychotherapy research worth engaging in is one that will eventually inform clinical practice. This is not to disparage either theoretical work or methodological research. On the contrary—I have done both. But ultimately, I believe, the most important consumers of psychotherapy research are psychotherapists. For therapists, I have come to value research on mid-level theoretical constructs over the more global theories of treatment. Volumes of comparative outcome research have been generated, showing few differences in efficacy rates. This research is, to my mind, less valuable to the practicing clinician than the development of theories of change within clearly identifiable episodes based on intensive microanalyses. While I might be assured in my belief that structural therapy (or Bowenian therapy or Milan systemic therapy or . . .) is efficacious for family work, I need to know exactly what to do when, for example, the couple I am working with reveals a long history of violence. Only change event research, of which task analysis is one variant, is equipped to develop the mid-level kinds of theory that can guide me toward effective therapeutic interventions in such a situation.

My research program has evolved over the years from experimental to non-experimental and from group research to small n studies, always in search of more clinically meaningful methods. This movement has not, however, led me to abandon traditional rigorous standards of methodology. Indeed, I have been concerned with finding statistical approaches and developing instruments, particularly verbal coding systems, that are not only theoretically compatible with systems thinking but are also adequately supported psychometrically.

One might also surmise, from the foregoing, that I have little use for either experimentation or hypothesis-testing. Such an assumption would not be accurate, however. I have relied on analogue experiments in the validation studies of the FRCCCS and CCCS described above as well as in various projects designed to test theory. I have tested theory both experimentally (Friedlander, Thibodeau, et al., 1985) and in small n studies (Friedlander et al., 1991; Friedlander, Thibodeau, & Ward, 1985; Raymond et al., 1993). While I believe that inductive, discovery-oriented research is valuable, particularly for delineating the salient aspects of the work of "experts," programs of psychotherapy research that incorporate experimental tests of theoretical hypotheses derived from detailed, inductive microanalyses (qualitative as well as quantitative) of successful treatments are potentially the most informative. Indeed, the creation and refinement of theoretical concepts and models is essential for knowledge to advance and ultimately be transmitted to our students and trainees.

Finally, I have long struggled with the problem of sampling therapists whose work can best carry out this mission. A fair amount of my research has involved expert therapists whose published work exemplifies a specific theoretical approach well known to a large audience of clinicians. While informative, research of this type has inherent limitations, notably the problem of generalizing to therapy as it is actually practiced in the field. Sampling skilled non-experts is exceedingly difficult, I have found, not only because there are many problems inherent in conducting research in a clinic or agency but also because most clinic staff are relatively inexperienced. The more seasoned therapists tend to be in administrative roles or in private practice settings that are generally off limits for research. Enticing skilled, experienced therapists to participate in research is an ongoing difficulty for process researchers. Hopefully, more clinicians will be eager to join a research effort as our methods and findings continue to improve in relevance.

Recently I completed a comprehensive review of all *ex post facto* process research in family therapy (Friedlander, Wildman, Heatherington, & Skowron, in press). In contrast to the hundreds, perhaps thousands, of studies of individual therapy, we located only 35 published process studies of family therapy. Clearly, there is much exciting work to be done in this area. I expect to continue, with the help of my predecessors and peers, to press on. Ultimately, the efficacy of the healing process is our concern—we can only hope to have contributed.

REFERENCES

Bateson, G. (1958). *Naven*. Stanford, CA: Stanford University Press. (Original work published 1936)

Boscolo, L., Cecchin, G., Hoffman, L., & Penn, P. (1987). *Milan systemic family therapy: Conversations in theory and practice*. New York: Basic Books.

Corrigan, J. D., Dell, D. M., Lewis, K. N., & Schmidt, L. D. (1980). Counseling as a social influence process: A review. *Journal of Counseling Psychology, 27*, 395–441.

Friedlander, M. L. (1984). Psychotherapy talk as social control. *Psychotherapy, 21*, 335–341.

Friedlander, M. L., Ellis, M. V., Raymond, L., Siegel, S. M., & Milford, D. (1987). Convergence and divergence in the process of interviewing families. *Psychotherapy, 24*, 570–583.

Friedlander, M. L., & Heatherington, L. (1989). Analyzing relational control in family therapy interviews. *Journal of Counseling Psychology, 36*, 139–148.

Friedlander, M. L., & Heatherington, L. (1993). *Assessing clients' constructions of family problems II: Cognitive Constructions Coding System*. Unpublished manuscript.

Friedlander, M. L., Heatherington, L., Johnson, B., & Skowron, E. A. (1994). "Sustaining Engagement": A common change event in family therapy. *Journal of Counseling Psychology, 41*(1), 438–448.

Friedlander, M. L., Heatherington, L., & Wildman, J. (1991). Interpersonal control in structural and Milan systemic family therapy. *Journal of Marital and Family Therapy, 17*, 395–408.

Friedlander, M. L., & Highlen, P. S. (1984). A spatial view of the interpersonal structure of family interviews: Similarities and differences across counselors. *Journal of Counseling Psychology, 31*, 477–487.

Friedlander, M. L., Highlen, P. S., & Lassiter, W. (1985). Content analytic comparison of four expert counselors' approaches to family treatment: Ackerman, Bowen, Jackson, and Whitaker. *Journal of Counseling Psychology, 32*, 171–180.

Friedlander, M. L., & Kaul, T. J. (1983). Preparing clients for counseling: Effects of role induction on counseling process and outcome. *Journal of College Student Personnel, 24*, 207–214.

Friedlander, M. L., & Phillips, S. D. (1984). Preventing anchoring errors in clinical judgment. *Journal of Consulting and Clinical Psychology, 52*, 366–371.

Friedlander, M. L., & Phillips, S. D. (1985, August). *Interactive counseling discourse as social control: Stochastic analysis and microanalysis*. Paper presented at the annual convention of the American Psychological Association, Los Angeles.

Friedlander, M. L., & Schwartz, G. S. (1985). Toward a theory of strategic self-presentation in counseling and psychotherapy. *Journal of Counseling Psychology, 32*, 483–501.

Friedlander, M. L., Thibodeau, J. R., Nichols, M. P., Tucker, C., & Snyder, J. (1985). Introducing semantic cohesion analysis: A study of group talk. *Small Group Behavior, 16*, 285–302.

Friedlander, M. L., Thibodeau, J. R., & Ward, L. G. (1985). Discriminating the "good" from the "bad" therapy hour: A study of dyadic interaction. *Psychotherapy, 22,* 631- 642.

Friedlander, M. L., & Ward, L. G. (1984). Development and validation of the Supervisory Styles Inventory. *Journal of Counseling Psychology, 31,* 541–557.

Friedlander, M. L., Wildman, J., Heatherington, L., & Skowron, E. A. (in press). What we do and don't know about the process of family therapy. *Journal of Family Psychology.*

Gaul, R., Simon, L., Friedlander, M. L., Heatherington, L., & Cutler, C. (1991). Correspondence of family therapists' perceptions with the FRCCCS coding rules for triadic interactions. *Journal of Marital and Family Therapy, 17,* 379–394.

Greenberg, L. S. (1984). Task analysis: The general approach. In L. N. Rice & L. S. Greenberg (Eds.), *Patterns of change: Intensive analysis of psychotherapy process* (pp. 124–148). New York: Guilford.

Greenberg, L. S. (1986). Change process research. *Journal of Consulting and Clinical Psychology, 54,* 4–9.

Haley, J. (1963). *Strategies of psychotherapy.* New York: Grune & Stratton.

Halliday, M. A. K., & Hasan, R. (1976). *Cohesion in English.* London: Longman.

Heatherington, L., & Allen, G. J. (1984). Sex and relational communication patterns in counseling. *Journal of Counseling Psychology, 31,* 287–294.

Heatherington, L., & Friedlander, M. L. (1987). *Family Relational Communication Control Coding System coding manual.* Unpublished manuscript. (Available from Laurie Heatherington, Department of Psychology, Williams College, Williamstown, MA 01267.)

Heatherington, L., & Friedlander, M. L. (1990a). Applying task analysis to structural family therapy. *Journal of Family Psychology, 4,* 36–48.

Heatherington, L., & Friedlander, M. L. (1990b). Complementarity and symmetry in family therapy communication. *Journal of Counseling Psychology, 37,* 261–286.

Heatherington, L., & Friedlander, M. L. (1990c). Couple and family psychotherapy alliance scales: Empirical considerations. *Journal of Marital and Family Therapy, 16,* 299–306.

Kruskal, J. B., & Wish, M. (1978). *Multidimensional scaling* (Sage University Paper Series on Quantitative Applications in the Social Sciences, No. 07-011). Beverly Hills, CA: Sage.

Laing, R. D., Phillipson, H., & Lee, A. R. (1966). *Interpersonal perception: A theory and a method of research.* London: Tavistock.

Minuchin, S. (1974). *Families and family therapy.* Cambridge, MA: Harvard University Press.

Pinsof, W. M. (1980). *The Family Therapist Coding System manual.* Chicago: Family Institute of Chicago.

Pinsof, W. M., & Catherall, D. R. (1986). The integrative psychotherapy alliance: Family, couple, and individual therapy scales. *Journal of Marital and Family Therapy, 12,* 137–151.

Raymond, L., Friedlander, M. L., Heatherington, L., Ellis, M. V., & Sargent, J.

(1993). Communication processes in structural family therapy: Case study of an anorexic family. *Journal of Family Psychology, 6,* 308–326.

Rogers, L. E., & Farace, R. V. (1975). Relational communication analysis: New measurement procedures. *Human Communication Research, 1,* 222–239.

Siegel, S. M., Friedlander, M. L., & Heatherington, L. (1992). Nonverbal relational control in family communication. *Journal of Nonverbal Behavior, 16,* 117–139.

Sluzki, C. E., & Beavin, J. (1977). Symmetry and complementarity: An operational definition and a typology of dyads. In P. Watzlawick & J. Weakland (Eds. & Trans.), *The interactional view* (pp. 71–87). New York: Norton. (Reprinted from *Acta Psiquiatrica y Psicologica de America Latina,* 1965, 11, 321–330)

Stiles, W. B. (1980). Measurement of the impact of psychotherapy sessions. *Journal of Consulting and Clinical Psychology, 48,* 176–185.

Strong, S. R. (1968). Counseling: An interpersonal influence process. *Journal of Counseling Psychology, 15,* 215–224.

Watzlawick, P., Beavin, J. H., & Jackson, D. D. (1967). *Pragmatics of human communication.* New York: Norton.

White, M., & Epston, D. (1990). *Narrative means to therapeutic ends.* New York: Norton.

CHAPTER 9

Strategic Choices in a Qualitative Approach to Psychotherapy Process Research

DAVID L. RENNIE

For the past decade I have been engaged in qualitative research addressing the client's subjective experience of an hour of psychotherapy. As an approach to research, this has been a radically new experience. I was trained in the tradition of the scientist-practitioner model of clinical psychology in which objectivism, quantification, and experimental and/ or statistical control are the norm of research practice. For several years I had applied this logico-empiricism to the study of variables involved in the training of counselors (e.g., Rennie, Brewster, & Toukmanian, 1985). As I came to learn, the values and practices of logico-empiricism were in many ways not compatible with an interpretive approach to method characterizing the new program.

I became disillusioned about the typical analogue research into counselor training. As I came to put it acidly one day, we were studying bogus counseling given by bogus counselors to bogus clients. Moreover, we were limited to quasi-experimental designs (Campbell & Stanley, 1966) and were thus further handicapped in making truth warrants. In my view, we burdened ourselves with multivariate analyses whose complexity outweighed the conclusions that we derived from them.

Underneath all of this was a deeper crisis in meaning. I found that I was not reading much because most of the literature threatened the integrity of the microcosmic research world that I was creating; I had become a narrow technician. Supporting this emptiness was a growing suspicion that in counselor training we may have been putting the cart before the horse. The training model was derived from the work of Carl Rogers and his students on the operationalization of the therapist "conditions" for positive therapeutic change in the client (Rogers, 1957). The research literature on this model of therapeutic change seemed less sound than its advocates claimed. I was struck by the finding that therapeutic change in a group of hospitalized patients was more related to their characteristic level of processing before the study began than to the level of therapist conditions proferred (Rogers, Gendlin, Kiesler, & Truax, 1967). I wondered if the therapist's side of the therapeutic transaction had been emphasized at the expense of the client's side.

This skepticism about the soundness of the therapy process research on which counselor training was based clinched the decision to shift from counselor training research to psychotherapy research proper. In this research, a group of my graduate students and I wanted to get a fresh perspective on therapy—the perspective of the client. We felt that this perspective had been insufficiently explored and we found that this impression was supported by a survey of the psychotherapy research literature (Phillips, 1984; for more recent reviews, see Elliott & James, 1989; McLeod, 1990). In deciding to access participants' subjective experience of therapy, we wondered about how to go about it. We also wondered how we could analyze information we obtained about the subjective experiential data and how we could justify our truth claims once we analyzed it.

As leader of the group, when mulling over how best to achieve such access, I was aware of the grounded theory (Glaser, 1978; Glaser & Strauss, 1967) form of qualitative analysis because a student in our graduate program had done a study using this method. Once I started reading about grounded theory, I was drawn to literature on what has been referred to as *the logic of justification in qualitative research.* As time went on, I developed a set of strategies for adapting the grounded theory method to psychotherapy research. As will become evident, gaining a clear sense of the logic of justification has proved more difficult, however. This aspect of the qualitative approach strikes at the heart of the philosophy of social science and, to complicate matters, currently is deeply contextualized within the sociology of this science. In any case, compared with my earlier work, I found that my framework had reversed. Previously, I had fitted content to method; now I was embarked on a program of trying to fit method to content.

This chapter is organized into four sections. It begins with a presentation of the main issues I faced and the strategies I developed during the unfolding of my intent to conduct an open-ended inquiry into the client's experience of therapy. As will be seen, this inquiry was directed toward the experience of a total of 16 therapy sessions. The interviews with the clients about their recollections of these sessions produced hundreds of pages of transcript, necessitating some difficult decisions about how these voluminous data could be analyzed, within the grounded theory framework, in a way that was both systematic and manageable. The second section of the chapter addresses in broad outline the main strategies developed to achieve these objectives. The third section is a presentation of the main findings that flowed from the study. Finally, the chapter ends with a discussion of the logic of justification of the approach as a whole.

THE STRATEGY OF INQUIRY

In planning to consult with clients about their experience of therapy, I wanted to get as close to the experience as possible. I had used extensively the replay of therapy tapes to interns as a way of helping them to remember what they had experienced in particular moments and their reasons for their interventions. Furthermore, I was familiar with Kagan's (e.g., 1975) use of videotape replay as a way of stimulating what he referred to as Interpersonal Process Recall (IPR) as an aid to counselor training. It seemed a natural step to replay therapy tapes to clients and to have them comment on what they saw and/or heard during the replay (although I did not know it at the time, Robert Elliott had chosen the same strategy; see Elliott, 1986). This decision entailed four main problems: deciding on the "sampling unit" when addressing the therapy experience, deciding on whether to study the client's experience only or that of both the client and the therapist, meeting the ethical requirements imposed by making the potentially reactive research intervention part of ongoing therapy, and deciding on the approach to the inquiry. Each of these problems and the strategies used to solve them are addressed in turn.

Choosing the Sampling Unit

I decided to study the moment-to-moment experience of a single therapy session. There were several reasons for this decision. Laura Rice was a member of my department and I was aware of her research on the resolution in therapy of a particular type of event occurring in everyday life (see Rice & Saperia, 1984). I was not part of her research group; doing something different helped to establish some autonomy now that I had moved into their research domain. Meanwhile, Robert Elliott became attached to Rice's group, and I became aware of his use of IPR as a way of studying the experience of the most significant event in a session. That strengthened my inclination to "get the lay of the land" by sampling

Strategic Choices in a Qualitative Approach

whole therapy sessions because it promised a different focus compared with Elliott's program (see Rennie, 1992).

Apart from being influenced by this sociology of my local research environment, I was uneasy about going too quickly to the study of a particular type of event, whether selected on theoretical or empirical grounds. I felt that, because insufficient attention had been paid to the client's subjective experience of therapy, the focus on specific types of events might be premature and that such a strategy logically should follow rather than precede a focus on the moment-to-moment experience of a fairly large unit of therapy (see Rennie & Toukmanian, 1992).

The decision was also influenced by the interests of my research group. Jeff Phillips wanted to interview former therapy clients about what in their judgment most influenced them, both in and outside of therapy, to change positively during the period of therapy (Phillips, 1984). Lynne Angus wanted to study both the client's and the therapist's experience of metaphor as a particular type of event in therapy (e.g., Angus & Rennie, 1989). At the time, we felt that if I went ahead with my plan to study the experiences within one therapy session, the three projects would form a continuum; the experience of a particular event and that of an entire course of therapy would anchor the two ends, and the experiences in an hour of therapy would fill in the middle. An indication of the strength of my resolve to study the moment-to-moment experience of a full hour of therapy was my response to a conversation with a colleague at a neighboring university. Within a community psychology framework, Ben Gotlieb was using interviews as his method of inquiry and a type of content analysis as his method of analysis. When learning of what I was planning, he urged me to focus on an aspect of the session to prevent getting swamped. I listened to his advice, then ignored it.

Deciding Which Perspective to Address

After a pilot study, I decided to focus on the client's experience alone rather than include the therapist's experience as well. The pilot study was with one of my own clients who consented to the two of us being interviewed by a colleague about our independent experience of one of our sessions. I transcribed both inquiries, as well as the therapy session, and made my debut as a qualitative researcher, attempting a grounded analysis of the two inquiry transcripts. I found it overwhelming. I weighed the scope of my focus against the richness of both perspectives. It seemed that looking at both sides across an entire session was too big a task (perhaps I was influenced by Ben Gotlieb after all). Faced with a choice between reducing the scope and forsaking the therapist's perspective, I opted for the latter. I also recall thinking, somewhat perversely, that we already knew a great deal about the therapist's perspective and that concentrating on the client's was the new frontier.

It was not until I supervised Lynne Angus's study of metaphor that my awareness of the dynamic richness of gaining access to both perspectives was brought home. However, she benefited from her focus on a particular type of event, which enabled her to look at both sides and still have a manageable study. On balance, I do not regret the decision to focus on the client's experience only, given the scope of my sampling of that experience. Currently, I have stopped gathering data and am devoting my efforts to doing refined analyses of the research protocols and, in general, writing up the returns. Nevertheless, in my most recent research inquiries, I have made an effort to interview both the client and the therapist. I am doing this in anticipation of carrying the project to its logical next stage—the integration of both the client's and the therapist's perspectives. I feel that it will be easier to do this once I have established a platform of understanding of the client's experience. There has been another development, as well, that reinforces the conclusion that I can begin to let go of the focus on the client's experience and shift to the dyadic interaction. Recently Watson (Watson & Rennie, in press) and Shaul (1993), studying both the client's and the therapist's perspectives on particular types of events in therapy, have conceptualized categories of the client's experience that replicate in many ways those conceptualized in my study.

The Ethics of the Study

This study was problematic in that, by virtue of the plan to interview clients who were actively in therapy, it invaded the therapy itself. What was to be made of this intrusion? Would it be disruptive or would it benefit the therapy? How would I know? If it proved to be disruptive, could I leave it to the members of the therapy dyad to sort it out, or should I offer to mediate, or, indeed, should I abandon the project? These were difficult questions.

I decided to address the ethical demands in two ways. First, I gave the customary assurance to the clients that, should they agree to participate, they could withdraw from the study at any time without jeopardizing their therapy. Second, I suggested that, if they decided to remain in the study, they could choose among three ways of dealing with the information that came from it (Rennie, 1990). They could assume the responsibility for communicating to their therapist what they learned from the inquiry, have me brief the therapist of my sense of their experience, or invite me to consult with them and their therapist about the therapy in the light of what emerged. Correspondingly, these options were part of the orienting information about the study given to therapists when I approached them for referrals from their caseloads. Thus, the acceptance of these alternatives was the condition for the therapists to nominate someone from their clientele and for the clients to participate in the study.

As it turned out, practically all of the clients elected to handle the decision about whether or not to debrief the therapist. Exceptions were two participants who were my own clients, of course, as well as a client of one of my students who agreed to have her therapist listen to the inquiry interview and to comment on it. More ambiguous cases were three other research interviews involving two clients (one client was interviewed separately about two sessions occurring several months apart), where the clients knew that I would be interviewing the therapist as well. I was not asked by either of these clients or their therapists to collaborate jointly with them on the implications of the research inquiries for their relationships with each other. Hence, they assumed control of the decision about what, if anything, to do in the way of talking about the impact of the research inquiry on the therapy.

I followed up with several of the clients to learn of the impact of the research on them and their relationship with their therapists. Both of my clients reported that it was useful because it enabled them to let me know of ways in which they felt I had misunderstood them. A frank sharing of the nature of these misunderstandings subsequent to the inquiry enabled us to establish a more effective working alliance (Bordin, 1979; Greenson, 1967). An interesting sequel was that, when I followed up one of these clients 2 years after he had finished therapy, he had forgotten the nature of the misunderstanding to the point of insisting that I was wrong when I pointed it out to him. It was only when I showed him the transcript of the inquiry session that he believed me.

Memory lapse was also shown by another client who, when I contacted her 2 years after she had ended with her therapist, could not remember much about the therapy, let alone the impact of the inquiry interview. (Martin and Stelmaczonek, 1988, found, however, that clients in counseling recalled significant moments in counseling 6 months after they occurred.) Another client reported long after her therapy had ended that she was seriously ill (physically, she implied) and did not wish to talk about the impact of the research. This follow-up was by telephone, and was brief, so that it was difficult to know whether her reluctance was for the reason she stated or because she felt bad about the research (in the inquiry interview she had indicated some dissatisfaction with the therapy—dissatisfaction that she had not shared with her therapist). Yet another client—the one who was seen by my student—had indicated in the closing moments of her inquiry session that, upon listening to the replay of the tape, she had realized that she needed to deliberate more when interacting with her therapist and had vowed to make that the theme of her therapy from that point forward. As indicated, in this case her therapist had heard the tape of the inquiry interview and so was in a good position to initiate a refined working alliance. At follow-up 3 years later the client revealed that she had been hospitalized for treatment of a manic-depressive disorder, according to her account, in the period since the therapy under study. She made no connection between the therapy and the hospitalization; indeed, she spoke very fondly of her therapist. However, she made no mention of her vow, and I had the impression that she had forgotten about it. Finally, I sent to another client a copy of a draft of a paper that I had written because I was inspired in part by her report on her experience of storytelling (Rennie, 1985a; 1994b). I wanted her impressions; in the course of her reply (which was positive) she gave no indication of adverse effects of the inquiry.

In summary, I followed up a number of the interviewees, and, with one possible exception, none reported adverse effects of the research inquiry. Hence, the decision to give the clients the option to control the feedback to their counselor evidently worked out well. At the same time, when I reflect on having interviewed just the client as opposed to both members of the dyad, I prefer the latter approach. It is more balanced and thus more likely to lead to clients discussing with their therapists the implications of the inquiry.

Deciding on the Structure of the IPR Interview

The final consideration about the inquiry was its structure. How active should I be as I conduct the interview? And should I be open-ended, structuring, or both?

In terms of activity, the nature of the endeavor made it difficult to be retiring, distant, and objectivistic. It took courage for the clients to come forward and, regardless of what they had learned about the project before actually seeing me, they were still unclear in many ways about what to expect. I appreciated their coming forward and wanted to make them as comfortable as possible; more specifically, I wanted to *engage* them, to strike up a good rapport and allow them to feel that I accepted and understood them. Above all, I wanted to *understand* them. These sentiments and desires inclined me to be active and co-constructive. Even though the interviewees had just emerged from the therapy session and had the benefit of watching and/or listening to the replay of the tape of the session, they still had to represent in words what they recalled experiencing.

We can surmise that several factors, such as defensiveness, ineffability of the experience they were attempting to recall, and inadequacy of language as a medium for the representation, impeded this representation. While the interviewees were struggling to catch their experience in words, I was struggling with them. I had *my* sense of what they were getting at and had to decide whether to convey that sense or not.

This decision always involved a dilemma. On the one hand, if I withheld my sense, there was a danger that I would be frustrated by lack of clarity when it came time to analyze the transcript. On the other hand, if I did convey my sense, there was the danger that I would be wrong.

I once discussed the problem with Robert Elliott. He felt that the IPR consultants should keep their activity as low as possible in order to minimize their subjectification of the interviewee's experience. He was even nervous about the effects of paraphrasing and reflecting feeling because they are inevitably interpretive at least to some extent (Elliott, personal communication, September 1988). Indirectly supporting the counterargument was Al Mahrer's remark to the audience, at one of my early presentations (Rennie, 1985a); "The first thing we have to do is to find out what Rennie did to get these people to tell him what they did." This was the rub. The more active and co-constructive I was, the more information I got; yet the more I got, the more I had to worry about the extent to which it was coming from me more than the client.

This is a complex matter and I do not feel that I have gotten to the bottom of it. In the broadest sense, it strikes at the heart of the issue of objectivism and constructionism in social science (e.g., Gergen, 1985; Polkinghorne, 1988; Rennie, 1993; Rennie & Toukmanian, 1992). Proponents of constructionism hold that it is a myth to believe that human experience can be represented independently of the social context in which it is communicated (Kurt Danziger, personal communication, October 1988). More narrowly, at the level of procedure, I have learned that skillful interviewing can mitigate the intrusions of the interviewer's subjectivity to a certain extent. With experience, I came to conduct myself in a manner that was more in keeping with the cautions put forward by Elliott. I increasingly reduced "content" interventions (such as paraphrasing) in favor of "process" interventions (like asking the interviewee to self-reflect) to ascertain if more could be said and to appraise the accuracy of what was said. I also drew more upon meta-communicative responses to check on the extent to which the client was feeling pressured or influenced by me. Finally, I learned that, while a protocol might seem barren prior to analysis, it invariably seemed less so upon analysis. As a consequence, I felt less pressured to be actively co-constructive (Rennie, 1992).

I believe that the meta-communicative initiatives allowed the interviewees to feel comparatively free to disagree with me. At the same time, I am aware from my research findings that clients have a great tendency to defer to their therapist (Rennie, 1994a; in press) and I have to assume that they feel the same way, at least to some extent, when interacting with an interviewer interested in their experience of the therapy. I often have said to my students that somebody should do a study of clients' experience of being interviewed about their experience of a therapy interview. Admittedly, such a study would be the leading edge of an infinite regress. Nevertheless, it would be useful to gain clients' reports of the extent to which they feel inclined to defer to the researcher vis-a-vis the therapist. (As a footnote to the question of the appropriate level of therapist activity in the inquiry, Elliott has indicated, in a personal communication in May 1993, that of late he has felt freer to be more active in the inquiry in the interests of facilitating rapport. If, during the analysis phase, he decides that the content of the interview came more from him than the client, then he does not analyze the material.)

Turning to the question of whether to conduct an open-ended or structured inquiry, I generally adhered to Glaser and Strauss's suggestion that, in the early stages of a grounded theory study, the inquiry should be open-ended in order to prevent foreclosure on potentially relevant information. As the analysis proceeds and a conceptualization of commonalities has been achieved, then the inquirer has the option of asking focused questions based on the conceptualization. Accordingly, when beginning the replay of the tape, I suggested to the clients that they should stop the tape at any point where they recalled experiencing something of interest, importance, or significance. It was this general focus that gave rise to a broader range of phenomena than would have been the case if I had inquired into particular experiences, such as the experience of moments of change, of the relationship with the therapist, of misunderstandings, and so on. At the same time, on occasion I stopped the tape and made an inquiry when something caught my attention and that seemed about to be passed over by the client without comment. And, in keeping with the Glaser and Strauss suggestion, I sometimes introduced phenomena to the client once it became apparent to me that they generally are widely experienced.

In conclusion, it was within the foregoing context that I interviewed the 14 clients, two of them twice, providing a total of 16 protocols of the client's moment-to-moment experience of an hour of therapy. The tape of the therapy session on which each research inquiry was based was transcribed, as was the tape of the inquiry session. The inquiry transcripts were the data upon which the grounded theory analysis was applied, with the therapy transcripts serving as context. As was true of the inquiry, the analysis required decisions about alternative strategies. It is to these decisions that I now turn.

STRATEGIC CHOICES IN THE ANALYSIS

The grounded theory form of qualitative analysis was developed by two American sociologists in expression of their concern that theory in sociology was too hypothetico-deductive and insufficiently grounded in primary subject matter (Glaser & Strauss, 1967). They proposed a method of induction that promised to lead systematically to theory that is grounded. The method in its progressive development has been described by its originators in a series of monographs (Glaser, 1978; Glaser & Strauss, 1967; Strauss, 1987; Strauss & Corbin, 1990).

As indicated, my group became interested in the method in the early 1980s and thus had as primary sources the early works of Glaser and Strauss. While we found that these sources outlined the general principles of grounded theory development, they did not specify in detail the procedures of the approach. This left us in the position of developing our own way of fashioning the details of the method. A recent review of grounded theory studies (Quartaro, 1993a) reveals that most researchers across a variety of disciplines similarly devised procedures in line with their styles and purposes. The broad outline of the procedures developed by my group is presented elsewhere (Rennie, Phillips, & Quartaro, 1988). This chapter provides an opportunity to describe the underlying reasons for developing those procedures. These considerations are organized under two headings: deciding on strategies for effecting constant comparison, and deciding the size of the "meaning unit" or portion of text to be analyzed.

The Constant Comparison Strategies

In grounded analysis, there are three main aspects. There are data, categories, and relationships within and between them. The data are typically but not necessarily verbal. In being verbal, they may be in the form of either recorded reports by respondents of their experience of a given phenomenon, or recorded observations by a researcher acting as a participant observer of a phenomenon. In either case, researchers have verbal text as the material to be analyzed. The task is to conceptualize a theory of the phenomenon by interpreting the meaning embodied in the text in a way that remains faithful to the text itself—in short, "grounded."

The royal road to theory development is constant comparison, which begins with the analyst breaking the text into units for the purpose of analysis. Glaser and Strauss recommend that the meanings in each unit then be summarized into what they refer to as "codes." They advocate that the critical step is to acquire two protocols and then to compare codes with other codes derived from within and between the protocols. This process is iterated as the protocols accumulate. This multiple comparison, effected by a series of sorting of codes, leads to coherent clustering of codes. The clusters are represented lexically by words or phrases referred to as "categories." Categories are in turn constantly compared, leading to the conceptualization of higher order categories. The relationships between codes and the categories colligated from them, and between higher order categories colligated from lower order ones, ideally lead to the conceptualization of a supreme or "core" category. The overall set of relationships between the categories at all levels is the basis for the conceptualization of the theory of the phenomenon.

The members of my group tried various ways of coding (e.g., Angus & Rennie, 1989; Rennie, 1992; Rennie & Brewer, 1987; Watson & Rennie, in press). The procedure developed for my own project departed from Glaser and Strauss's recommendation. I had difficulty accepting the prospect of sorting and re-sorting an accumulating mountain of codes, especially given the complexity of my data. I decided to forgo the coding stage and to move directly to categorizing. Furthermore, instead of categorizing by conceptualizing the meaning apparent in clusters of codes, I categorized the meaning(s) in each unit of analysis as I worked through a given protocol. (Henceforth, the unit of analysis, now termed "meaning unit," will be given the acronym MU.) Thus, when dealing with a given MU, which might be a few sentences in length, I pondered over the unit and wondered, "What meaning is contained here?" This was continued until I could come up with no more answers. The result could be a single answer, or several. Each answer was represented by a word or phrase that was tied to the meaning of the text constituting the unit; in each case the result was a category. In some instances, the language of the category was identical to the language of the unit, such as conceptualizing the category "client's track" when interviewees used the terms "on track" or "off track" in commenting on their processing and/or on the work of the therapist. In other cases, the language of the category was not actually contained in the language of the unit, as when the category "concern about the therapist's approach" was derived from a unit in which the interviewee reported having difficulty with the therapist but did not express it precisely in terms of "concern" and "approach." After developing this strategy, I belatedly learned that Turner (1981) had earlier suggested a similar way of doing grounded analysis.

Hence, we developed a strategy of bypassing Glaser and Strauss's coding stage and instead of moving directly to categorizing as we worked from one meaning unit to the next. Within the framework of this strategy, the analysis was complete once we worked out a set of tactics for representing, organizing, and filing the emerging set of categories, as well as the relationships between them and the meaning units (for details, see Rennie, Phillips, & Quartaro, 1988).

Some members of my group have preferred my overall tactic of doing the analysis "by hand" with the aid of index cards, and so on (e.g., Quartaro, 1993b; Shaul, 1993). Other members have developed modifications of existing mainframe software (Dolhanty, 1990; Mainwaring, 1992) and microcomputer software (Johnston, 1994) that seem to work reasonably well. The advantage of using computers in grounded analysis is that the main burden of typing is limited to entering the meaning units into the computer's memory; once that is done, they do not have to be retyped when assigning them to categories. This saves time because, as explained above, in grounded analysis a given meaning unit needs to be assigned to as many categories as seem fitting given the meaning embodied in the unit.

The matter of the amount of information dealt with in a grounded analysis takes us to the second challenge in the analysis requiring the development of a strategy—the determination of the size of the meaning unit.

Deciding on the Size of the Meaning Unit

Glaser and Strauss (1967) recommend that the text be analyzed line by line. This suggestion never made much sense to my group because people represent meaning in words, phrases, sentences and combinations of sentences, rather than in lines of a transcript. Thus, we were inclined to decide on analytical units on the basis of the *meaning* evident in the text. Having said that, it is not easy to define exactly what we meant by a "unit of meaning."

In my early work, I attempted to define it as a single thought or concept. This definition meant that the MUs were usually short—up to three or four lines of text. However, as the analysis proceeded, I got impatient with the work that categorizing such short MUs entailed. Furthermore, I found that there was often repetitiveness in the assignment of categories as I moved from one MU to the next.

I began with small MUs because I wanted to be sure that in the analysis I dealt with all of the information, and thoroughly. I also had the feeling that the narrower I maintained my focus, the more I would be prevented from imposing a narrative gloss on my interpretation of the MU (see Spence, 1986). My students were inclined toward the same strategy and for the same reasons. Later on in the analysis I moved toward larger MUs, to the point where they might be a page or two of text. I found that I preferred to work with MUs that represented what we could refer to as episodes, themes, or topics. As I grew more experienced at analyzing text, I came to realize that the interviewees usually had something that they wanted to tell me, that there was a *point* that they were trying to make. When they made it, they moved on to talking about something else. I increasingly tended to look for these episodes and to declare them to be my MUs.

A consequence of this new strategy was that many more categories were assigned to these larger MUs (up to 10 in some instances), but I found that I could work with that complexity because it helped me to understand how the categories interrelated. Furthermore, the strategy saved time because it entailed less redundancy.

As I look back, I believe that the movement from small to large MUs was developmental. I felt more secure in working with larger units once my taxonomy became reasonably stabilized. However, I now think that I need not have been so careful. My present students are putting this belief to the test because I am urging them to move more quickly than I did toward the selection of larger blocks of data as their MUs; I am awaiting their judgment on the soundness of the strategy.

It is not the intent of this chapter to follow the foregoing depiction of the method of inquiry and of analysis with a detailed presentation of the results of the study. At the same time, it is important to give an overview of the results in order to indicate the kinds of returns made possible by this approach to research.

OVERVIEW OF THE RESULTS OF THE RESEARCH

Once the participants in this study were given an opportunity to describe freely what they recalled experiencing from moment-to-moment in an hour of therapy, they revealed an inner world of thinking and feeling that exceeded its representation in their actual discourse with the therapist. These reports indicated that, as would be expected, the clients' main interest was in focusing on themselves (see also Phillips, 1984). This was, after all, why they came to therapy. In this self-focus, they attended to whatever they were prepared to think about, which, in most instances, was something that was troubling. Once within this focus, they entered a path, or track, leading to their inner experience. Meanwhile, they were aware of the therapist. When their inner exploration was going smoothly, it was important for the therapist to be with them but not intrusively; otherwise, they had to deal with the therapist. Alternatively, when their inner quest was not going smoothly, it was important for the therapist to help them along the path. In either case, they often thought more than they revealed in the discourse.

When the process was going well, many thoughts were unspoken because the clients did not want to take time out to try to express them in words; furthermore, they often did not feel particularly obligated to express them because these were *their* thoughts, *their* therapy, and there was no particular reason why the therapist need know them. Alternatively, when the process was not going well, the clients harbored unspoken thoughts about the therapist and his or her approach to the therapy, and about the relationship with the therapist. They kept silent because, for a number of reasons, they felt deferential to the therapist and were loath to challenge or criticize.

Thus, the clients' reports revealed that they were much more active in their therapy than could be gleaned from an analysis of the discourse with the therapist. In this activity, as discourse analysts might expect, there was often a one-to-one correspondence between what the clients were thinking and what they were saying. However, there were also many moments when they thought about their own thoughts and chose to express some thoughts and not others, either for the sake of expediency or for the health of the relationship with the therapist.

Perhaps because the moments of inner deliberation were more salient than the moments of discourse that were not deliberated, in their reports the clients chose to address the former more than the latter. Consequently, in the grounded analysis, I conceptualized *clients' reflexivity* as the most pervasive, or *core,* category representing the client's experience of an hour of therapy. Expanding on its treatment in the literature on the philosophy of mind (e.g., Harré, 1984; Husserl, 1913/1976; Lawson, 1985; Mead, 1934/1962), I defined reflexivity as self-awareness and agency within it. This core category subsumes four main clusters of categories—client's relationship with personal meaning, client's perception of the relationship with the therapist, client's experience of the therapist's operations, and client's experience of outcomes. They subsume subclusters beneath which are a total of 51 categories. Elsewhere, the taxonomy is outlined in the context of the core category (Rennie, 1992) and various aspects of the taxonomy are presented (Rennie, 1990, 1992, 1994a, 1994b, in press).

We now turn to the final section of this chapter, which addresses the rhetoric involved in justifying claims to understanding arising from the grounded theory approach to research in general and my version of it in particular.

JUSTIFYING CLAIMS TO UNDERSTANDING

The early works by Glaser and Strauss that were the foundation of my approach to qualitative research gave a heady sense of freedom. In contrast to the "thick description" (Geertz, 1973) goal of psychological phenomenologists (see Giorgi, 1970; Polkinghorne, 1989), Glaser and Strauss were after theory—theory grounded in the phenomenon it addresses. As indicated elsewhere (Rennie, Phillips, & Quartaro, 1988), the emphasis of the grounded theory approach, at least in this period of its development, was on the generation of theory more than on verification. This is not to say that theory-verification was excluded by Glaser and Strauss from the mandate of the grounded theory approach.

In providing guidelines for staying grounded as an analyst, Glaser and Strauss evidently drew upon the notion of the phenomenological reduction put forward by Husserl (e.g., 1913/1976) and encouraged researchers to assume a naive attitude when addressing the phenomenon of interest. This attitude could be fostered, they suggested, by attempting to put aside biases and preconceptions; by not reading relevant literature about the phenomenon until the grounded analysis was completed; and by writing "theoretical memos," or a research journal, during the course of the analysis as a way of separating speculation from grounded contact with the phenomenon.

The justification for the approach thus rested on the principle of groundedness. Glaser and Strauss suggested in their early work that if theory resulting from the application of the method was grounded, then it would make sense to the reader and ring true. Furthermore, extensive illustration of the categories was not recommended; the theory had to make sense as a coherent whole, and examples were given for clarification, not justification. The important task was to develop good theory; verification was to come later, either at the hands of the primary investigator or at the hands of others.

A shift in position on the place of verification in grounded theory is found in Strauss (1987) and in Strauss and Corbin (1990). In these more recent monographs, Strauss suggests that grounded analysis is conceived best as a process of shifting back and forth between theory-generation and -verification during the analysis itself. He advocates that analysts actively raise hypotheses as to why the respondent gave a particular response, and that they use subsequent responses by the respondent as evidence in support of some hypotheses and against others until, by the end of the analysis, the model that is conceptualized has been verified internally.

This is a departure from the emphasis on theory-generation as opposed to theory-verification that marked the early works by Glaser and Strauss and that was the catechism guiding my analysis as well as that of many other investigators (Quartaro, 1993a). However, there is a debate going on that eases the feeling of being left behind by developments because, ironically, one side of the debate is in line with the original position taken by Glaser and Strauss: This is the debate on the logic of justification in qualitative research.

The Debate on the Logic of Justification in Qualitative Research

I have a rather chronic anxiety about the acceptability of my work by the community of mainstream psychotherapy process researchers. This anxiety is symbolized by a conversation with Clara Hill. She told me that she frequently cited a paper that I presented at a convention—a paper on clients' deference in the therapy relationship (Rennie, 1985b). She wondered why I had not published more. She suggested that I might try the *Journal of Counseling Psychology* (in which she played an editorial role), but gently pointed out that I would have better luck if I could demonstrate the validity of my categories (Hill, personal communication, November 1991).

Meanwhile, it has been suggested that a variety of validities are appropriate to qualitative research (Stiles, 1993), and criteria to aid reviewers in assessing the publishability of qualitative research have been proposed (Elliott, 1993). These developments are occurring in the context of debates about the commensurability of quantitative and qualitative research (e.g., Giorgi, 1988; Guba & Lincoln, 1982, 1989; Miles & Huberman, 1984; Smith & Heshusius, 1986). More broadly, polemics are maintained between what has been referred to as the "natural science" (see Makkreel, 1975/1992), "paradigmatic" (Bruner, 1986; Polkinghorne, 1988), "rationalist" (Mahoney, 1991), or "empirical foundationalist" (Gergen, 1988) approach to social science, on the one hand, and the "human science" (see Makkreel, 1975/1992), "narrative" (Bruner, 1986; Polkinghorne, 1988), "constructivist" (Mahoney, 1991), or "constructionist" (Gergen, 1985, 1988) approach, on the other hand.

Some have argued that quantitative and qualitative approaches are commensurable (e.g., Guba & Lincoln, 1982; Miles & Huberman, 1984). The rationale for this position is that in many respects the canons of the conduct of natural science can be applied to human science. This commensurability may be established through the application of procedures such as the triangulation of different types of data and the achievement of conventionally acceptable criteria of intersubjective agreement on categories, and so on.

The contrasting argument is that the two approaches are incommensurable because each draws upon a different logic of justification (Guba & Lincoln, 1989; Smith & Heshusius, 1986) or, more appropriately, rhetoric (Rennie, 1993; Russell, 1991; Weimer, 1979). It is held that the canons of natural science do not hold for human science. Instead, human science is an interpretive discipline conducted within particular social contexts dealing with a subject matter that in turn is contextualized. While it is the case that even in natural science "truth" is understood within the context of the intellectual climate of the time, the interpretive nature of human science places its credibility much more in the arena of social consensus. This is because both the "object" and the "instrument" of inquiry in human science is the subjectivity of human experience. Human science is thus about meaning, and any quest for objective truth that is independent of the subjectivity of the researcher is misplaced. Instead, the credibility of human science comes from the extent to which the meaning conveyed by the researcher is either shared by his or her audience (e.g., Smith & Heshusius, 1986) or receives endorsement from the audience on the strength of the researcher's rhetoric (Russell, 1991).

I continue to wrestle with the issues raised in this debate. I am siding with constructionism (Rennie, 1992, 1994, in press) but am not as sure of my ground as I would like. I wince when reminded by therapy researchers whom I respect that, when working alone, it is easy to miss some data and to misinterpret others. At the same time, I wonder if I could have done my analysis much differently even if I had desired it. Elliott points out that he uses multiple judges when generating categories, but then he analyzes single events in therapy—events represented by a few lines of text (e.g., Elliott, 1983; Elliott & Shapiro, 1992). My data set is much larger (see Rennie, 1992, for details). The analysis was conducted over a course of several years, and I lacked sufficient grant support to pay a companion analyst.

Nevertheless, there is a difference between validity and reliability, to use the language of natural science. While it would have been difficult to establish indices of interjudge agreement on the original category generation in my study, this did not preclude an investigation of the reliability of the categories. And indeed, succumbing to concern that I may have been overconfident in my belief that my use of my categories was basically sound, I instituted a series of studies on the reliability of my taxonomy (Kovac, 1990; Morris, 1992; Solish, 1989). I developed a manual of definitions of the categories (Rennie, 1989). Two judges received up to 25 hours of training in the use of the manual and then independently assigned categories to 15 MUs taken from the protocols of each of five clients. The task was to draw upon the taxonomy of 51 categories and to assign as many categories as seemed appropriate to each MU (the number of categories that I had assigned to the same MUs, in my original analysis, ranged from 1 to 11, with the average being around 3 or 4).

The two assistants and I thus made up a trio of judges who had made their judgments independently: My judgments had been made during the analysis itself, while those of the two research assistants were made after being trained on the manual. The three sets of judgments were compared in the three combinations. In the most recent study (Morris, 1992), we found that the agreement ranged from 51% to 57% and the corresponding Cohen's *kappas* from .49 to .56. The fact that in this analysis multiple categories were assigned to the same MUs doubtless violated the assumption of independence of entries underlying the statistic. Nevertheless, if we can put that reservation aside, the z values associated with these *kappas* were from 51.0 to 55.7 (a z score of 5.3 is significant at the $p < .000005$ level).

I do not know what to do with this finding for two reasons. First, I do not know how to interpret it in its own right. In studies of interjudge agreement on categories, the convention is to look for *kappas* of .80 or so (Stiles, 1993). However, such studies always involve taxonomies with far fewer categories than those making up the present taxonomy. It seems to me that to get *kappas* of .49 or more when judges assigned multiple categories drawn from a 51-category set is impressive, but to win the day would perhaps require the establishment of a new standard of acceptable reliability in the use of complex taxonomies.

This is not my main difficulty, however: I am not sure that I want to do anything with the finding (and for this reason have not attempted to get the answer to the first question). I feel that proclaiming my findings would be tantamount to a decision that I accept the Miles and Huberman type of position on the rhetoric of human science. Like Smith and Heshusius, I prefer to *keep the conversation open* (Rennie, 1993). In supporting my claims to understanding made from my study thus far, I have used as rhetoric descriptions of the phenomena conceptualized in the light of the grounded analysis and supported by illustration. I cannot feel confident that the credibility of claims to understanding is necessarily improved by demonstrating that the research fulfills the canons of natural science. Furthermore, I worry that if such a decision contributed to the development of the standards for human science, then it could serve to shut down the inquiry into complex phenomena involving large data sets—the type of inquiry for which human science is so aptly suited within its rhetoric.

CONCLUSION

This chapter has described choices among strategies in the application of the grounded theory method to psychotherapy research. It has also disclosed my struggle to find my position in the debate on paradigm choices and the place of qualitative research, or, more broadly, human science. In taking stock of these two themes, it is difficult to be objective. The strategies once applied have involved a lot of work and commitment. Thus, that I resist a radical alteration of them is perhaps to be expected. Nevertheless, putting that aside, as I enter the phase of writing up the returns from the study, I do find that the strategies have provided a base of information that is both rich and easy to use. As indicated, while recognizing that an alternative workable base might have been created through an alternative set of strategies, it is gratifying to discover that my base has proved functional.

As for the rhetoric of claims to understanding arising from the method, I suspect that my present difficulty in feeling totally committed to constructionism, even though that is where my "heart" is, has more to do with the sociology of social science as practiced in psychotherapy research than with a more fundamental conflict about the right way to go. In psychotherapy research, and most areas of research in psychology, the natural science approach to method is still the norm. As a constructionist, one has the feeling that one is knocking on the door of the pale, asking to be admitted. The appeal of the natural science side of the debate is that it promises to facilitate admittance. Nevertheless, when I manage to quiet the feelings arising from the struggle for social acceptability, I conclude that adopting the canons of natural science to facilitate the acceptability of human science would be a bad bargain. It would reduce the benefit to the discipline that constructionism can offer when based on systematic strategies of inquiry and analysis.

The author wishes to express his thanks to Robert Elliott, Gary Johnston, and Georgia Quartaro for commenting on an earlier draft.

REFERENCES

Angus, L. E., & Rennie, D. L. (1989). Envisioning the representational world: The client's experience of metaphoric expressiveness in therapy. *Psychotherapy, 26*, 373–379.

Bordin, E. (1979). The generalizability of the psychoanalytic concept of the working alliance. *Psychotherapy: Theory, Research, and Practice, 16*, 252–260.

Bruner, J. (1986). *Actual minds, possible worlds.* Cambridge, MA: Harvard University Press.
Campbell, D. T., & Stanley, J. C. (1966). *Experimental and quasi-experimental designs for research.* Chicago: Rand McNally.
Dolhanty, J. (1990). *The urge to overeat: A qualitative analysis of personal accounts.* Unpublished master's thesis, York University, North York, Ontario.
Elliott, R. (1983). "That in your hands . . . ": A comprehensive process analysis of a single event in psychotherapy. *Psychiatry, 46,* 113–129.
Elliott, R. (1986). Interpersonal process recall (IPR) as a process research method. In L. S. Greenberg & W. M. Pinsof (Eds.), *The psychotherapeutic process: A research handbook* (pp. 503–527). New York: Guilford.
Elliott, R. (1993, June). Criteria for reviewing qualitative research manuscripts. In R. Elliott (Chair), *Proposed criteria for reviewing qualitative psychotherapy research: Empowerment or premature closure?* Panel conducted at the annual meeting of the International Society for Psychotherapy Research, Pittsburgh.
Elliott, R., & James, E. (1989). Varieties of client experience in psychotherapy. *Clinical Psychology Review, 9,* 443–467.
Elliott, R., & Shapiro, D. A. (1992). Client and therapist as analysts of significant events. In S. G. Toukmanian & D. L. Rennie (Eds.), *Psychotherapy process research: Paradigmatic and narrative approaches* (pp. 163–186). Newbury Park, CA: Sage.
Geertz, C. (1973). *Interpretation of cultures.* New York: Basic Books.
Gergen, K. J. (1985). The social constructionist movement in modern psychology. *American Psychologist, 40,* 266–275.
Gergen, K. J. (1988, August). *Toward a post-modern psychology.* Paper presented at the International Congress of Psychology, Sidney, Australia.
Giorgi, A. (1970). *Psychology as a human science: A phenomenologically based approach.* New York: Harper & Row.
Giorgi, A. (1988). Validity and reliability from a phenomenological perspective. In W. Baker, L. Mos, H. Rappard, & H. Stam (Eds.), *Recent trends in theoretical psychology* (pp. 167–176). New York: Springer-Verlag.
Glaser, B. G. (1978). *Theoretical sensitivity: Advances in the methodology of grounded theory.* Mill Valley, CA: Sociology Press.
Glaser, B. G., & Strauss, A. (1967). *The discovery of grounded theory: Strategies for qualitative research.* Chicago: Aldine.
Greenson, R. (1967). *The technique and practice of psychoanalysis.* New York: International Universities Press.
Guba, E., & Lincoln, Y. (1982). Epistemological and methodological bases of naturalistic inquiry. *Educational and Communication Technology Journal, 30,* 233–252.
Guba, E., & Lincoln. Y. (1989). *Fourth generation evaluation.* Newbury Park, CA: Sage.
Harré, R. (1984). *Personal being: A theory for individual psychology.* Cambridge, MA: Harvard University Press.
Husserl, E. (1976). *Ideas: General introduction to pure phenomenology* (W. R. Boyce Gibson, Trans.). New York: Humanities Press. (Original work published 1913)

Johnston, G. (1994). *Structured vs. unstructured group therapy in partial hospitalization: The client's subjective experience over time.* Doctoral dissertation in progress, York University, North York, Ontario.

Kagan, N. (1975). *Interpersonal process recall: A method of influencing human action.* East Lansing: Michigan State University.

Kovac, V. (1990). *Combining the qualitative and quantitative research paradigms: A case study.* Unpublished honours BA thesis, York University, North York, Ontario.

Lawson, H. (1985). *Reflexivity: A post-modern predicament.* La Salle, IL: Open Court.

Mahoney, M. J. (1991). *Human change processes: The scientific foundations of psychotherapy.* New York: Basic Books.

Mainwaring, L. (1992). *The psychological response of athletes to sport-related knee injury rehabilitation.* Unpublished doctoral dissertation, York University, North York, Ontario.

Makkreel, R. A. (1992). *Dilthey: Philosopher of the human studies.* Princeton: Princeton University Press. (Original work published 1975)

Martin, J., & Stelmaczonek, K. (1988). Participants' identification and recall of important events in counseling. *Journal of Counseling Psychology, 35,* 385–390.

McLeod, J. (1990). The client's experience of counselling and psychotherapy. In D. Mearns & W. Dryden (Eds.), *Experiences of counselling in action* (pp. 1–19). London: Sage.

Mead, G. H. (1962). *Mind, self, and society* (C. W. Morris, Ed.). Chicago: University of Chicago Press. (Original work published 1934)

Miles, M., & Huberman, M. (1984). Drawing valid meaning from qualitative data: Toward a shared craft. *Educational Researcher, 13,* 20–30.

Morris, R. (1992). *Exploring the borderland between paradigmatic and narrative explanation.* Unpublished honours BA thesis, North York, Ontario.

Phillips, J. R. (1984). Influences on personal growth as viewed by former psychotherapy patients. *Dissertation Abstracts International, 46,* 2820B.

Polkinghorne, D. E. (1988). *Narrative knowing and the human sciences: Systems of inquiry.* Albany: State University of New York Press.

Polkinghorne, D. E. (1989). Phenomenological research methods. In R. Valle & S. Halling (Eds.), *Existential-phenomenological perspectives in psychology: Exploring the depth of human experience* (pp. 41–60). New York: Plenum.

Quartaro, G. K. (1993a). *Seeds on the wind: A review of Glaser and Strauss' grounded theory method as implemented by other researchers.* Unpublished manuscript, York University, North York, Ontario.

Quartaro, G. K. (1993b). *The use of self help books: A grounded theory approach.* Unpublished doctoral dissertation, York University, North York, Ontario.

Rennie, D. L. (1985a, February). *An early return from interviews with clients about their therapy interviews: The functions of the narrative.* Paper presented at the annual meeting of the Ontario Psychological Association, Ottawa.

Rennie, D. L. (1985b, June). Client deference in the psychotherapy relationship. In D. Rennie (Chair), *The client's phenomenological experience of psychotherapy.*

Panel conducted at the annual meeting of the International Society for Psychotherapy Research, Evanston, IL.
Rennie, D. L. (1989). *Taxonomy of the client's experience of psychotherapy.* Unpublished manual, York University, North York, Ontario.
Rennie, D. L. (1990). Toward a representation of the client's experience of the psychotherapy hour. In G. Lietaer, J. Rombauts, & R. Van Balen (Eds.), *Client centered and experiential therapy in the nineties* (pp. 155–172). Leuven, Belgium: Leuven University Press.
Rennie, D. L. (1992). Qualitative analysis of the client's experience of psychotherapy: The unfolding of reflexivity. In S. G. Toukmanian & D. L. Rennie (Eds.), *Psychotherapy process research: Paradigmatic and narrative approaches* (pp. 211–233). Newbury Park, CA: Sage.
Rennie, D. L. (1993, June). Homage to Smith and Heshusius: Let's keep the conversation open. In R. Elliott (Chair), *Proposed criteria for reviewing qualitative psychotherapy research: Empowerment or premature closure?* Panel conducted at the annual meeting of the International Society for Psychotherapy Research, Pittsburgh.
Rennie, D. L. (1994a). Clients' accounts of resistance in counselling: A qualitative analysis. *Canadian Journal of Counselling, 28,* 43–57.
Rennie, D. L. (1994b). Storytelling in psychotherapy: The client's subjective experience. *Psychotherapy, 31,* 234–243.
Rennie, D. L. (in press). Clients' deference in psychotherapy. *Journal of Counseling Psychology.*
Rennie, D L., & Brewer, L. (1987). A grounded theory of thesis blocking. *Teaching of Psychology, 14,* 10–16.
Rennie, D. L., Brewster, L., & Toukmanian, S. G. (1985). The trainee as client: Client process measures as predictors of counselling skill acquisition. *Canadian Journal of Behavioural Science, 17,* 16–28.
Rennie, D. L., Phillips, J. R., & Quartaro, G. K. (1988). Grounded theory: A promising approach to conceptualization in psychology? *Canadian Psychology, 29,* 139–150.
Rennie, D. L., & Toukmanian, S. G. (1992). Explanations in psychotherapy process research. In S. G. Toukmanian & D. L. Rennie (Eds.), *Psychotherapy process research: Paradigmatic and narrative approaches* (pp. 234–251). Newbury Park, CA: Sage.
Rice, L. N., & Saperia, E. P. (1984). Task analysis of the resolution of problematic reactions. In L. N. Rice & L. S. Greenberg (Eds.), *Patterns of change: Intensive analysis of psychotherapy process* (pp. 29–66). New York: Guilford.
Rogers, C. R. (1957). The necessary and sufficient conditions of therapeutic personality change. *Journal of Consulting Psychology, 21,* 95–103.
Rogers, C. R., Gendlin, E. T., Kiesler, D., & Truax, C. B. (1967). *The therapeutic relationship and its impact: A study of psychotherapy with schizophrenics.* Madison: University of Wisconsin Press.
Russell, R. (1991, October). *The context of discovery versus the context of justification: Deconstructing a mythic dualism.* Paper presented at the annual meeting of

the North American Chapter of the International Society for Psychotherapy Research, Panama City, FL.

Shaul, A. (1993). *Therapist's symbolic visual imagery: A key to empathic understanding.* Unpublished doctoral dissertation, York University, North York, Ontario.

Smith, J. K., & Heshusius, L. (1986). Closing down the conversation: The end of the qualitative–quantitative debate among educational inquirers. *Educational Researcher, 15,* 4–12.

Solish, A. (1989). *Intersubjective credibility of a taxonomy derived from a grounded theory analysis.* Unpublished honours BA thesis, York University, North York, Ontario.

Spence, D. P. (1986). Narrative smoothing and clinical wisdom. In T. Sarbin (Ed.), *Narrative psychology: The storied nature of human conduct* (pp. 211–232). New York: Praeger.

Stiles, W. B. (1993). Quality control in qualitative research. *Clinical Psychology Review, 13,* 593–618.

Strauss, A. (1987). *Qualitative analysis for social scientists.* New York: Cambridge University Press.

Strauss, A., & Corbin, J. (1990). *Basics of qualitative research: Grounded theory procedures and techniques.* Newbury Park, CA: Sage.

Turner, B. (1981). Some practical aspects of qualitative data analysis: One way of organizing the cognitive process associated with the generation of grounded theory. *Quality and Quantity, 15,* 225–247.

Watson, J. C., & Rennie, D. L. (in press). Through the looking glass: Analyzing clients' reflections of change to illuminate their cognitive-affective processes in psychotherapy. *Journal of Counseling Psychology.*

Weimer, W. B. (1979). *Notes on the methodology of scientific research.* Hillsdale, NJ: Lawrence Erlbaum.

PART III

Toward a Model of Knowledge for Research on Practice

CHAPTER 10

Summary and Analysis

LISA T. HOSHMAND AND JACK MARTIN

This project has grown since it was originally conceived. Our intentions became more clear as we reflected on our communications with each other and the contributing authors. We discovered new ways of looking at the efforts of our colleagues and our own. It is perhaps in the nature of human endeavors that our purposes and understandings would change with experience and reflection. What was intended as an analysis of method choice and inquiry process in research programs became a process of learning at several levels. We found ourselves searching for common criteria and frames of reference among all participants, against which to articulate our own values and perspectives. We were frustrated with the inevitable incompleteness of dialogue and the social inhibitions on the type of interaction that would lend itself to a genuine meeting of the minds. We became sensitive of the fact that we are inadvertently evaluating individual research careers, in a profession that pays attention to published research as its tally of achievements. We were drawn to the human drama conjured up by each story that was told, and humbled by the sensibilities that one must develop as fellow travelers on the same journey. In the end, we asked ourselves to critique our own assumptions and reactions, in the hope of being at peace with the nature of our responsibilities.

The summary and analysis that follow represent our present interpretations of the researchers' accounts given in Part II of this book. These conclusions are the result of extensive dialogue on our respective interpretive stances and the counterposing of narrative and analytical modes of understanding. We have asked the researchers to react to our analysis of their accounts in their postscripts. We also invite readers to derive their own interpretations and to critique ours. It is our hope that a continuation of dialogue will occur, and that personal as well as collective purposes will be served.

COMMONALITIES IN THE RESEARCHERS' ACCOUNTS

It appears that all of the researchers have undergone some changes in their orientation to inquiry. Part of the observable change consists in learning to apply different means to answering research questions and solving conceptual or methodological problems. This is an area on which we shall comment further in a subsequent consideration of the heuristics of method choice. While the six examples represent considerable methodological diversity, the movement in each toward the choice of new methods and strategies has been gradual and halting. In the cases of Martin, Hill, Howard, and to a certain extent Friedlander, there has been a lag between the apparent shift to an alternative epistemological or ontological perspective and the actual use of alternative methods consistent with such perspectives. In the cases of Rennie, McMullen, and also Friedlander, the lag appears to have been between the use of new methods and the development of procedures and processes of consensus for justifying their use. Altogether, our researchers' experience of paradigm and method change suggests that researchers in therapeutic psychology may be undergoing a gradual evolution of their praxis, and that the process is probably mediated by personal circumstances and other factors in one's professional environment.

Another common theme we infer is that every researcher has experienced moments of uncertainty and/or dissonance between personal epistemology or beliefs and the prevailing methodology or ideology of the profession. Hill acknowledged her earlier doubts in 1984 on research methodology for the study of counseling process. McMullen reported experiencing tensions between competing epistemological beliefs and values, as well as recurrent changes in her confidence in theory-driven and discovery-oriented strategies. Martin described a private interest in the cognitive paradigm while following a behavioristic emphasis in the early part of his research career. Friedlander expressed doubts about the practice relevance of her research yields in spite of her active contributions to the body of research on practice. Rennie relayed his disenchantment with traditional research methodology and, at the same time, continuing doubts about being accepted by the profession in his use of qualitative research methods. In their more recent work, Martin, Friedlander, and Rennie are faced with the epistemological problems of applying constructionist conceptions of therapeutic phenomena and human inquiry. Howard exemplified a challenge to the ontological assumptions of deterministic science and a dissatisfaction with the lack of prior efforts by psychological researchers in demonstrating the presence of human agency. To different degrees, each of the contributing authors seems to struggle with issues of personal faith in the prevailing ideology and practices of scientific psychology. While this also is true for ourselves, we are uncertain as to how far we should go in speculating on the personal dilemmas and private beliefs of our colleagues.

The various accounts share common features of professional rhetoric. Arguments are put forth to convince the reader (and perhaps oneself as well) of the rationale and appropriateness of the inquiry conducted. This is especially clear in the accounts given by Howard and Rennie. Through persuasive prose, the reader is asked to follow the thinking process and actions of the researcher in solving the problem at hand and to agree with the standards applied in judging the success of such efforts. In the case of Rennie, the researcher's task seems arduous by virtue of the fact that the standards of acceptability for qualitative methods are less clear than those of more commonly used methods. The described methodological approaches in all the accounts can be regarded as rhetorical devices in justifying the knowledge claimed. Every researcher depends to some extent on certain shared understandings with the reader regarding the philosophical assumptions and practical implications in the use of particular procedures. This is supplemented by explicit efforts in educating the reader about the logic-in-use in the inquiry. In following the methodological reasoning of Friedlander, for instance, one develops a clear notion of the next logical step in her investigation.

Against the common patterns that we have identified are various types of individual characteristics. These differences are broadly conceived as prototypes.

PROTOTYPES OF APPLIED EPISTEMOLOGY

If we were to use the researchers' accounts as a reflection and reconstruction of their epistemologies in action, it is possible to identify several distinct patterns. These patterns seem to be associated with interactions between particular ontological, ideological, or methodological commitments and the substantive and epistemic questions addressed. We conjecture that the type of issue with which each researcher wrestles, and the domain(s) from which a research path originates and to which it returns, are a function of the philosophical stances and professional interests represented. Furthermore, as proposed in Chapter 1, differences in epistemic style among researchers may be manifested in the type of criteria or warrants used, as well as the methods preferred. We also can discern different voices in the accounts given, depending on the role each person seems to adopt. These voices probably represent different kinds of knowledge interests, with particular constituencies. Each prototype identified here is probably recognizable as an existing role model for students and fellow researchers.

Hill's research program on therapist techniques reflects a realist, reductionistic approach. The choice of the units of analysis essentially has been measurement-driven and guided by the procedural requirements of operationalization. Instruments of observation and self-report measures were used as the tools of access to the phenomena of interest and to set the research agenda. Her approach is largely inductive in that empirical regularities are taken as a basis of scientific understanding. In extending her methodology from experimental analogues to case study designs and naturalistic observation, she has shifted to a more contextualist conception of therapist techniques. Although Hill has referred in her writing to the role of intentions and covert processes in mediating the effects of therapist interventions, her apparent epistemological and methodological stance has confined her investigation of these variables to the documentation of essentially linear patterns of association, albeit with exacting instantiations of her own design. Like many researchers in the field, for much of her career she has maintained a dedicated program of research by applying the standard methodology of the profession to those questions that can be addressed with it. Her final message is that new methods are needed to enable us to conduct research on the multiple dimensions of therapist techniques and further to understand other variables from which therapist techniques cannot be dissociated. In pushing her own methodological and epistemological commitments to their limits, Hill, through her pioneering work, has opened the field to investigation by fellow researchers with similar as well as different philosophical and methodological commitments.

Martin's research program is an example of hypothetico-deductive research in which ontological assumptions about the focal phenomenon are translated into a conceptual model of practice that is tested empirically. The inquiry originates from the ontological domain and always returns to a reconceptualization of the substantive domain. Research questions are framed according to an evolving understanding informed by data. By posing these questions and continuously refining the conceptual model based on substantive findings to each cycle of questions, a working model is being developed. The agenda here is one of theory-building. There is an interest in the causal mechanisms of therapeutic change and in understanding the interaction of therapist and client factors in the naturalistic context of practice. The conceptual yield of each study seems to sustain the continuing inquiry. The fact that ecological validity is empha-

Summary and Analysis 227

sized would seem to qualify Martin's efforts as generating theoretical knowledge of local relevance.

Howard's research consists of a sustained effort in demonstrating the presence of personal agency as a factor in human action. This ontological assumption of free will is manifested in a soft determinism that he chose to verify with the experimental paradigm by ruling out total determinism by external factors. Whereas one might have expected Howard's methodological practice to follow from his ontological position, it is characterized instead by the very methodological orientation that is typically associated with a mechanistic and behavioristic perspective. His work suggests that an ontology of human free will is not necessarily incompatible with experimental methodology. The research questions are framed according to the ontological assumptions of human agential control and are tested with the experimental paradigm. At the same time, this ideological agenda and choice of strategy seem to have placed constraints on the conceptual flexibility that might have been afforded by other methodological approaches. Within the chosen experimental protocol, Howard's work provides many examples of creative problem solving, such as combining the roles of experimenter and subject, or allowing subjects to engage in external conditions outside of the explicit awareness of the experimenter. The standard tools of experimental research are effectively used as rhetorical devices.

McMullen's research illustrates the use of both a descriptive, discovery-oriented strategy and a theory-testing strategy, within the realm of multiple case studies. Like Friedlander, Hill, and Martin, who have found it necessary at certain points to first develop a descriptive understanding of the phenomenon of interest before returning to theory-testing, she has put considerable effort into the discovery phase of her work. To complement this approach, she also has found it appropriate to draw upon existing conceptual models and to apply a more standard experimental paradigm. This shift has coincided with a change in focus from the specific phenomenon of metaphoric language to a more general interpersonal theory. The character of McMullen's research program seems to be a function of her own developmental process as a researcher, as well as the relatively undefined nature of her domain of interest. She has clearly identified the enduring influences of her original training and how her own reflections on method choice have paralleled the increasing sophistication of research in her substantive area of interest. Her research strategies, while always thoughtfully constructed and carefully implemented, appear to be tentative, awaiting further development.

Like McMullen's, Friedlander's research also reflects the challenges of investigating language phenomena in therapy. A pluralistic approach is demonstrated, with a flexible use of descriptive, case study strategies and focal hypothesis-testing and modeling. There is close attention to measurement issues, reflecting a similar methodological heritage to Hill's. The systemic nature of Friedlander's domain of interest, namely, family therapy, has posed additional challenges at the conceptual and methodological levels. Methods have to be developed that are consistent with a system's ontology and capable of generating clinically meaningful data. In common with Martin, Friedlander appears to be interested in refining theoretical formulations to match the substantive domain. Questions continue to spring from an unfailing curiosity about the unfolding phenomena. For her, the questioning always returns to the practice domain. She evaluates the conceptual yield of her research by its local relevance to practitioners. Her problem solving reflects the wisdom gained from extended experience in psychotherapy research and practice. Her research program is faithful to both theory and practice.

Rennie's account of his work has focused on the epistemic and ethical problems encountered in the type of phenomenological inquiry he has conducted. For him, substantive questions, such as clients' experience of therapy, represent only one of several types of problems that a psychotherapy researcher should be concerned with. Like Friedlander's, Rennie's approach reflects the seasoned experience of a therapist, trainer, and psychotherapy researcher. Consistent with the interpretive tradition, he gives appropriate attention to his own involvement in the process of data gathering and data analysis. His personal view of criteria and warrants allows for more intuitiveness and subjectivity than most of the other researchers whose works are featured here. Foremost in the criteria for choosing method and approach is experience-nearness. The reflections in Rennie's account are highly reflexive. At the same time, they are never disengaged from the professional contexts in which he struggles with issues of generativity, credibility, and responsibility. Rennie's research program exemplifies the challenges and accomplishments of a qualitative researcher. He has effectively demonstrated how qualitative inquiry can be systematic and disciplined, how one should be faithful to the focal phenomenon as presented in text, and what we may gain from a genuine collaboration with informants. Serving as a conscientious voice of the uncertainties of human science practice as an alternative to traditional science, he models an openness to continuing dialogue about the basis of all epistemic claims.

Our researchers have spoken with voices that represent particular interests. As a trainer of counseling psychologists, Hill shows an interest in understanding therapist techniques for the purpose of teaching students how to conduct therapy. The trainer's interest and the practitioner's voice are found in McMullen's and Friedlander's accounts. The conceptual and instrumental yield of research for practice seem clearly important to them. As suggested above, Howard and Rennie appear to speak with the voice of an ideologue, on behalf of humanistic beliefs in free will and human science methodology, respectively. Finally, Martin's account of model building reflects the interests of a theoretical researcher. In this case, research serves to inform our ontological model of human functioning as manifested in therapeutic practice. These characterizations are to be qualified, of course, by the author's self-identification and comments in the postscripts to their chapters. It is understood that all of the researchers have theoretical and practice-related interests, and have tried to write in a teaching voice for the benefit of students and fellow researchers.

Our assumption is that the various kinds of interest voiced, and the types of research practice modeled, have their respective constituencies. Research on psychotherapeutic practice can serve the interests of theory, ideology, training, and practice. These respective interests may have differential appeal to members of the profession and the public that we serve. Method choices reflect different philosophical commitments and epistemic styles, as well as learned attitudes and repertoires. Each type of choice has its following. Furthermore, as foreshadowed by our discussion in Chapter 3, there are diverse positions on, and approaches to, the various issues encountered in research on psychotherapeutic and other human practices. Those persuaded by a given position would tend to agree with the corresponding approach adopted. We may think of each mode of research practice and its constituency as a subculture, particularly within academic circles. It is possible that membership in each subculture involves certain recognition and security that, in time, become intrinsically rewarding. What may be at stake in questioning or abandoning a given mode of research practice may include not only the particular professional interest and public interest concerned, but certain personal interests as well.

THE HEURISTICS OF METHOD CHOICE

The pragmatist frame directs our attention to the nature of problem selection and problem solving in the researchers' work. The reader may recall the depiction of research paths given in Figure 2.2 of Chapter 2. Among our group of researchers, we found considerable variation in the starting point of inquiry and the type of questions that seem to engage each researcher's efforts. For example, Friedlander's problem finding seems to have originated from the context of practice, and her problem solving typically begins with an effort to conceptualize the focal phenomenon in the interest of practice. A range of methodological tools and research designs are employed in the process, with continuing inquiry guided by data, theory, and measurement possibilities. In the case of Rennie, the problems that appear to have been in the foreground consist of second-order epistemic questions and ethical questions. Problem solving has included conducting reliability studies, developing an elaborate procedural protocol for verification of interpretations, deriving an empirical understanding of the ethical implications of the research, and asking clients to control which part of the tape to focus on. He has utilized intersubjective processes while continuing to reflexively question the co-constructive approach and the wisdom of applying traditional standards to complex co-constructive processes of interpretation.

At other times, researchers may begin with ontologically based conceptual problems and focus on demonstrating the fit of their conceptual frame with the substantive domain. The work of Howard and Martin are similar in this respect, but the method choices involved in their problem solving differ. Howard has chosen to demonstrate human agency with the experimental paradigm and to solve the problems he has encountered by working within the same paradigm. Each of his studies seems designed to build the case in a workman-like series of demonstrations. To counter criticisms that the subjects might be showing experimenter-pleasing behavior rather than actual free choice, he rules out rival explanations by such means as arranging for the participants to engage in external experimental conditions outside of the awareness of the experimenter. By contrast, Martin's conceptual puzzle solving in the face of new data has involved extending his methodological strategies to discovery and hermeneutic alternatives, and revising his working model. As tight determinism gives way to more complex conceptions, methods and designs are continually adjusted. The divergence in method choice between Howard and Martin cannot be explained on heuristic grounds alone, as both have been systematic in following a pragmatic logic of problem solving.

It also may be the case that researchers will choose to engage in problem solving of a certain type and not others, either because of the constraints of their preferred paradigm or because of what they regard as personally interesting. Hill's research questions reflect an interest in inductive problems of categorization and measurement, using more or less standard methodological assumptions and methods, albeit with exacting psychotherapeutic instantiations of her own design. McMullen's shifts in

Summary and Analysis

problem focus and concomitant conceptual and methodological strategies suggest the personal influence of collaborating colleagues on her research direction. It is probably unrealistic to expect every researcher to give equal attention and energy to problems of a conceptual-ontological and epistemic nature, and problems framed as substantive or practice-oriented in nature.

On the other hand, we should expect a research program that follows a heuristic logic to reflect the application of criteria and warrants appropriate to a particular stage of inquiry. As discussed in Chapter 2, beyond making initial judgments about the usefulness of their conceptual categories, researchers subsequently should be concerned with the interrelatedness and correspondence among elements and networks of relationships from more than one domain. In other words, inductive empirical inquiry ideally should give way to reconceptualization and ontological deduction, in a dialectical interplay. Furthermore, as a program of research progresses to a mature stage of development, one cannot escape from questions about generalization validities or boundary search for the limits of one's findings. These problems and concerns experienced by the present group of investigators may serve as developmental indicators of their research programs.

In general, our researchers have demonstrated problem-solving wisdom where heuristic reasoning is evident. Changes in research strategy or methods have been determined by the needs of the task at hand. For example, when there is insufficient descriptive understanding of a phenomenon, focal hypothesis-testing is postponed and a descriptive strategy is used. This flexibility is consistent with the view that method choice should be adapted to context and that certain methods and strategies are more appropriate than others for certain uses and at certain times. It would seem that the learning reported by our researchers—from how to conduct skillful interviewing so as to mitigate researcher bias, to knowing when to trust one's native ability to organize meaning units that involve larger categories than would have been the case with reductionistic analysis—adds to practical wisdom. This kind of knowledge derived from the experience of research practice is probably an integral part of the personal knowing that guides researchers in their work. Much has been said in our profession about the reciprocal influence of research and practice. The present accounts of research programs also illustrate how research decisions were guided by clinical sense or experience of therapeutic practice. In such instances, the meta-reasoning applied seemed to be informed equally by the particular research context and the researcher's personal knowledge of practice.

ALTERNATIVE FRAMES AND THE LIMITS OF METHOD

We have viewed the work of our colleagues from the standpoint of method choice and the interaction among ontological, epistemological, and ideological commitments in shaping research programs. This is our particular window on research practice in therapeutic psychology. We have also considered alternative interpretive frames to the purely heuristic one, as permitted by the information available. It has become clear in the process that we cannot approach the question of method choice without considering the overall personal and professional context of each researcher. Our researchers generally acknowledge the professional influences and personal circumstances that have contributed to the development of their research programs. The sociology of their work environment and the zeitgeist of the profession are background factors to be considered. Practical constraints of time and resources have been noted in some cases, as have ethical considerations.

What can we say about the psychology of each researcher as constructed from their personal accounts? Our understanding is limited to the extent that we have only partial accounts and incomplete dialogue with our colleagues. We have commented on the uncertainty and learning process that our researchers seem to have experienced. Their apparent methodological and ontological stances do seem to point to different epistemic styles. Their inquiry approaches range from the behavioristic and reductionistic to the phenomenological and contextualist, and from the measurement-driven to the theory-driven. While there is diversity of method within each research program, the degree of pluralism has differed. To varying degrees our researchers seem to have been bound by their original training, and to varying degrees they have been influenced by alternative methodological perspectives.

Our pragmatist analysis requires a focus on the meta-reasoning followed by each researcher and the type of heuristic problem solving demonstrated. The clarity of the meta-reasoning involved seems to vary. Perhaps partly due to how it is communicated, the researcher's meta-reasoning is easier to discern in some cases than others. As analyzed above, there is heuristic problem solving in all cases. However, the problems are not all of a substantive nature. Some researchers have emphasized ontological/conceptual problems, and others, epistemic and ideological problems. The intensity of their quest is as evident as the diversity of their apparent intentions. This leads us to believe that research programs can be based on different kinds of meta-goals, and that these meta-goals reflect particular personal motives and thematic issues in one's career. A contrast was made earlier between Howard's single-paradigm approach and Martin's multiple-paradigm approach to heuristic problem solving. The respective method choices here may be understood more fully in terms of the apparent meta-goal of each researcher. Howard's personal agenda is revealed by his comments about William James and the unfulfilled empirical mission of humanistic psychology in support of the belief in free will, in an historical period when experimental methodology reigns. His choice of the experimental paradigm would seem to serve this ideological agenda of setting history right. Martin's stated agenda is theory-building in the therapeutic domain, a domain that has not been researched satisfactorily with any single conceptual or methodological strategy. His meta-goal demands the kind of conceptual and methodological flexibility made possible by pluralistic paradigm choices.

Whether the applied epistemology of each researcher is consistent with his or her expressed rationale and professional stance remains somewhat in question. Given our observation of struggles with personal doubts and apparent discrepancy or lag between private and formal commitments of either an ontological or a methodological nature, we will have to conclude that applied epistemology may not always be consistent with one's formal stances or private beliefs. Another way of interpreting this less than tidy picture is to revise our definition of applied epistemology, from one that is based solely on cognitive epistemic criteria to a broadly pragmatic conception of knowledge as serving both epistemic and non-epistemic ends. The constructionist in us can readily see our researchers' accounts as biographical sketches, and their work as evolving identity projects mostly in a mid-life and mid-career context. We do not pretend to fully understand the purposes and values that inform these accounts and projects. Each of us has limited access to the others' personal mythologies, at least in the types of relationships that have shaped our current interpretations.

Like our researchers who have attempted to study therapists' beliefs and intentions, we are faced with similar problems of understanding. Do we depend on the researchers' own accounts? Should we focus mainly on their actions and research practice? Can we reconcile discrepancies through dialogue? Will expressed beliefs and intentions illuminate actions and inform us as to the nature of actual practice? Can we assume that the researchers' constructed accounts of their work represent the same cognitive schemata that they are likely to bring to their continuing research? We are no less constrained by the limits of our own method than are the researchers whose work we have tried to understand. In the end, the reader will have to judge the coherence of our meta-narratives and analyses, and to consider what may be the most viable approach to understanding researchers' beliefs and intentions, if the latter are assumed to be an important aspect of their research practice and epistemology-in-action. Our exploratory efforts suggest that the naturalized study of research practice should be based on a comprehensive understanding of the psychology of the researcher that includes beliefs, intentions, as well as actions in their personal and historical contexts. Furthermore, this understanding should be informed by an awareness of the nature of rhetoric and scientific ideology in the profession. To the extent that we can involve our colleagues in a reflexive conversation about, and continuing deconstruction of, our personal and professional beliefs, we may be a little closer to understanding the nature of our knowledge enterprise.

CHAPTER 11

Concluding Comments on Therapeutic Psychology and the Science of Practice

LISA T. HOSHMAND AND JACK MARTIN

THEMATIC ISSUES IN RESEARCH ON THERAPEUTIC PRACTICE

In choosing to conduct our project in the area of research on therapeutic practice, we have hoped to illustrate some of the thematic issues of inquiry in the human domain. The accounts in Part II of this volume are replete with examples of how ontological, epistemological, and axiological considerations interact in entering into the manner in which a given study is carried out and a research program develops. One may revisit some of the issues raised in Chapter 3 by recalling a few examples from the researchers' accounts.

With respect to the issue of rigor versus relevance, the researchers have made different choices. Friedlander, Hill, and Martin seem to have opted, at least in major portions of their research programs, for a combination of ecologically valid (high relevance) and quasi-experimental, sometimes post hoc, designs and analytical strategies. Additional attempts at safeguarding rigor in these programs are reflected in these researchers' development and attempted validation of rather exacting measures of therapeutic responding and processing, with known psychometric properties. Other researchers, like McMullen and Rennie, seem, for the most part, to have opted for generally high levels of ecological validity and relevance in their adoption of more consistently idiographic, qualitative methodologies. The rigor of their work derives from the depth and elaboration of the experiential understanding it reveals, rather than from adherence to more formalized, traditional notions of experimental and quasi-experimental rigor. These generalizations undoubtedly are oversimplified and are intended only to provide the reader with a way of thinking about the nature of psychological research in this and other human domains.

The manner in which researchers have dealt with the issues of verification versus discovery, and choice of holistic versus reductionistic units of analysis, is also instructive. Although most of the researchers seem to have assumed some form of theory-testing agenda at one point or another in their work, they have felt the need for descriptive and discovery modes of inquiry to assist them in defining their focus. Friedlander and Martin, for example, have acknowledged the conscious shift into a discovery mode to gain a descriptive understanding of the phenomena they wish to probe with specific theoretical formulations. The formal distinction between verification and discovery becomes blurred by the fact that evaluative judgments and the concern for validation are found in all instances. Hill's work, for the most part, does not involve theory-testing per se, but is always guided by concerns for validity. Rennie's work, while more qualitative and discovery-oriented, is similarly burdened with the issue of justification. There is an interplay of strategies and frequent shifting of the contexts of verification and discovery in the research programs. This also is probably true for other areas of psychological research.

The contrast between holism and reductionism is found in both the conceptual units and the methodological procedures used. Hermeneutic and case study approaches are used in the interest of preserving holism, whereas operational and measurement efforts are necessarily reductionistic. Each researcher has striven for the meaningful investigation of therapeutic realities. No researcher seems to be entirely satisfied with the adequacy of his or her units of analysis, as far as capturing the focal phenomenon of interest. All rely on categorization or higher levels of psychometric scaling to bring some order to what they are studying. The underlying concern here is not unrelated to the issue of rigor versus relevance discussed earlier. It seems to be a matter of finding a balance between competing demands and of seeking validity in terms of reliability, meaningfulness, and intelligibility. McMullen, Friedlander, and Rennie have illustrated further the use of specific qualitative criteria for judging the interpretive aspects of their work.

We have stated previously that the validity of knowledge is to be evaluated by its functional value and consequential nature. This is the issue behind the question regarding the type of yield that we can expect from research such as in the therapeutic domain. Each research program here may be considered fruitful in producing information of potential use. The programs of Friedlander, Hill, and McMullen seem to be aimed at instrumental, prescriptive yield, while those of Martin, Rennie, and Howard seem more clearly conceptual and philosophical in the type of yield intended. This is not to cast doubt on the fact that most researchers have hopes of contributing to therapeutic practice in both an instrumental and a conceptual way. It is up to other theorists, researchers, and practitioners to judge the usefulness of the information these programs have generated. Ultimately, the real test of the consequential nature of the various types of yield will be their impact on therapeutic practice and the clients served by such practice.

The issue of determinism versus agency is one that originates from the axiological and ontological domains, and translates into conceptual and methodological choices as well as intimations of moral agenda. The work of Howard and Rennie represent diverse methodological choices in spite of similar commitments to human agency, partly for reasons that we have proposed in Chapter 10. To varying degrees, intentionality of therapists and/or clients is granted in the research programs of Martin, McMullen, Hill, and Friedlander. This brings us to reconsidering some of the non-epistemic questions raised in Chapter 3. Conceptual models that include client agency and intentionality may be presumed to support the empowerment of clients. Modes of inquiry that treat clients and therapists as knowing subjects who can impart their own meanings and experiences, and elucidate their own actions, are likely more empowering than those that do not. Researchers' ethical awareness may be deduced from their procedures and the extent to which they reflect upon, and attempt to address, ethical problems. The fact that we have left it open to our researchers to comment on these non-epistemic issues does not, however, guarantee that their accounts represent adequately their personal stances on these issues.

We believe that these various issues encountered by researchers of therapeutic practice are thematic in psychological research on other domains of human practice as well. The most important question that remains concerns what kinds of human possibilities are being envisioned by the collective efforts and intentions of our researchers. This is a question worth asking of all psychological inquiry. It is central to the topic of progress, which we will address after some additional comments about what we have learned in terms of the inquiry process and ways of gauging the current state of our research praxis in the therapeutic domain.

INQUIRY PROCESS, METHODOLOGICAL PLURALISM, AND PROGRAMMATIC RESEARCH

One of our main goals has been to illuminate the nature of the inquiry process. We have learned that it is a recursive process involving many false starts, struggles with understanding, and repeated cycles of questioning and problem solving. All of our researchers provide phenomenological accounts of their inquiry in these terms. They also illustrate the developmental nature of the process, with their own learning and reflection, and the undiminished tenacity of their problem-solving efforts as analyzed in Chapter 10. We have confirmed the role of personal knowledge in guiding the decisions and actions of the researchers throughout the process of inquiry. What is warranted at a given point depends on the particular context of inquiry and the criteria used by the researcher, based on his or her contingent understanding of the requirements of the research task at hand. The concept of stage of inquiry seems to apply more to the temporal sequence of problem finding and problem solving in a developmental sense than to a distinction between discovery and verification. In fact, this progression seems to be brought about by a dialectical interplay of the modes of thought and strategies associated respectively with discovery and verification.

In relation to method choice, we have learned that what works, or is supposed to work, during the process of inquiry also must be placed in the overall context of the meta-goal of each researcher. Soundness of method choice is supposed to keep alive an inquiry process, just as the intentions and motivation of the researcher would seem to sustain its movement. In Figure 2.1 of Chapter 2, we delineated the various paradigmatic positions in relation to method choice and knowledge criteria. In our sample of researchers, we have found a certain degree of diversity in method choice, and evidence of increasing pluralism. This methodological pluralism has allowed some of the researchers to bring more flexibility to the inquiry process, both conceptually and procedurally. It is not, as demonstrated by Howard's work, a necessary condition for programmatic research. This observation, however, is not an argument against methodological pluralism in programmatic investigation. In our judgment, there is much to be gained from a sustained, conceptually related series of studies with pluralistic methodology that is guided by sound meta-reasoning and well-articulated purposes.

Our conception of the inquiry process and research methods has been a pragmatic, social, and psychological one. It draws our attention to the functional and embedded nature of method choice. The pressures and constraints experienced by researchers are to be recognized, as are the support and rewards provided by professional colleagues and the work environment. In trying to deduce the logic-in-use behind the applied epistemologies of our researchers, we have confirmed the non-neutral nature of method choice and the presence of more than one logic-in-use. As discussed previously, a heuristic logic is clearly at work in most of the research programs. For others, there have been decisions informed by the researcher's meta-goal and ideology, as much as the requirements of the problem task at hand. Overall, the apparent logic-in-use seems to be more complex than what may be expected of a formal, linear logic. In other words, the progression of inquiry as depicted in the various accounts is less straightforward and more fluid than the implied structure of the standard research report.

DEFINING PROGRESS IN A SCIENCE OF PRACTICE

What may we conclude about ways of judging progress in a human science of therapeutic practice? We can perhaps suggest two basic ways of evaluating progress in the science of psychological practice, such as in theory and research on therapeutic practice. One is in terms of the evolution of the research praxis itself. What we have observed as far as the learning gains of the researchers, the increasing pluralism in the use of quasi-experimental and hermeneutic paradigms (in addition to the experimental), the flexible or combined use of discovery and verification strategies, as well as the new attention given to criteria and methods of validation in the discovery context—all point toward a gradual evolution of the praxis. The willingness of researchers to revise their concepts and methods in the light of their findings and experience of research practice may be considered another sign of progress. Conversely, the inability or unwillingness to overcome the limits of one's rationality (ideas, methods, and cognitive values) may constrain progress.

It seems appropriate to define progress also by an increasing ability and willingness to ask meaningful and fruitful questions, and greater sophistication in solving not only problems of a substantive nature, but ontologically and axiologically entailed conceptual, methodological/epistemic, and ethical problems. As the inquiry process is fueled by curiosity and problem finding, there remains a balance of solved and unsolved problems. This state of affairs may be indicative of a healthy science. Our group of researchers has certainly demonstrated a quest attitude and remarkable energy in sustaining inquiry efforts. While the judgment is not completely in yet on the types of yield reported, there is reason for optimism, especially since we have examined the work of only a small sample of research practitioners in the area of therapeutic psychology.

A second approach to addressing the question of progress is in terms of the overall contribution to the field and to society at large. Several of the questions of a non-epistemic nature that were posed in Chapter 3 have not been definitively answered. Nonetheless, we can discern a moral tone in some of the accounts, such as in urging the profession to adopt an agential conception of humankind and to empower our human clientele and subjects, or calling on the profession to join efforts in solving the substantive, conceptual, and methodological problems encountered in this type of research, or seeking a collaborative conversation about the basis of all epistemic claims. These calls seem to be aimed at promoting idealistic and cooperative goals for professional psychology and psychological science. At the same time, realizing the power of professional rhetoric and its impact on ourselves and the public, we hasten to emphasize the importance of an ongoing critique of research accounts and the metanarratives of research accomplishments. In answering questions about merit and worth in a democratized culture and professional climate, it is easy to settle for politically correct answers without sufficient moral reflection and commitment.

Whether the type of work described here, and the efforts our researchers hope to inspire, will contribute to social progress and other goods of a personal and cultural nature is for all to judge in due time. The merit and worth of a knowledge enterprise such as the psychological science of practice cannot be evaluated simplistically or unilaterally. We can begin by engaging in a reflexive discussion and critical evaluation of our collective intentions and efforts. This includes reflection on the kinds of needs and interests being served, relative to others that may be neglected or undermined. All relevant constituencies must be given voice, just as all contributors to the enterprise should be encouraged to articulate the basis of their commitment and what they believe to be the social value of their efforts. It is our hope that a fusion of horizons would be possible as we set our sights and concentrate our efforts on future possibilities.

THE PLACE OF META-METHODOLOGY IN A CONTINGENT THEORY OF KNOWLEDGE

The eventual aim of our project is to evolve a theory of knowledge for the psychological science of practice, granting that it can be only a contingent one. Having reached far in exploring this challenging goal, we wish to return to the more imminent one of developing a meta-methodology of research practice. We have confirmed that focusing on the researcher's meta-reasoning and personal knowing in the apparent logic-in-use, such as discussed in the previous chapters, can be helpful in understanding the actual practice of research. It allows us to follow the heuristic problem-solving process, to identify epistemic and non-epistemic values that inform the research praxis, as well as to evaluate the fruitfulness of the inquiry in terms of the meta-goal(s) of each program.

Concluding Comments

Our seeking of meta-methodological principles stems from a concern with current problems of a divergent pluralism in the absence of consensus. The kinds of meta-methodological understanding we have attempted to derive may illuminate the applied epistemology of researchers and provide a common basis for adjudicating their work. In our case, commonalities were found across researchers with different philosophical and methodological commitments. The lessons learned by the researchers conceivably can benefit all who engage in psychological inquiry, regardless of epistemic orientation. Overall, the pragmatist frame that we have employed, together with the narrative, constructionist perspective brought to the accounts studied, seem to permit meaningful renditions of the various contexts of inquiry and the appropriate criteria for the evaluation of method choice in each type of context. Obviously, we need meta-theoretical analyses to complement this kind of meta-thesis on research methodology. Other naturalized approaches to our human science of practice, such as conducted by historians, sociologists, and anthropologists, can further shed light on our knowledge enterprise.

A meta-methodology must be constantly revised with the benefit of experience and the growing wisdom of the research community. It should be an honest reflection of our intellectual adaptability over time; of our potentials and realistic constraints. In providing us with tentative, contingent visions of how we may progress in our inquiry, it has an important role in the development of a theory of knowledge for the psychological science of practice. It cannot, in the end, usurp the place of a comprehensive model of human inquiry that is informed by both epistemic and nonepistemic values, and the evaluation of our professional efforts in a fully human and moral context.

Postscripts

AUTHOR'S POSTSCRIPT TO CHAPTER 4

After reading Lisa's and Jack's summary and analysis of the six different research programs, I had a number of reactions. First, I was impressed by the awesome task they had in trying to learn something from the different research programs. Second, I felt wounded about the characterization of my research as using a "realist, reductionistic approach" and about the comment that "her apparent epistemological and methodological stance has confined her investigation of these variables to the documentation of essentially linear patterns of association." I felt that my research was devalued because I do not adhere to the philosophical and methodological approach that Lisa and Jack espouse. Undoubtedly, I took it all much too personally because I am certainly aware, and am a central player in, the critical nature of our scientific endeavor.

My third reaction is that perhaps we need to step back and try to understand where we are in the area of therapist techniques from an historical perspective. As we discussed in Hill and Corbett (1993), the study of therapist techniques began in the 1940s and has been dominated by the verbal response modes (VRM) paradigm. With the surge of interest in counselor skills training in the 1970s, VRMs were used to operationalize what counselors do with their clients. The interest in skills training has decreased substantially in the past 20 years because many training programs were too simplistic. Concurrently, there has been a rise of interest in the therapeutic relationship as a mechanism of change and in diagnosing client pathology. I think that these factors, combined with the difficulties in measuring therapist techniques and assessing their effects on the therapeutic process and outcome, have led researchers to turn to studying other, more promising areas using other, more exciting methodologies.

But I cringe when I hear of therapists who graduate from our doctoral programs without ever receiving any skills training. I think we have thrown the baby out with the bath water. By assuming that therapist techniques are not important, we miss the opportunity to teach therapists to learn more effective modes of communication and to test out the effects of their interventions with clients. Even though some people get bored when they contemplate the idea of a cookbook of different therapist techniques that have been shown to be effective in specific situations for specific client types, I think we need to have that kind of information for training therapists. We also need to teach therapists how to use their clinical intuition in conjunction with information about effective techniques when they interact with clients.

In sum, I think we need to keep studying therapist techniques. I also think we need to work on developing more effective programs to teach basic as well as advanced therapy skills. We need to have the pendulum swing back to where techniques are again considered important in conjunction with the therapeutic relationship and client dynamics.

Should our research on therapist techniques be theory-driven? My response to this query is that theory-driven research can certainly be helpful, although I think building a theory on the basis of what seems to work is a more efficient and ultimately practical exercise.

Should we use qualitative methods rather than quantitative methods? I think we should use all sorts of methods, but my main caveat is that we stay close to the clinical phenomena. For example, we need to be aware that the effects of therapist techniques are not all immediate, that not all effects are observable, and that clients do not tell us everything they are feeling.

Clara E. Hill
University of Maryland

AUTHOR'S POSTSCRIPT TO CHAPTER 5

My dual role in the production of this volume, as co-author/co-editor and contributor of one of the case studies in Part II, has been uniquely challenging. Probably more than others who contributed case studies, I am committed to the purposes, and believe in the utility and importance, of this work. Nonetheless, I think I share the ambivalence I believe other contributors must have felt, with respect to communicating my personal sense of my own work to an anonymous audience of readers, some of whom are likely to be professional colleagues, students, journal editors, referees for granting councils and professional awards, and current and possibly future employers. In this context, it seems inevitable to me that my account of my work is somewhat "watered down" for public consumption. I have attempted to be honest about my work and my intentions and reactions to it. Nonetheless, I know that I talk somewhat (although not completely) differently about these matters to my spouse than I have done on these pages, expressing more doubt, insecurity, and frustration than I was able to insert in my chapter.

Perhaps my greatest worry is that my discussion of my own work may have received more sensitive and generous treatment by Lisa and me than we were able to extend to the contributors of the other case studies. As much as possible, Lisa and I tried to treat my case study in a manner identical to that in which we received, considered, and interpreted the others. The most significant formal deviation was that Lisa always prepared and distributed her interpretations of my work prior to my communication of my own interpretations to her. The sequencing of these exchanges was less structured with respect to the other case studies. However, the informal constraints that Lisa (and I) might have experienced, given our partnership in the creation and conduct of this work, are easy to imagine. Of course, we discussed such matters at some length on several occasions, attempting to guard against the kind of "reactivity" that might issue from such constraints. In the final analysis, I think my work may have been treated with greater ease and generosity on these pages as a consequence of a partial convergence of the warrants and judgments Lisa and I eventually employed and the way in which they interacted with my account. Consequently, I still worry greatly about the possible lack of impartiality. Such, seemingly, is my nature.

With the various interpretations of my work that appear in Chapters 10 and 11, I have little quarrel. I am pleased that these interpretations emphasize my concerns for developing and testing theory, and for "getting the ontology right." This latter concern relates to my firm belief that the focal phenomena of psychology and psychotherapy (i.e., human actions and experiences) are both socially located and represented in the personal theories and intentions of actors in those locations. All researchers of psychotherapeutic practice somehow must face the epistemological difficulties entailed by these ontological considerations (see Chapter 3).

I am, however, not sanguine about the progressiveness of my work. There may be real limits to what we can come to understand about psychotherapeutic processes and change mechanisms through the vehicles of social science (positivist or hermeneutic). Recently, I have begun to wonder if the fundamental coins of therapeutic exchanges might earn richer dividends of understanding if considered more as "moral goods" than "discursive data for social scientific dissection." But this way of construing threatens to replace empirical psychology with transcendental and moral philosophy. Perhaps a more genuine merging of these horizons might eventually be possible, one that will eclipse anything any of us have yet managed with respect to understanding and explaining psychotherapeutic practice.

Jack Martin
Simon Fraser University

AUTHOR'S POSTSCRIPT TO CHAPTER 6

I'd never been called "an ideologue" in print before. It gave me quite a jolt to have Lisa and Jack call me one in Chapter 10. However, the more I thought about that characterization of my work, the more correct it felt. Undoubtedly, part of my initial, negative reaction was conditioned by the unsavory associations I have with the concept of ideology. Surely one would be better off not being an ideologue. Instead one ought to be ... what? Honest! Unbiased! Dispassionate! Impartial! Objective! Fair! Evenhanded! In short, to possess all those superhuman attributes that we associate with "the perfect scientist." However, our fantasy of perfectly fair and rational scientists represents the heart of the sin of scientism. The philosopher Richard Bernstein (1976) helps us to understand how an uncritical belief in scientism brings us full circle: "Scientism in social and political studies has become a powerful, albeit disguised, ideology" (p. 106). Simply stated, I cannot object to being called an ideologue because there is no alternative—we are *all* ideologues of one stripe or another. Some of us have owned up to that reality in ourselves, others have not yet done so.

My ideology is said to be for the humanistic belief in free will. That much is correct. However, I must admit that I also believe in a second ideology—the improvability of scientific knowledge. While I do *not* believe that science yields unbiased, objective, and unvarnished Truths, I do believe that it is by far the best knowledge-securing game on the block. Therefore, I continue to practice science, to argue for its special virtues, and to suggest changes in our notion of proper science itself. There is a sense in which I am devoting my life to the belief that science is worth improving. I look toward a day when we will possess a science truly capable of appreciating human nature in all of its complexity, subtlety, and richness. Our capacity for free will (or self-determination) surely will be an important part of our scientific appreciation of human nature. Thus, I see any improvement (whether theoretical, epistemological, axiological, methodological, etc.) as a step in the right direction. Of course, given that definition of progress, this book also must be judged a success.

George S. Howard
University of Notre Dame

AUTHOR'S POSTSCRIPT TO CHAPTER 7

As I reflect further on my own contribution to this book and on Lisa Hoshmand and Jack Martin's analysis of each contributor's account, I am aware that I have broken many of the rules of research praxis that were taught to me. First, I have not really engaged in bona fide hypothesis-testing. Most often, I have a general query in mind at the beginning of a research project, but rarely do I test specific hypotheses. Even in our most recent work on the themes of dominance and nurturance in clients' figurative language, the specific questions from interpersonal theory were formulated at the point of data analysis and were used as a guide in determining the heuristic value of the theory.

Second, I rarely know in advance how I am going to analyze the data. If ever there was a rule that was entrenched in my psyche it was that one *must* determine before data collection how the data are to be analyzed. In my own research, I sometimes do not decide how the data will be analyzed until they have been collected and even coded. Sometimes this delay seems necessary because I do not have a clear sense of how a coding scheme will work. Other times, I feel that I need to have a familiarity with the data before deciding what to do with them.

Third, I never know in advance what the next study is in my research program. There is no logical next step that I am able to delineate in advance of conducting a particular study. I do not know where the results of a particular study will take me.

While breaking the rules has resulted in my being in a state of uncertainty a good deal of the time, it also has been an important part of my own evolution. I am pleased that Lisa Hoshmand and Jack Martin have highlighted the intimate connection between the development of my research program and my development as a researcher. For me, this connection is the most salient part of my account. Grappling with method choice and dealing with the uncertainty of how to proceed has brought me face to face with the crucial importance of constantly returning to the research question(s); of fitting the method to the question (and not vice versa); of knowing my own needs, talents, and interests as a researcher; and of appreciating the influence of the casual suggestion.

In our teaching and writing, we typically have not paid enough attention to these aspects of research praxis, preferring instead to present it as a preset, lock-step sequence that is relatively free from the influence of personal characteristics and circumstances. Lisa Hoshmand and Jack Martin are to be commended for focusing our attention on the lived experience of the researcher, however unconventional it might be.

Linda McMullen
University of Saskatchewan

AUTHOR'S POSTSCRIPT TO CHAPTER 8

In my first research seminar as a doctoral student at Ohio State, Ted Kaul asked each member of the class to free associate to the words "counseling research." My response was roughly the following: The process of counseling—talking with people about their feelings, their thoughts, needs, values, and relationships—has, throughout most of history, been the primary domain of women. Once Freud got involved, I said, psychotherapy became a very manly thing to do. And, maybe to justify their involvement in this feminine activity, men invented the idea of *researching* it. Hence, the Science of Psychotherapy. (It was the late 1970s and I was, of course, an unabashed feminist.) In a playful but provocative tone, I asserted that psychotherapy is an *art*, not a science, and that I doubted it could ever be understood from a scientific perspective.

It's a wonder I was allowed to complete my degree following that performance!

Well, this embarrassing memory came to mind after reading Hoshmand and Martin's reflections on the six accounts in this book. The anecdote may have come to mind for a number of reasons. First, my career seems to reflect an attempt to *disprove* my own pronouncement on the field. I have, indeed, spent a good deal of time trying to infuse some science into this "art." Second, as Hoshmand and Martin note, my research autobiography suggests some loosening up—I've followed a path from the strict rights and wrongs of traditional, hypothetico-deductive methods toward more fluid and subjective qualitative methods. So, of late I have been working hard at infusing some art into this science.

Finally, the gender thing. I was amused by Hoshmand and Martin's conclusion that Hill, McMullen, and Friedlander (the three women of the group) have been more practice-oriented than Martin, Rennie, and Howard (the three men), who are described as more "conceptual" and "philosophical." Hmm. . . . Yes, this business is indeed intensely personal. When studying human behavior we can hardly leave our humanness aside. And we shouldn't.

Myrna L. Friedlander
University at Albany
State University of New York

AUTHOR'S POSTSCRIPT TO CHAPTER 9

In reading their review of my chapter, I feel that the editors are correct in their appraisal that its main thrust is epistemic and I am encouraged by their understanding and support of what I am trying to achieve. The one quibble I have about their evaluation is their comment about a lag in the development of procedures for the use of my methods. The lag has pertained more to the development of my understanding of the rhetoric of qualitative research than to procedures; in the main, the latter have been in place from the beginning of my research program. Also, I am pleased that the editors have teased out my preoccupation with ontology despite my having given it a minor place in the chapter. Being led to the importance of reflexivity has thrust me into the timeless debates on the concept of mind. I am still trying to sort out whether or not conceptualizing clients' reflexivity as the core category has been useful because all it really does is say that the core category is the quality of being a person. Yet, in the context of reductionism marking so much of thinking in psychology—the so-called cognitive revolution notwithstanding—I feel that it is important not to lose sight of the importance of personhood as a root metaphor.

A lot has happened since the chapter was written. The three articles that I cite as being in press were accepted for publication after the body of the chapter was completed. I have been actively involved in a debate on guidelines for adjudicating the publishability of human science studies in counseling and psychotherapy journals. This debate began and is continuing in the International Society for Psychotherapy Research and is being extended to the Counseling Division of the APA. The central issue in the debate is the matter of verification of categories conceptualized in a human science analysis. I have concerns that the modernist position on this issue is too dominant, although very recently there appear to be signs of a softening of this position—a development that I think is vital if human science in its several genres is to be given a place in the mainstream. As I read my chapter in the light of these recent developments, I feel that it is somewhat more impassioned than would have been the case if I had written it today, but not greatly so. Human science is not out of the woods yet, at least in the discipline of counseling and psychotherapy research.

David L. Rennie
York University

EDITORS' POSTSCRIPT

Having concluded the current project, but by no means having exhausted the work that we envision, we find ourselves reflecting on the nature of our own inquiry process. One question that we have concerns the precise manner in which our conceptual frames have interacted with the data contained in the case accounts we examined during this project. Although we feel that our analyses and conclusions in Chapters 10 and 11 have been informed in significant ways by our examination and interpretation of these accounts, we realize that our *a priori* knowledge and presuppositions inevitably have entered into our interpretations in numerous ways. Given the necessary interaction between "theory" and "data," and between discovery and verification, we hope that our inquiry has been consistent with our own beliefs about how open and disciplined it should be. Clearly, our method (including our contingent understanding and working assumptions) has been refined and articulated by the very process of interpreting the case data. Just as our researchers have learned from the application of their methods, we have benefited from our experience of method use over the duration of this project.

From the outset, we have acknowledged our philosophical orientation in using a pragmatist framework, together with a constructionist perspective and critical realism. Our own bias has been in favoring methodological pluralism and programmatic inquiry as guided by a reflective, quest attitude that is sensitive to the needs of both theory and practice. These stances have undoubtedly influenced our analysis and evaluation of the work of our group of researchers. In retrospect, we feel somewhat compromised by the fact that one of us has had a dual role as editor and contributor. We hope that we have been fair in our interpretive comments and have been able to maintain an integrity of judgment and purpose throughout.

This project has been enriched by the diversity represented in our group of researchers and their work. The differences in background and initial perspectives between us as editors have also enabled a dialectical approach to inquiry, with a certain provision of checks and balances. This experience of collaboration between ourselves and with our contributing authors has affirmed for us the synergistic value of pluralism (of world views and epistemic orientations) in maintaining the health of our enterprise as we work toward common goals. At the same time, we know that we cannot expect from others an equal commitment to the positions we personally hold. We did not expect, nor did we experience, a complete harmony of values or professional outlook with one another.

The present work may be viewed as an attempt to bring contemporary philosophical understanding to applied psychological inquiry in general, and psychotherapy research in particular. Simultaneously, we have tried to provide a naturalized understanding of epistemology by studying researchers in action and embedding research practice within its multifaceted human context. In so doing, we hope to have contributed to the two separate disciplines of philosophy of science and psychology. If this should come to pass, this volume may prove to be of value to philosophical psychologists, methodologists, and researchers of therapeutic practice and other domains of applied psychology and human sciences. Students, in particular, may benefit from a vicarious apprenticeship with the researchers whose accounts of their work bring to life the philosophical issues and psychological realities of inquiry in the human realm.

A remaining concern that we share is whether we have practiced reflexivity sufficiently in maintaining a critical stance toward our own values and the knowledge purposes our project has presumably served. This skepticism compels us to raise new questions—about the moral dimensions of the psychological research enterprise, the appropriate grounding for meta-level methods of analysis that are necessarily transcendental in nature, and how the common good may yet come from a continuing quest for knowledge and understanding.

Lisa T. Hoshmand
California State University, Fullerton

Jack Martin
Simon Fraser University

Author Index

Ackerman, Nathan, 178
Addison, R. B., 14
Aleksandrowicz, D. R., 154
Allen, G. J., 181
Allender, J. S., 14
Allport, Gordon W., 52, 141
Altman, I., 13
Angus, Lynne E., 115, 123, 201, 202, 208
Anthony, William A., 81, 83
Aristotle, 56, 69
Arlow, J. A., 154
Asch, Soloman E., 127
Ashcraft, M. H., 112
Avner, R., 97

Banaji, M. R., 50
Bandura, A., 56
Bannister, D., 14
Barker, C. B., 84
Barlow, D., 63, 64
Barlow, J. M., 154–155, 158
Barrett-Lennard, G. T., 95
Bass, D., 13
Bateson, Gregory, 13, 181, 182
Bauer, R., 154
Beavin, J. H., 174, 181
Bennett, V. L., 129
Berdie, R., 64
Berg, D. N., 18
Berger, P. L., 130–131
Bergin, A. E., 63, 82
Berkson, W., 11
Bernstein, Richard J., 54, 246
Best, S., 72
Bhaskar, R., 54, 69
Bordin, E., 203
Boring, E. G., 73
Boscolo, L., 191

Bowen, Murray, 178
Brace, L. J., 84
Brandtstadter, J., 62
Brewer, J., 16, 34
Brewer, L., 208
Brewster, L., 198
Brinberg, D., 9, 20, 32, 40
Bruce-Stanford, G. C., 81
Bruner, J., 163, 213
Busse, T. V., 31

Campbell, D. T., 8, 9, 21, 36, 37, 71, 198
Carkhuff, R. R., 81, 82, 83
Carter, J. A., 85
Caskey, N., 84
Catherall, D. R., 183
Cecchin, G., 191
Chenail, R. J., 19
Chodorow, N. J., 14
Cohen, L. H., 66
Colaizzi, P. F., 18
Conway, C. G., 57, 136, 137, 138, 139, 142
Conway, J. B., 153, 165, 166
Cook, T. D., 9, 138
Corbett, M. M., 82
Corbin, J., 92, 98, 207, 212
Cornfield, J., 50
Corrigan, J. D., 172
Coulehan, Robin, 192
Craik, F. I. M., 117
Cronbach, L. J., 9, 37, 51, 65, 71, 129, 135
Crowder, R. G., 50
Cumming, J. D., 91
Cummings, Anne L., 116, 118, 123
Curtin, T. D., 136, 140–141, 143, 144
Cutler, C., 185

Daniels, J. A., 84
Danziger, Kurt, 5, 49, 60, 205

Davidson, D., 58
Davis, B., 38
Dell, D. M., 172
Dewey, John, 34
DiGangi, M. L., 136, 139
Dilthey, W., 52
Dobson, K. S., 64
Dolhanty, J., 209
Dooley, D. A., 84
Dunfee, E. J., 148

Edwards, L., 85, 91
Egan, G., 96
Elkin, I. E, 91
Elliot, Robert, 13, 61, 63, 65, 84, 85, 92, 93, 94, 110, 123, 160, 199, 200–201, 205, 206, 213, 214
Ellis, Albert, 178
Ellis, M. V., 177, 184
Epston, D., 191
Ericsson, K. A., 60–61, 69

Farace, R. V., 181
Feyeraband, P. K., 73
Fine, H. J., 154, 157
Firth-Cozens, J., 93
Fishbein, S. S., 136
Flood, R. L., 15, 16
Frank, J. B., 97
Frank, J. D., 97
Frankl, Viktor, 141, 145
Fransella, F., 14
Freeman, A., 111
Friedlander, Myrna L., 62, 90, 171–197, 173, 174, 175, 176, 177, 178, 179, 180, 181–183, 184, 185, 186, 190, 191, 192, 194, 224, 227–228, 229–230, 235, 236, 237, 248–249
Fromm, Erich, 141
Fuller, F., 123

Gabbard, Clint E., 148, 149
Gadamer, H. G., 54, 71
Gallimore, R. L., 20, 21, 30, 36
Garfield, S. L., 63
Gaul, R., 185
Gavey, N., 14
Gee, J. P., 119
Geertz, C., 13, 212
Gendlin, E. T., 15, 199

Gergen, Kenneth J., 7, 54, 58, 71, 129, 205, 213
Gibbs, J. C., 13
Giorgi, A., 13, 129, 212, 213
Glaser, B. G., 13, 199, 206–207, 208, 209, 212
Goetz, J. P., 13
Goldman, A. I., 8
Good, R. H., 38
Goodman, G., 84
Gordon, D., 154
Gore, N., 154
Gormally, J., 83, 84
Gotlieb, Ben, 201
Greenberg, Leslie S., 13, 52–53, 61, 63–64, 65, 98, 110, 123, 184, 186, 187–189
Greenson, R., 203
Greenwood, J. D., 54, 69
Guba, E. G., 9, 12, 13, 213, 214
Gulanik, N., 83
Gurman, A. S., 95
Gutting, G., 31, 53

Hadley, S. W., 161
Haley, Jay, 174–175, 181
Hallberg, E. T., 116, 118, 123
Halliday, M. A. K., 175
Hammond, S. G., 84
Hanfling, O., 7
Hanson, N. R., 5, 129, 135
Hardy, G., 93
Hare-Mustin, R. T., 9
Harper, F. D., 81
Harper, R. G., 94
Harré, R., 57, 60, 113, 129, 156, 211
Hasan, R., 175
Hayes, S. C., 63, 64, 87, 138–139
Heatherington, Laurie, 181–182, 183, 184, 185, 186, 188, 190, 191, 192, 194
Heaton, K., 85, 91
Heidegger, M., 73
Henry, W. P., 166
Heraclitus, 132
Hermans, J. M., 57
Hernandez, H. V., 129
Heshusius, L., 213, 214
Hesse, M., 5
Highlen, P. S., 177, 179, 180, 182
Hill, Clara E., 36, 59, 64, 81–103, 82, 83, 84, 85, 86, 87, 88, 89, 90, 91, 92, 93, 98, 123, 213, 224, 226, 227, 228–229, 230–231, 235, 236, 237, 243–244

Author Index

Hoffman, L., 191
Hollon, S. D., 91
Horowitz, M. J., 91
Hoshmand, Lisa T., 3–28, 8, 11, 12, 13, 14, 18, 29–47, 30, 48–78, 49, 145, 223–234, 247, 250–251
Houghton-Wenger, B., 84
Houts, A. C., 18
Howard, George S., 6, 9, 13, 49, 57, 63, 64–65, 71–72, 123, 127–152, 129, 136, 137, 138, 139, 140–141, 142, 143, 144, 146, 147, 148, 150, 224, 225, 227, 229, 230, 232–233, 237, 238, 246–247
Howard, K. I., 82, 91
Howe, K. R., 17
Huberman, A., 14
Huberman, M., 213
Hunter, A., 16, 34
Husserl, E., 211, 212

Jackson, Don D., 174, 178
Jacob, E., 119
Jacobson, N. S., 13
James, E., 199
James, William, 52, 149–150, 233
Johnson, A. J., 136, 139, 143, 144
Johnson, B., 190
Johnson, M., 167
Johnston, G., 209
Jones, E. E., 91
Jorgensen, D. L., 13
Jung, Carl, 141

Kagan, N., 89, 160, 200
Kaplan, A., 30
Kaul, T. J., 171–172, 173, 177, 248
Kazdin, A. E., 13, 87
Keeney, B. P., 13, 19, 23
Keller, Evelyn Fox, 153, 167–168
Kellner, D., 72
Kelly, G., 112
Kempen, H. J. G., 57
Kerlin, J. R., 154
Kiesler, D. J., 91, 166, 199
Kilmann, R. H., 19
Kimble, G. A., 19, 161
Klemm, W. R., 31
Kneller, G. F., 31
Koch, S., 9
Koestler, A., 31
Kovac, V., 214

Kozulin, A., 112
Krasner, L., 18
Krathwohl, D. R., 19, 20
Krumboltz, J. D., 97
Kruskal, J. B., 178
Kuhn, T. S., 7, 10, 11, 15, 129, 135
Kvale, S., 9, 13

Labadie, D., 115
Laing, R. D., 192
Lakatos, I., 11, 31, 39
Lakoff, G., 167
Lamb, R., 156
Lambert, M. J., 82, 92, 98
Lassiter, W., 177, 179, 182
Latour, B., 43
Laudan, L., 11, 21, 37
Lawson, H., 211
Lazarick, D. L., 136, 143
Leary, T., 165
LeCompte, M. D., 13
Lee, A. R., 192
Lefcourt, H. M., 56
Lenrow, P. B., 154
Lewis, K. N., 172
Lincoln, Y. S., 9, 12, 13, 213, 214
Llewelyn, S. P., 93
Loiello, M. J., 136
Lonberg, S. D., 84

MacCorquodale, Kenneth, 104–105
Mahoney, M. J., 7, 111, 141, 156, 213
Mahrer, A. R., 13, 15, 54–55, 61, 65, 92, 110, 111–112, 113, 123, 205
Mainwaring, L., 209
Makkreel, R. A., 213
Mandler, J. M., 112
Manicas, P. T., 111
Mann, J., 96
Mansfield, R. S., 31
Maracek, J., 9
Margolis, J., 21, 60, 73
Martin, Jack, 3–28, 29–47, 48–78, 55, 59, 61, 64, 65, 66, 67, 88, 89–90, 93, 104–126, 106, 107, 108, 109, 110, 112, 113, 114, 115, 116, 117, 118, 119, 203, 223–241, 224, 226–227, 228, 229, 233, 235, 236, 237, 244–246, 247, 250–251
Martin, W., 59, 90, 107, 108, 110
Marx, Ron W., 105
Maslow, Abraham, 141

Matarazzo, J. D., 94
McClintock, Barbara, 153
McGovern, T., 83
McGrath, J. E., 9, 20, 32, 40
McKay, D. G., 15, 38
McLeish, John, 104, 112
McLeod, J., 199
McMullen, Linda M., 115, 153–170, 156, 161, 165, 166, 224, 227, 229, 230–231, 235, 236, 237, 247–248
McMullin, E. D., 129
McNeilly, C. L., 91
Mead, G. H., 211
Meehl, P. E., 51
Merleau-Ponty, M., 13
Merton, R. K., 10
Messick, S., 9, 51
Meyer, M., 90, 107
Michaels, S., 119
Miles, M., 14, 213
Milford, D., 177
Milgram, Stanley, 127, 131
Minuchen, Salvador, 176, 177, 178, 180, 188, 190–191
Misiak, H., 13
Mitroff, I., 19
Modarressi, T., 154
Morgan, G., 18
Morris, J., 13, 19, 23
Morris, R., 214, 215
Morrow-Bradley, C., 63
Mosher, D. L., 154
Moustakas, C., 14
Mulkay, M., 10
Musgrave, A., 11, 31, 39
Myers, Pennie R., 136, 140–141, 143, 146

Nadler, W. P., 13, 61, 65, 110, 111–112, 113, 123
Nagel, E., 58
Nance, Don W., 136, 146
Neeman, R., 97
Neimeyer, G., 6, 14
Neimeyer, R. A., 112
Neisser, U., 49, 50
Nelson, R. O., 63, 64
Nersessian, N. J., 22
Nichols, M. P., 176
Nickles, T., 9, 21, 31, 53
Nisbett, R. E., 60

O'Connor, M. C., 119
O'Donohue, W., 5, 23
O'Farrell, M. K., 85, 86
O'Grady, K. E., 88, 89, 90, 91, 123
Okrent, M., 21
Orlinsky, D. E., 82
Orne, M. T., 138

Packer, M. J., 14
Paivio, S., 115
Patton, M. Q., 14
Patton, S., 86
Paul, G., 97
Penn, P., 191
Pepinsky, Harold, 173
Perls, Fritz, 141, 178
Peters, R. S., 57
Phillips, D. C., 54
Phillips, Jeff R., 13, 199, 201, 207, 209, 210, 212
Phillips, S. D., 174
Phillipson, H., 192
Pinsof, W. M., 65, 123, 179, 183
Pistrang, N., 84
Polanyi, M., 73
Polkinghorne, D. E., 10, 12, 13, 14, 49, 66–67, 71, 145, 163, 205, 212, 213
Pollio, H. R., 154–155, 157
Pollio, M. R., 154
Pope, Alexander, 127
Popkewitz, T. S., 14
Popper, K., 9, 11, 21
Potter, J., 162, 163, 164
Poulin, K., 123

Quartaro, G. K., 13, 207, 209, 212, 213

Raymond, Lily, 177, 184, 194
Reason, P., 12
Reichenbach, H., 4, 52
Rennie, David L., 13, 14, 51, 115, 123, 198–220, 201, 202, 204, 205–206, 207, 208, 209, 211, 212, 213, 214–215, 224, 225, 228, 229, 230, 235, 236, 237, 249–250
Rescher, N., 16
Resnikoff, A., 6
Rhodes, R., 93
Rice, Laura N., 13, 49, 61, 63–64, 65, 110, 123, 154, 186, 188, 200
Richards, R. J., 37

Author Index

Richter, C. P., 31
Rogers, Carl R., 82, 141, 178, 198, 199
Rogers, L. E., 181
Rogoff, B., 13
Rorty, R., 21, 71, 73
Rosenthal, R., 97
Rossel, R. D., 154
Rowan, J., 12
Royce, J. R., 9
Russell, R. L., 85, 214
Rychlak, J. F., 57, 58, 64, 69, 129

Sacks, H., 160
Salner, M., 19
Sanday, P. R., 13
Saperia, E. P., 200
Sarason, S. B., 9
Sarbin, T. R., 13
Sargent, John, 184
Sargent, M. M., 66
Schacht, T. E., 166
Schachter, S., 144
Schaffer, N. D., 94
Schmidt, L. D., 172
Schön, D., 66
Schroeder, K., 83
Schultz, D., 141
Schwartz, G. S., 173
Schwartzman, J., 23
Sechrest, L. B., 66
Secord, P. F., 129
Seiber, S. D., 34
Sexton, V. S., 13
Shapere, D., 5
Shapiro, D. A., 13, 61, 93, 214
Shaul, A., 202, 209
Shaw, B. F., 64
Shoham-Salomon, V., 97
Siatczynski, A. M., 136, 137, 138, 139–140
Siegel, S. M., 177, 185
Siegel, T. C., 13
Simon, H. A., 60–61, 69
Simon, L., 185
Simons, H. W., 10
Simpkinson, C., 157
Skinner, B. F., 30, 32, 104
Skowron, E. A., 190, 194
Slemon, Alan G., 59, 90, 107, 108, 110, 118, 123
Sluzki, C. E., 181

Smedslund, J., 62
Smith, J. K., 213, 214
Smith, K. K., 18
Snyder, J., 176
Snyder, W. U., 84
Solish, A., 214
Spence, D. P., 210
Spradley, J. P., 13
Sprenkle, D. H., 19
Stanley, J. C., 9, 198
Steibe, S. C., 136, 143
Stelmaczonek, Karl, 93, 111, 113, 114, 115, 116, 117, 119, 203
Stiles, W. B., 14, 84, 85, 89, 97, 118, 175, 183, 213
Strauss, A., 13, 21, 92, 98, 199, 206–207, 208, 209, 212
Strong, S. R., 66, 67, 172
Strupp, H. H., 84, 161, 165, 166
Super, D. E., 64

Taggart, M., 9
Taylor, C., 72
Tharp, R. G., 20, 21, 30, 36
Thibodeau, J. R., 175, 176, 177, 194
Thompson, A. S., 64
Thompson, B. J., 93
Thoresen, C. E., 141
Toukmanian, S. G., 14, 51, 198, 201, 205
Toulmin, S., 11, 21, 37, 73
Truax, C. B., 82, 199
Truax, P., 13
Tucker, C., 176
Tukey, J. W., 50
Tulving, E., 117
Turner, B., 208
Turner, T. B., 129

van Loon, R. J. P., 57
Van Maanen, J., 13
Vygotsky, L., 104, 112, 113

Wampold, B. E., 38, 123
Ward, L. G., 175, 177, 178, 194
Wartofsky, M. W., 53
Watson, J. C., 202
Watzlawick, P., 174, 181
Weber, S. J., 138
Weimer, W. B., 129, 214
Westcott, M., 56

Wetherall, M., 162, 163, 164
Wexler, D. A., 49, 107, 156
Whitaker, Carl, 178, 180
White, M., 191
Wiens, A. N., 94
Wiggins, J. S., 165
Wildman, J., 185, 194
Williams, R. N., 56, 57, 69
Wilson, T. D., 60

Winch, P., 57
Winne, Phil H., 105
Wish, M., 178
Woolgar, S., 43

Yin, R. K., 10, 42
Youngs, W. H., 136, 137, 138, 139–140

Ziman, J., 32

Subject Index

Action research, 36
Adaptive Counseling and Therapy (ACT), 146–149
Agency, determinism versus, 56–58, 227, 237
Analogue research, 83–84
Axiology, 9, 40, 71, 239

Barrett-Lennard Relationship Inventory, 162
Behavioral freedom. *See* Determinism
"Bracketing," 16

Case study research, 13, 85–88
Category system, 83, 84–85
Causality, 57–58
Clients' Constructions of Family Problems Scale (CCFPS), 191
Cognitive Constructions Coding System (CCCS; Friedlander & Heatherington), 191–192, 194
Cognitive-mediational paradigm for research, 105–123
Collaborative Study Psychotherapy Rating Scale (CSPRS), 91
Commensurability, method choice and, 10, 15
Conceptual yield, instrumental yield versus, 62–68
Constructionism, 205, 214
 method choice and, 7
 in model of psychotherapy, 111–118
Context of discovery (Reichenbach), 4–5, 31
Context of inquiry, 9, 29, 66
Context of justification (Reichenbach), 4–5, 31, 53
Contextualism, method choice and, 12
Control, in psychological research, 6
Creativity in science, 11, 31

Critical realism, 43–45
Critical theory analysis, 14

Deconstruction, 14
Deductive logic, 3–4
Determinism, 128–149, 227, 246–247
 agency versus, 56–58, 227, 237
 evidence for, 136–149
 experimental approach to, 131–136
Discourse Activity Analysis System (DAAS; Friedlander), 173–175
Discovery, verification versus, 52–56

Empathy, research on, 60, 68–69, 82–83, 95–96
Empiricism, inquiry process and, 32–33, 35, 40–41
Episodic memories, in model of psychotherapy, 111–118, 121
Epistemology
 applied, prototypes of, 36–37, 225–229
 epistemic style, 18–19
 epistemic standards and warrants, 9
 epistemic values, 6, 19
 inquiry process and, 32–33, 35, 40–41, 42
 method choice and, 8, 19
 in research on psychological practice, 70–71, 73
Ethics, in qualitative research, 202–204
Ethnography, 13, 30
External validity, internal validity versus, 50–52, 185

Family Relational Communication Control Coding System (FRCCCS; Friedlander & Heatherington), 182–186, 188–189, 194

259

Family Therapist Behavior Scale (FTBS; Pinsof), 179
Family therapy, 19, 176–194
    cognitive constructions in, 190–192
    convergence hypothesis and, 179–180
    interpersonal influence in, 177–180
    relational control in, 180–186
    task analysis in, 186–190
Foundationalism, 7

Generalizability, 6
Grounded theory framework, 13, 199–213

Hermeneutics, 14, 239
Heuristics, 21, 22, 224, 229–231
Hill Counselor Verbal Response Category System (HCVRCS), 84, 85, 91–92
Hillcrest series, 178–181
Holistic units of analysis, 58–62
Hypothesis-testing methods, in psychotherapy research, 113–116
Hypothesis validity, 38
Hypothetico-deductive methods, 3–4, 22, 226

Ideology, 35–36, 73, 224
Inductive logic, 4
Inquiry process, 29–45, 237–239
    problem-solving view of, 32–36
    for qualitative research, 200–207
    reconstructing, 42–45
    researcher's role in, 36–37
Instrumental yield, conceptual yield versus, 62–68
Intention, verbal response modes (VRMs) and, 88–90
Intentions List, 89
Internal validity, external validity versus, 50–52, 185
Interpersonal Process Recall (IPR), 200, 204–207
Interpersonal theory
    in family therapy, 177–180
    metaphor in psychotherapy and, 165–166
Issues of research on psychological practice
    determinism versus agency, 56–58
    epistemology, 70–71, 73
    holistic versus reductionistic units of analysis, 58–62, 236
    instrumental versus conceptual yield, 62–68, 236–237
    ontology, 68–70
    rigor versus relevance, 49–52, 235
    verification versus discovery, 52–56

Knowledge,
    claims, 10
    criteria of, 10–11
    model of, 9, 240
    personal nature of, 19

Logic, 4, 21, 30

Meaning units (MU), 207–210, 215
Memory mediation, in model of psychotherapy, 111–118
Meta-methodology, 16, 32, 73, 240–241
Metaphors, in psychotherapy, 116–118, 153–168, 202
Meta-reasoning, 15, 20, 31, 232
Method, defined, 4–5
Method choice, 3–23
    appropriateness of, 6–7
    commensurability and, 10, 15
    constraints on, 19–20
    constructionism and, 7
    contextualism and, 12
    epistemological difficulties in, 8, 19
    heuristics of, 229–231
    as inherent in research, 5–6
    isolationist position and, 15–16, 38
    ontological assumptions and, 8, 23
    paradigmatic positions and, 7, 12–17, 18–19
    pluralistic methods and, 11, 14–15, 16–17
    positivistic science and, 7, 9–10, 13, 14, 17
    pragmatist framework for, 21–23, 37, 38–39
    problem-solving view of, 32–36
    progressive research programs and, 11
    for qualitative research, 199–200, 206–207
    reflexivity and, 17–18, 22
    validity and, 6, 8–9

Subject Index

Methodology, 3, 4–7
Methodological pluralism, 14–15, 38, 237–239
Minnesota Multiphasic Personality Inventory (MMPI), 162
Model of psychotherapy, 104–123, 226–227
    cognitive mediation and, 106–111
    constructionism and, 111–118
    Martin's model described, 118–121
    memory-mediation and, 111–118
    neopositivism and, 109–111
    reflections on, 121–123
Multidimensional scaling (MDS), 178–180

Narrative-hermeneutic approach, 13
Naturalistic observation, 13
Neopositivism, in model of psychotherapy, 109–111

Objectivism, 156, 157, 205
Ontology
    inquiry process and, 32–33, 35, 40–41
    method choice and, 8, 23
    in research on psychological practice, 68–70

Paradigms, 3, 7, 12–17
Person-centered therapy, evaluation of, 108–110
Perspective, research on therapist techniques and, 95–96
Phenomenology, 13, 18
Pluralism
    inquiry process and, 35, 38–39, 237–239
    method choice and, 11, 14–15, 16–17
Positivism, method choice and, 7, 9–10, 13, 14, 17
Post-positivism, 7
Pragmatism, 11, 21–23, 38–39. See also Heuristics
Precision, in psychological research, 6
Problem-solving, 11, 22, 32–36, 230
Programmatic research, inquiry process and, 34–35, 39–40, 237–239
Progressive research programs, 11
Psychiatric Status Schedule, 162
Psychotherapy Q-Set (PQS), 91–92

Qualitative research
    grounded theory in, 199–213
    logic of justification in, 213–215
    quantitative research versus, 213–215
Quasi-experimental designs, 13

Rational-emotive therapy, evaluation of, 108–110
Reductionistic units of analysis, 58–62
Reflexivity, method choice and, 17–18, 22, 43
Relevance, rigor versus, 49–52
Reliability, method choice and, 6
Research on psychological practice, 48–74, 235–237. See also Issues of research on psychological practice
    non-methodological considerations and, 71–73
Rigor, relevance versus, 49–52, 235
Rogers's Relational Communication Control Coding System (RCCCS; Rogers & Farace), 181–182, 185

Science
    creativity in, 11, 31
    rationality in, 4, 37
    progress in, 11, 37, 42, 239–240
    rhetoric in, 10, 236–237
Self-determination. See Determinism
Semantic cohesion analysis, 176
Sequential analysis, 86, 98, 174–175
Session Evaluation Questionnaire (Stiles), 118, 175, 183
Sociolinguistics, 173–176
Stage models of treatment, 96
Stimulated recall, in model of psychotherapy, 107–108
Structured content analysis, 107–108
Supervisory Styles Inventory (Friedlander & Ward), 178

Task analysis, family therapy and, 186–190
Theory, 4. See also Model of psychotherapy; Interpersonal theory
Therapeutic events, in model of psychotherapy, 113–114
Therapeutic Interventions Scale of the Therapeutic Procedures Inventory–Revised (TPI-R), 91–92
Therapy techniques, 81–99, 226, 243–244
    defined, 81
    empathy scales and, 82–83

Therapy techniques (*continued*)
   global measures of, 91–92
   issues to consider in measuring, 94–96
   open-ended methods of defining, 92–94
   relative importance of, 82
   testing efficacy of, 96–98
   verbal response modes (VRMs) and, 83–91

Units of analysis, 236
   in grounded theory, 207–210, 215
   holistic versus reductionistic, 58–62

Validity
   concept of, 135
   external versus internal, 50–52, 185
   inquiry process and, 38, 40
   method choice and, 6, 8–9
Vanderbilt Psychotherapy Process Scale, 162
Verbal response modes (VRMs), 83–91, 92, 244
   analogue research, 83–84
   case study research, 85–88
   category system, 83, 84–85
   other process variables and, 88–91
Verification, discovery versus, 52–56
Volition. *See* Determinism

About the Contributors

Myrna L. Friedlander is Professor of Counseling Psychology at the University at Albany, State University of New York. Her areas of interest include counseling research and independent practice with individuals, couples, and families. A member of the editorial board of *The Counseling Psychologist*, she has published on language phenomena and social influence processes in psychotherapy.

Clara E. Hill is Professor of Psychology at the University of Maryland. Her areas of interest are psychotherapy process, counselor training, and dream interpretation. She is the current Editor of the *Journal of Counseling Psychology*. She has published over 80 articles, and is the author of *Therapist Techniques and Client Outcomes: Eight Cases of Brief Psychotherapy*, published by Sage, 1989.

Lisa T. Hoshmand is Professor of Counseling at the California State University, Fullerton. Her areas of interest are epistemology, human science methodology, issues in professional psychology, and the teaching of philosophy of science and psychological inquiry. She has served on the editorial board of *The Counseling Psychologist* and the *Journal of Counseling Psychology*. She is the author of *Orientation to Inquiry in a Reflective Professional Psychology*, published by the State University of New York Press, 1994.

George S. Howard is Professor of Psychology and Director of the Laboratory for Social Research at the University of Notre Dame. His areas of interest include the theoretical, methodological, and philosophical problems in applied psychological research in counseling, clinical, educational, industrial, ecological, and sport psychology. A fellow of several divisions in the American Psychological Association and of Notre Dame's Kroc Institute for International Peace Studies and the Reilly Center for Science, Technology, and Values, he has published four books and over 130 articles.

Jack Martin is Professor of Counseling and Educational Psychology at Simon Fraser University. His areas of interest include the philosophy of applied psychology, research in counseling and therapy, and the psychology of education. He has served on the editorial board of *The Counseling Psychologist* and the *Journal of Counseling Psychology*. His most recent major work is *The Construction and Understanding of Psychotherapeutic Change: Conversations, Memories, and Theories,* also published by Teachers College Press, 1994.

Linda M. McMullen is Associate Professor and Director of Clinical Training in the Department of Psychology at the University of Saskatchewan. Her areas of interest are psychotherapy research and human verbal interactions. She has published on the use of figurative language in psychotherapy, and the influence of status, familiarity, and gender on dyadic interactions.

David L. Rennie is Associate Professor in the Department of Psychology at York University. His areas of interest are qualitative methodology, psychotherapy research, and the study of counselor training. His recent publications have been on the epistemology of qualitative research and the client's experience of psychotherapy. He was the co-editor of the book *Psychotherapy process research: Paradigmatic and narrative approaches,* published by Sage, 1992.